MOTHERS AND DAUGHTERS

SIAN O'GORMAN

B

Boldwood

This edition first published in Great Britain in 2020 by Boldwood Books Ltd.

A CIP catalogue record for this book is available from the British Library.

Paperback ISBN 978-1-80048-547-1

Hardback ISBN 978-1-80426-186-6

Large Print ISBN 978-1-80048-550-1

Ebook ISBN 978-1-80048-551-8

Kindle ISBN 978-1-80048-549-5

Audio CD ISBN 978-1-80048-543-3

MP3 CD ISBN 978-1-80048-544-0

Digital audio download ISBN 978-1-80048-548-8

Boldwood Books Ltd
23 Bowerdean Street
London SW6 3TN
www.boldwoodbooks.com

For Sadhbh

THE FORTY FOOT

For centuries people have been swimming in the Forty Foot, stepping into the cool waters of the Irish Sea from a tiny tip of rock at the southern end of Dublin Bay. In the shadow of a Martello tower, the swimmers gather, even on the coldest winter's day. Some arrive in dressing gowns over their togs, others with towels under their arms, ready to wobble and wriggle into their swimsuits before gingerly picking their way down the steps and into the cold (always so cold!) sea, only ever deterred by large swells or big waves churned up by storms. The last time I swum there was the morning of my grandmother's funeral, when I was twenty-five; years ago now. And these days, when I drive past and see the hardy swimmers making their way down, all I feel is relief that it's not me submerged in those unknown depths.

Rosaleen, my grandmother, was one of those daily swimmers at the Forty Foot. She had no time for 'namby-pambies' her word for people who *didn't* swim in the sea in all weathers, in other words the rest of the world.

'I go in with a head full of problems,' she used to say, pulling on her flower-strewn swimming cap and red swimsuit, 'and come out with the clarity of John the Baptist himself.' She wasn't remotely religious, and had brought up her daughter without the encumbrance of a man or even marriage, but often she would invoke the name of a holy person or holy event to make a point. The Irish emphasis. 'Mother of the divine Jesus' was as exciting her swearing ever got, and usually when she had lost her purse or burned a stew or when the sea was particularly cold. But a swim in icy water cured everything. Colds, headaches and even namby-pambyism. 'Come on, Tabitha,' she'd urge while I teetered on the edge. 'Sure, you'll be grand once you're in.'

And I always was. With her anyway. She was the nicest person I knew, always laughing and chatting with people, and I her little shadow. She'd bring me down to the sea on a Sunday morning and in we'd plunge, laughing and screaming at the cold until we'd float out, stretching our arms towards the horizon, feet kicking madly. Away we'd go, a tiny propeller of a girl and a fine-figured woman slicing through the Irish Sea. 'Holy water,' Rosaleen used to say. 'We're swimming in the holy water. That feeling of stepping into the sea. It was like nothing else. I remember the icy water, the camaraderie of the other swimmers, the feeling of zingy invincibility when you got out, as though you'd been reborn, made anew, and we'd emerge, skin bright red, singing and stinging and tingling.

I remember being very little and sitting on one of the old stone benches while Rosaleen bent over me, drying my feet carefully and gently, and then putting on my socks and shoes. Years later, on the very last day we swam together, I returned the favour. Her breathing was bad and bending down was difficult, so I dried her feet and pulled on her stockings and slipped on her shoes. 'Thank you, loveen,' she'd said. 'You're a pet.

Sometimes my mother, Nora, would join us, if she wasn't off somewhere working, protesting, righting wrongs; as an 'environmentalist and political agitator', as she likes to call herself, her life spent protesting, placard waving, and heel-digging in. These days, as she's grown older and since she's retired she too has become a daily sea communicant. For years and years, Nora worked for various environmental groups as a press officer, spending her life calling journalists and trying to make them care about the planet. Oil spills, Sellafield, tree cutting, forest fires, rezoning were all in a day's work. Just last year she was on the front page of the *Irish Times* protesting about a car park which was being built beside a tuft of gentian orchids. Hair flying in the wind, Barbour flapping, she looked like the pirate queen I remembered from when I was growing up. Nora, my accidental mother, always engaged, forever concerned and outraged, saving slugs, fungi and flowers from the farmer's spade, always standing up for her beliefs.

'You should come down,' she goes on, even though she *knows* why I don't. But she never gives up. Ever. 'It'll do you good,' she keeps saying. 'Your grandmother said it was a cure-all, and like in most things, she was right.'

'But I don't need to cure anything.'

Nora gives me a look as if to say, she knows better. I could still see the appeal. The icy water, the camaraderie of the other swimmers, the zingy invincibility when you remerged, as though you'd been reborn. But the reason I never swim there is not a fear of cold water or sharks or jellyfish. It's something else. You see, for me, the water isn't holy and magical anymore but dark, disapproving... there's an ominous power to that water, as though I can't quite shake off all those droplets that cling to my skin.

1

A summer morning, early May, the sky blue, the air still. Ireland at its most beautiful. Driving back from the supermarket, I took the coast road, through Sandycove, past the Forty Foot, worrying about my daughter. Rosie was all I really thought about now, anyway. For the last two years, she had done nothing but revise. The Leaving Cert are the set of tough, gruelling exams at the end of your school days that you fervently believe will dictate the rest of your life. They wreak such havoc on the psyche of every Irish citizen, instilling such fear and horror, no one ever quite recovers. Your whole life hangs in the balance of knowing particularly difficult Irish grammatical tenses, impenetrable maths equations and the exact movements of Padraig Pearse during the Easter Rising. I still remember that sick feeling in the pit of my stomach, the dread... and then, when they are over, you do miraculously move on with your life but like traumatised elephants, you never forget.

But we were so close to Rosie's liberation from all this tension and pressure. She was pale and seemed to be fading fast. She just had to cling on and the old Rosie, the confident happy girl, would return. As I indicated to turn left to continue on to home, in Dalkey, I spotted my mother on the road ahead, creakily, rustily, slowly pedalling home from her swim, dressed in her usual charity-shop purchases. Her old men's sandals and knitted socks, her legs bare under her long skirt, her trusty battered Barbour and an old cloth bag slung over her shoulder. Her long hair, damp from her dip, hanging over her shoulders to dry. Instinctively I thought of my husband Michael and what he would make of her and mentally cheered her on. She stood for everything he didn't and Nora was the part of me which he found most difficult to accept. She didn't fit in with his idea of an acceptable extended family. She would cheerily tackle him on any issue, good-naturedly holding him personally accountable for everything from home-lessness to the closure of the Dun Laoghaire bowls club.

He believed in the individual, that anyone can make it if given the right support. She believed in welfare and community. But when I decided to marry him, it seemed, to be the most rebellious thing I could do and I don't regret it – I wouldn't change a thing about Rosie, after all – but it had been rash, not a love match but what I had thought was a pragmatic and sensible choice.

As I passed Nora's bike, I slowed down and tooted my horn. 'That's it!' I called through the open window. 'Keep it up! Nice to see you getting a bit of exercise!'

'Thank you, Tabitha,' she said, 'You're very kind. But your encourage-ment is unnecessary.' But she was smiling. 'How's Rosie? Not still at those books?'

'You know what's she's like, takes after you. Never gives up!'

There was a car behind me. 'See you later, Mum.' I said, pressing on the accelerator and moving forwards. But her face suddenly lifted as though she'd just remembered something.

'The trees!' I think she shouted. In my rear-view mirror, she waved again, mouthing something. 'The trees!'

* * *

The black ministerial car was parked outside the house, which meant Michael was home. Terry, his driver, reading a paper in the front seat of the Mercedes. Michael rarely made domestic appearances these days, arriving unexpectedly and disappearing just as quickly, shunting daily life out of its rhythm and he often asserted himself into the household in some way.

Usually it was that the garden needed tidying at the front or he had been shocked to see a dead cheese plant in the hall.

After hopping through the ranks from local councillor to member of the Progressive Conservatives and a front-bench position, Michael had now made it to the giddy heights of Europe. He spent more time in Brussels than Dublin and all his talk, when he did come home, was about EU directives, policies and late-night votes and dining on steak and red wine and crème brûlée. He was good at the mechanics of politics, remembering every name of anyone he had ever shaken hands with, able to differentiate between constituents, who had the brother in hospital and who had the issue with the damp. And after being submerged in Bill Clinton's autobiography, he emerged pale and drawn but excited by all the new techniques he had absorbed, such as finding a face in the crowd and waving, the double handshake and the disconcerting never breaking eye contact.

Politics was his passion; the deal making, the risk taking, the prestige, power and perks, along with a flat in Brussels and a studio in Dublin city centre. His was important work. The *most* important work, changing the world, one EU directive at a time.

Michael had grown up in the shadow of his father, Michael Sr, also a politician. He never watched children's television, only the news, had never worn jeans, and saw politics as the family business. And he wanted Rosie to continue the family dynasty and do exactly what he did. Go to Trinity to do Law, get into local politics and then... well, next stop Brussels.

I harboured secret and treasonous thoughts that Law in Trinity was too much like hard work (and far too boring) and that no one – and definitely not my daughter - should be subjected to it. But then I wasn't a Fogarty. After giving up her dreams of acting, Rosaleen, my grandmother had been front of house manager at the Gaiety Theatre all her life. Nora gave no credence to academic qualifications but everything to the ability to chain oneself to railings in protest. The only time I can remember feeling she was *really* proud of me was when I won first prize for my poster in a competition against Sellafield when I was twelve.

Unministerially, Michael was eating Weetabix. 'Morning Mammy!' he said. 'Cold milk on cereal! Breakfast of champions. It's the milk, though *Irish* milk from Irish farmers that makes it! Am I right?'

'Hi Michael,' I said, not bothering to tell him for the billionth time to call me Tabitha, rather than Mammy, and that he already had his own mother and didn't need another one. 'Um...' I tried to formulate an opinion on milk.

'Caught the red-eye from Brussels and needed my farmers' association tie for the meeting in Dundalk,' he went on blithely. 'You need...' he spooned the last drops of milk from his bowl into his mouth, 'the right tie. Bill Clinton says it's the killer move. Get it wrong and no one will trust you. Get it right, and putty in the hand!'

'I suppose the same could be said for the handbag,' I said, putting away the shopping, 'too expensive and everyone mistrusts you...'

'It's an art,' he said, as though I hadn't spoken. 'You have to think of who you are meeting and with farmers, it can't be too flashy. It has to be just right. I'm thinking of a Donegal tweed. Well, that's what Lucy has decreed.'

Michael's best perk was Lucy, his secretary. Over the last two years she'd made it her life's work to overhaul not just his office but also his image. There is now a more contemporary look to his hair and the cut of his suit. His fringe pushed up, lapels more city slicker than fusty politico. And his teeth have undergone a bleaching more thorough than any toilet and now gleam brighter than those of Tom Cruise's.

'I'm sure Lucy's right,' I said, trying to keep a facetious tone out of my voice. 'She always is, isn't she? That's what you say.'

'She's a marvel,' he said, smiling broadly. 'Yes, yes, quite the marvel.' His eyes went misty for a moment as we both contemplated the myriad ways Lucy was a marvel.

'Now,' he said, breaking focus, 'where's herself?' He meant Rosie.

'Upstairs. You know, Michael, the exams,' I said, 'I've been wanting to talk to you about it. If there's anything we could do, anything we should be doing to make it easier for her. They're so awful. I think they might even be worse than when we did them. I mean, they seem to be even harder these days ...'

'She'll be grand,' he said, dismissing me. 'Us Fogartys always are. I sailed through mine. She's got a good brain, that's all you need.' Rosie, he believed, was more Fogarty than Thomas – the politics, the clear head, the methodical way of doing things. Chip off the old block. He'd been talking about Rosie going to Trinity, his alma mater, since before she was born, and as Rosie had done exceptionally well in her mock exams and had been offered a place, it was a case of just passing the finals and she'd be in.

'Trinity College! She's on her way.' Michael put down the cereal bowl and *actually* rubbed his hands with sheer excitement. 'I was just onto my old professor yesterday and we had a good chat about Trinity and how it's changed. He said to bring Rosie in one of these days for a look round the place. Thought I would show her a few sights. The library. The old lecture hall, that kind of thing.'

'She's already been round...'

'Ah, but not with me. An old boy, so to speak. Not that I'm old. Just *older* than I was.' Michael was the same age as me, 42, but gave what he might think was a boyish grin and ruffled his own hair. Which he then quickly smoothed back in place.

'Michael, it was more than twenty years since you were there.'

'Technically, yes.' He helped himself to another two Weetabix sprinkling them liberally with sugar and splashing on the milk. He took a mouthful. 'The Fogarty name still opens doors, you know. We are not nobodies. We belong there and Rosie will be the fourth generation. Now...' His face suddenly looked grave, like a headmaster disappointed in the child who had been caught smoking. 'I need to talk to you...'

'Really?' What had I done now?

'The hall light was on,' he said. 'Why? It's a summer morning? There's really no need.'

'I must have flicked it by mistake...'

'It's not the expense,' he said, shaking his head at my absent-mindedness. 'But the waste. If I am seen as wasteful, then I am not setting a good example for my constituents. They expect me to have the highest of standards, Mammy. We must live up to that ideal.'

'Yes, Michael.' Over the years, I had learned to nod and agree.

'I am a public figure,' he went on, 'and must be beyond reproach. SIPL!'

'Sipple?' Was this some new, utterly perplexing, mind-bending, borderline-barmy EU policy?

'Standards in Public Life. It's my latest directive. I've *told* you about it before...'

'Oh yes,' I said weakly, glancing at my unread paper and thinking of the croissant I had just bought and had been looking forward to for the last hour. 'So...?' I tried to stay focussed on what Michael was saying but, as usual, when he held forth on Europe, my concentration wavered. Where was my nice pot of jam? I hoped Rosie hadn't finished it *all* off.

'Now *this* is really exciting,' he was saying, 'It's going to be very popular with voters, I just know it. All politicians, across Europe, will sign up to this agreement, declaring that they are beyond reproach. Voluntary self-regulation and a move towards a different relationship between people and politicians. Bring back respect.' He chattered away confidently in that way he had that what he was saying was of great interest to the listener. 'We shouldn't behave like ordinary people, *civilians*, the ones doing ordinary jobs, leading ordinary lives, like going to the park, or making dinner, or watching Strictly Come Whatever. Instead, we non-civilians will be shining lights, exhibiting impeccable human behaviour, so that others, the civilians know how to behave.'

'Is that really what you politicians think is a good way to spend taxpayers' money?'

'Yes! Everyone hates a sleazy politician, the one who accept backhanders or are just in it for the perks and the free lunches...'

'It sounds like you are asking for trouble, Michael,' I said. 'Setting yourself up as a beacon of respectability.'

'Well...'

'You won't be able to put a foot wrong,' I said, thinking that life with Michael was just one extended episode of Politics Today. 'You can't forget to put something through on the self-service tills or drive in a cycle lane or park in a disabled space...'

'I have no intention of such things,' he said. 'I never go self-service and I am meticulous about staying out of cycle lanes. Anyway, it's the idea – the *ideal!* – which is the thing. Striving to be better, that's it. Upholding common, decent values. Morals are too easily running down life's plughole.'

'It seems as though you are setting yourselves a very high bar,' I said. 'Beyond reproach? It doesn't give you much room to be human.'

'Ah, but we aren't human. Well, we are, technically. But we are above human... I mean, superhuman...'

I looked at his face. He was entirely serious. 'As in Superman, super-human?' I had to make sure he was saying what I thought he was saying. 'Actually super-human, or just super humans?'

He looked confused. 'Super-human,' he said. 'More than human.'

'Right. Michael...' I toyed with trying to discuss this with him but, as I usually did, I gave up. 'It sounds like a complete waste of EU money, if you ask me.'

'Well, I don't and nor do many – very many – of my EU colleagues.' He sounded annoyed. 'It's going to be voted on in a few weeks. Before we break up for summer. It's the directive that's going to make my name.'

Not for the first time, I thought that Michael's pomposity would be his undoing.

'Hi Dad,' Rosie came into the kitchen and again I saw how pale she was. She'd lost weight, she was just wearing leggings and a long top, her hair scrunched up onto her head.

'What are you doing home?' she said, surprised but not displeased to see him. He was like a forgotten-about lodger, sometimes. We never knew when we would be graced by his presence but neither of us minded either way. Michael didn't try to parent too heavily or husband too deeply, and we never complained about his peripatetic attitude to the home, so it all worked quite well. He loved Rosie, that was clear, albeit in his own way. She knew it and had, I thought, never felt a particular lack. He just wasn't one of those rough-and-tumble dads or even the bedtime-story dads... and that seemed okay. Good enough.

'And how's Daddy's little politician?' He ruffled her hair affectionately.

'She's fine,' said Rosie, flatly. He glanced at me, as though he had heard my concerns. Rosie was normally far chattier and full of life. But this had become her usual way of late, low-enthusiasm and energy.

'Now, I hope you're working hard. Mammy says you are.' He looked at her intently. 'Is everything all right? Are you eating properly? There's some Weetabix in the cupboard.'

'Weetabix!' she said. 'Is that your answer to everything?'

'It's a good, healthy cereal,' he said, looking hurt. 'It's a good stomach-settler.'

'Can we just stop the inquisition? Am I working, am I eating? Yes I am and no I would rather chew my own Ugg boots than eat Weetabix. I eat granola. You should know that.'

Michael wasn't an emotions man. He liked rationality and reason. No crying, slight hysteria or shaky voices. Rosie, being a normal teenager, would display every human emotion in just one conversation, which always had a slightly destabilising and unnerving effect on Michael.

'I do know that, Rosie,' he said, a politician's smile plastered on his face. 'I just merely forgot your breakfast preferences for one moment. And anyone is allowed to do that from time to time.' He was desperately trying to bring the conversation back to *Politics Today* but things were often far more *Loose Women*.

'Now, I was just saying to Mammy here that we should pop into Trinity together. I can show you around... the library, the cafeteria, that kind of thing. My old favourite lecture theatre... Trinity's hallowed gates.'

'So you keep saying...' she said, the slightly terrified look in her eyes reappeared anytime Trinity was mentioned.

'Next stop for you, Rosie,' he pressed, 'is politics. What do you say?' But before Rosie could answer there was a beep of a horn outside. 'Right, time to go,' he said. 'Meeting in Drogheda. Right,' he said, clicking his heels together and giving us a salute. 'I'm off. Had my Weetabix... your *favourite*, Rosie...'

'Da-aad...'

'I'm joking,' he said. 'But I might bring you back a bumper box of 72 when I'm next home. You will like them... much better than fannying around with muesli...'

Rosie was smiling, despite herself.

'By the way, Mammy,' he said. 'Was that ordinary milk I just had?'

'Supermarket's finest,' I said.

'It wasn't organic or from goats or anything strange like that.'

'No... Why?'

'Just had an idea,' he said. 'You don't get anywhere without ideas.' He kissed Rosie on the head, gave me a friendly tap on the arm and gathered his briefcase and rushed outside. 'Remember, lights off!' he shouted behind him as the door slammed. 'Standards must be upheld!'

* * *

The Thomas family was rather different to the Fogarty's political dynasty bursting with heirs all born to rule. In my family, the only destiny we seemed to follow was having one-daughter. Both my mother, my grandmother and I had just the one girl but Rosaleen, and Nora had their babies out of wedlock. My rebellion was to do it within the conventional confines of marriage.

Rosaleen was an unmarried mother at a time when it was possibly the most shocking thing anyone could do apart from eat garlic or refuse to go to Mass. When she discovered her pregnancy, she told no one anything. Not a word. Not even Nora's father who was a boy from back home in West Cork... but already married. She left home, saying she was heading off to Dublin to work, but kept her pregnancy a secret, kept her baby and brazened it out. It takes a tremendous amount of guts to do that, to stare down the gossips and the whisperers and the elbow-nudgers. Force of personality and determination got her through.

My paternity was never up for much of a discussion. As far as I know, I was conceived at a music festival so the chances of me discovering who he was were lost in a haze of hallucinogenic substances. Not the most conventional start to my life. But that was Nora. She didn't do normal.

I thought Nora was going to faint when I told her that I was getting married. To Michael. 'What?' She looked horrified and didn't try to hide her shock. 'You can't. Tab, you can't... he's...'

'He's what?'

'He's not like us...' was all she managed. And she was right. He wasn't like us, at all. 'He's a Progressive Conservative.' But I wanted a child and he wanted a wife.

And Nora got over it. Not enough to *embrace* Michael (he wouldn't have actually embraced her, anyway, as he always said, with a slight shudder, there was the whiff of Oxfam off her), but enough not to go on about it. Anyway, we all had Rosie to think about now.

But whenever I walked on the pier in Dun Laoghaire, I'd look at the couples, the ones who looked like they'd been married for years and years, the ones brimming with love and lustre, chatting nineteen to the dozen, holding hands, and I would feel a tug of loneliness. I used to have that, once, but life had taken a different direction and Rosie was the centre of my universe. Michael and I, when he was home, didn't share a bedroom and we had used the fact that he had the nasal capacity of a jet engine as the reason for his moving to the spare room. Michael and I weren't perfect, but it wasn't bad. Certainly not *bad enough* to leave.

'Mum...'

'Yes sweetheart?' I said, looking up from the fridge from where I was putting the shopping away.

'Nothing,' she said, turning away. 'Forget it.'

'No, what is it? Is everything all right?'

This school year hadn't started well for Rosie when her boyfriend, Jake, ended things. And now, with the pressures of exams, the light had gone out of her. It was awful to see. She had even retreated from her best friends, Alice and Meg.

'Yeah, fine.' She turned to go.

'Have you eaten?' I said, in an attempt to keep her with me.

She shrugged. 'I had some granola earlier.'

'Would you like something else? Poached eggs? I bought some nice bread.'

'No, it's fine.'

'Do you fancy doing something? A walk? Or we could go the farmers market? Or into town? Do some shopping. Get you something nice?' The bribe fell flat.

'No, you're grand. I've got to get back upstairs.'

'Ro...' I eyeballed her, parent face on. 'You don't go out. I can't remember the last time you left the house... what about Alice, Meg... I bet they are still going outside...' I smiled, to let her know I was still on her side.

'So?' Suddenly, she was furious, on the brink of tears. 'I'm trying to work, okay? That's all. I'm just trying to work.'

'I know, I know,' I soothed, quickly. 'But don't you think it might be nice? Why don't you go and see Alice? I'm sure she could do with a break too.'

She held up her hand. 'Mum, can't you just give me a break. Leave me to it. Okay? Everyone's doing it,' she told me. 'We're all working away. Stop fussing.'

'Stop fussing? I'm your mother. This is what we do. We fuss. And if mothers stopped fussing, where would we be then?'

'Happier?'

I pressed on. 'Have you even talked to Alice? Texted her?'

'You should be pleased I'm working so hard. Not nagging me. God, anyone would think you would want me to fail.'

'Of course I don't want you to fail but...' What exactly did I want? I liked the fact that she was a hard worker. This very fact had made my parenting so much easier. She was the kind of child you didn't have to worry about. Conscientious, successful. She made me look good. But... but... something was nagging at *me*, something wasn't quite right. It was too much. 'You need a break,' I said. 'At least from time to time. You've shut yourself away like...'

'Like what? A madwoman in the attic?' She had her arms crossed, challenging me.

'No...' I tried to keep it neutral. These days all I seemed to do was upset her. I was losing her. 'You're hibernating, like a... like a...'

'Squirrel?' She almost laughed.

'Like a hermit.'

'Mum, hermits don't hibernate. Maybe you should have studied harder.'

'Listen,' I said, 'obviously, I'm not quite sure what I'm trying to say but I don't want you to stop being you. Having fun. Seeing your friends. It's like life is on hold. There's no such thing as a pause button. Not when it comes to being alive. However much you might want there to be.' For a moment I thought of the times when I wished I could press pause, when life seemed to move too fast for me. 'What about seeing if Alice or Meg would like to go to the cinema with you,' I persisted. 'I'll drop you. And collect. I'll give you money for sweets.'

She rolled her eyes, defiance and anger had returned. 'Mum, I'm doing my Leaving Cert. And you want me to go and eat sweets. Or press pause. Or be a squirrel...' She was looking at me as though I was mad.

'Forget the squirrel bit...'

'Have you any idea how stupid you sound?'

'No... I mean I just think you deserve a bit of a break. You don't leave your bedroom. Surely, you know it all by now.'

'You see! That's typical of all of you. None of you get it. I can't just take time off.' She began to cry. 'How else am I going to get to Trinity? To do *Law*.' She spat it out. Up until this moment, I had thought she wanted it just as much as Michael. But maybe it was just pre-exams nerves, the fear of this huge culmination of 14 years of full-time education... the feeling of being out of control. Inevitably she was going to doubt herself and her choices.

'You don't have to,' I said. 'If you've changed your mind about Trinity or Law or anything, it's not too late.'

'Oh yes it is!' she said. 'But there's nothing I can do.'

2

I'd been principal of the Star of the Sea girls' primary for the last five years. Every day as I drove in to work, I couldn't believe that I was leading the school where I had been a pupil – as had Rosie and even my own mother.

Every single day our pupils made me proud, from hearing them sing in assembly, to just seeing them dressed in their uniforms, eager to please and to learn. The school had seen many changes since I played skipping games and wrestled with my times tables to when, years later, I was made school principal. So far, we were doing well. We retained our 100% approval rating from the local authority year on year and had several commendations, including those for our anti-bullying attitude and the green school scheme.

We did, however, have one problem. Well, two, if you counted the fact that Sixth class didn't actually have a teacher, since Ms Samuels had disappeared after winning €50,000 on the lottery and was last seen heading for Departures with a copy of *Let's Go South East Asia*.

But the other big, equally pressing, problem occupying my waking thoughts was cash flow. Or rather the lack of. We weren't a private school and relied on the local authority, whose budget seemed to decrease every year. Instead, we were encouraged to do as much fundraising as possible. But however many cake sales, bring-and-buys, raffles or parents' cheese and wine evenings we enthusiastically held, we never had enough money to fix the things that we really needed. The other local school, Willow Grove had recently presented each child with their own iPad. Willow Grove was a private school and the fact that the fees had recently been upped by a whopping €2000 a year might partly explain where the extra dosh had come for to pay for all this. Our parents' committee had even held a whole meeting on this very subject, and the result had been retuned that we had to provide our children with the very same. We just had to keep on fundraising. More cake sales were prescribed, along with sponsored walks and swims and no school uniform days. Anything sponsorable was in. Except for the human pyramid idea suggested by one pupil which would definitely end in tears, broken bones and probably a barring order from never running a school again.

We just couldn't stand there and allow Willow Grove kids to become the world's future software billionaires. But also, as well as the new iPads, we needed money for our leaky roof and for resurfacing the playground ... My wish list of improvements was long and constantly growing and each sponsored event inched us forward. What we needed was a leap. We needed someone to invest in us.

With the school teetering on the edge of sponsor fatigue, one idea was gathering enthusiasm from me. It had been proposed by one of our board of governors, Brian Crowley. It was always a struggle to find a parent with enthusiasm coupled with spare evenings to join our not-particularly merry throng, but Brian, when he joined in January, seemed very eager. Very eager indeed. He had come up with a cunning plan and it didn't involve sponsor forms or baking cakes or reading piles of books or sitting in a bath of baked beans. He wanted us to sell a slice of school land, the Copse, a wooded area, at the far end of the school, beyond the hockey pitch.

When I was a pupil at the school, I remembered playing there, but now it was overgrown with brambles, the trees covered with ivy, the odd squirrel darting from branch to branch. It was part of the school grounds that I admit I didn't give much thought to. It wasn't out of bounds to the children, but neither did we encourage them to play there. So selling it, went Brian's logic, made perfect sense. The tricky part, he said, was finding someone who would take it off our hands. The land was a worthless, odd-shaped site, and it would be difficult to find a buyer, but he had to try. And he'd succeeded. He'd found someone.

* * *

At his very first board of governors meeting during the winter, Brian Crowley had spotted Sister Kennedy was the one to butter up. There were only five of us: Me, Sister Kennedy, (nun and former school principal), retired teachers Noleen Norris and Brendan Doherty, Mary Hooley (school secretary and friend) and Brian Crowley, spokesperson for the parents.

Sister Kennedy's faith tended to dominate her conversation as she found God to be a reliable source of talk, both small and large, and introduced Him into most conversations, how He always *found a way* and *worked in mysterious ways.*

At that meeting, Brian first raised the idea of selling the Copse. He waited - impatiently (drumming fingers, looking around the room, reading the small print on the wall posters, checking his phone for messages) - until I had run through points of interest, the relative success of a recent tombola raffle to the trialling of a new healthy eating campaign.

'God,' said Sister Kennedy in approval, 'has found His way again.'

'We are edging closer to our €20,000 target,' I said. 'Mary, what are we up to now?'

She glanced down at her notes. 'More than €3,156 is in the kitty. Some of that could be used to buy a complete set of Harry Potters for the library but, yes, Tabitha, you could say we are edging closer. But, I should say, at a rather subdued pace.'

Finally, Brian saw his opening. 'Well,' he said, 'that brings us to my rather interesting - though I may say so myself - proposal. Plan. Plot. Call it what you will but it's big, it's bold... and it's beaut-i-ful.' He beamed at us all, confident in our imminent excitement. 'Sister Kennedy, if I may be so bold, I think God may have found a way. He may well be the source of my inspiration.'

'Go on,' I said.

'Well, it's the scrubland. Over yonder. At the back of the school.'

'You mean the Copse?'

He nodded. 'Is that what you call it? I call it the waste ground, the patch of trees. Whatever it's called. It is the answer to our little problemmo re financing.'

I quickly translated for the sake of Sister Kennedy who had been rootling around in her bag for her glasses. 'Mr Crowley thinks he might be able to help us with the plan to buy computers,' I explained.

'God willing,' she said, smiling back at him, putting her large spectacles on her face and pulling back as though startled by him in close up.

'Ah, but Sister Kennedy,' he said. 'It's not God that's going to solve this problem but me, with your blessing. Anyway, I've had the thinking cap on, the old brain box in gear. We can't produce rabbits out of hats, we've got to be creative, think outside of our boxes, throw potatoes in the air.'

'Try something new,' I translated.

'God will advise,' said Sister Kennedy confidently. 'He always knows exactly what to do.'

'We will ask Him most certainly,' assured Brian, 'but first we must come up with a plan and then we will see if God will bless it. We are, after all, talking about a pointless, meaningless piece of land. Something that has no use. But could have real and long-lasting value and change the lives of the youngsters. We need to find a fella, someone who will take it off our hands. Now, I don't know if such a person exists. We need a charitable sort of person, someone who would do it not for his own gain but for that of the school.'

Sister Kennedy, Noleen and Brendan nodded enthusiastically. Beside me, Mary paused from taking the minutes, shuffled uncomfortably.

'Now doesn't that sound like a lovely plan?' said Sister Kennedy. 'The kindness of strangers is a beautiful notion. Reminds me of the Good Samaritan. Are you suggesting Mr Crowley that you have found a Good Samaritan, someone who will be able to provide our children with computers?'

Brian made deep and meaningful eye contact with her. 'I'm going to try,' he said, in a quiet, intense voice. 'I don't know if I'll succeed. But it's a good plan, I think. If I may be so immodest, it's even a great one...'

'Then I'll pray for you,' she said. 'And you'll do it, I know you will.' She looked at us around room. 'We'll all pray for you. We'll pray that this Good

Samaritan turns up. Won't we?' She eyeballed us beadily and urgently. 'Won't we?'

'Yes, Sister Kennedy,' we all said.

Brian promised us all he would do his best, for the good of the school, for the good of our children. He would do it for Ireland, for our proud benighted nation. He would do it for love. By the time he finished, Sister Kennedy, Noleen and Brendan were moist around the eyes, swept up by his words. Mary rolled her eyes at me.

'Protocol states that any proposals regarding anything that would affect the school must first be approved by the board,' I said, 'but that the current principal of the school has the final say. So, Brian, it's an interesting proposal but the ultimate blessing must come from me.'

'Indeed it does,' said Sister Kennedy. 'But God moves in mysterious ways. I find that when one asks Him for guidance He bestows wisdom on those who must make the decision.'

'*Most* mysteriously,' said Brian, nodding with the humility and wisdom of a living saint. 'I ask God for His guidance when I am making *all* my decisions. And He never fails to show me the way. Just this morning, I was ordering a breakfast roll in the Spar, two rashers, and two sausages, my usual. I asked God, if that was the right choice. And He answered me. Today, He guided me to ask for black pudding as well. And I must say, it was a revelation.' He winked at me.

Noleen smiled slightly uncertainly. Brendan looked utterly confused. Only Sister Kennedy smiled. 'That's exactly right, Brian,' she said. 'God is everywhere, even at the hot food counter of Spar.'

* * *

Mary Hooley, my school secretary, was a beacon of good-sense and intelligence. And although I sensed that she wasn't sure about Brian's Great Idea, I was determined that I could talk her round. After all, it would mean a break from raffles and bring and buys and *bric a brac* stalls. Our great economic leap forward.

'Morning, Mary!' I said. 'How are we doing? Are we millionaires yet?'

Mary was counting the takings from the sponsored readathon from the previous week. 'Morning, Tabitha,' she said, eyes on the change. 'We're up on last year. So that's good news.'

'Have we broken the €100 yet?'

'Not yet, but look there's another ice cream tub of coppers to go.' She gave it a good shake, the sound of no more than a fiver's worth of coins.

'We'll get there, Mary,' I said. 'One day we'll have enough to fix the roof, resurface the playground and invest in some technology. If we... if we give Brian's idea a go.'

'Hmmm.' Mary was the cousin of Lucy, Michael's political perk. Ireland being a small place where everyone is separated by a mere three or four degrees.

'I'm starting the think that this could be the best thing for the school, Mary,' I said. 'People are selling bits of land all over the place; for house building in gardens or development in other ways. We would just make sure it was unobtrusive... anyway,' I went on, talking despite her obvious lack of enthusiasm for the proposal. 'I've had another phone call from Brian Crowley. He's found someone who'll give us the money for the Copse.'

'Has he now?' Mary's eyebrows were raised to her hairline. 'Dress a goat in silk and he's still a goat.'

'What?' I laughed.

'Well,' she said. 'It's just that he is very fond of his own voice and he's all cufflinks and a hard handshake. And he takes up a lot of space. More than he needs. He really likes to spread out.'

I laughed again. 'But that doesn't mean it's not a good plan.'

She nodded. 'It's the man-spreading and the arm waving. I like people who take up the right amount of the world. Not more than their fair share. And he speaks far louder than he needs to, like what he is saying is so important that it needs to be said at a higher volume.'

'Tedious,' I agreed. Living with Michael, I had a thicker skin when it came to the overly-confident male. And anyway, I was blinded by the money and all we could achieve. And not for the first time did I banish thoughts of my socialist mother from my mind. Sometimes we all had to welcome our inner capitalist. For the greater good, I kept repeating. For the greater good.

'My mother,' said Mary, 'always said don't trust men who fancy them-selves more than you.'

'Good advice. I'll remember it.'

'Or women, in my case,' she smiled. 'But I know what she was trying to say.'

'Just think of the money. New chairs for the Sixth class girls, instead of the rickety ones they have. A new surface for the playground, books for the library, whiteboards for every classroom, fix the front gate...' What else? 'And a disco for the kids. We haven't had an end-of-year party for them in five years... that would be nice... And... well, there's just so much we could do.'

'If you think it's a good idea, Tabitha. But I don't mind all the sponsoring, the cake sales...'

'But there's only so many cake sales we can hold. At this rate, we're going to turn the entire population of Dalkey diabetic.'

She shrugged and went back to her counting.

'Tea?' I said.

'Oh yes, please, Tabitha,' she said. 'If only to soak up the biscuits I've brought in.'

'Pass me your mug,' I said. 'And I'll go and give it a wash.'

As I took it from her, I knocked a pile of books off her desk and, scrambling to put them back, I picked up *Chinese for Beginners: Mastering Conversational Mandarin.*

'Chinese, eh, Mary?' I said, teasing her. 'Your next exotic holiday destination? Or perhaps a job in international finance...'

Her face froze as she tried to smile. 'I don't think counting these coppers will get me a high-flying job,' she said, quickly slipping the book into her handbag. 'And I am quite happy with my annual trip to Florence to visit the galleries.'

'So, Brian's found his Good Samaritan, eh?' said Mary. 'And what will this Good Samaritan do with the land?'

'A house? A community centre?' I said hopefully. 'Whatever it is, we'll make sure that it's something positive. Not a casino or a strip club or a...'

'Oh, Tabitha!' she said suddenly, looking up. 'I'm forgetting everything lately. We've had a letter. From the Department. Staffing issue solved.

They are sending a new teacher next week. Richmond somebody. Funny name.'

The letter had been tucked behind her telephone and she passed it to me and I scanned the words on the letter. *We are pleased to inform you, et cetera, that Redmond Power will be available to join Star of The Sea National School, he comes very highly recommended...*

'It's Redmond,' I said, finding my voice. 'Not Richmond.' He was back. Red was back. 'He's just Red, though. No one calls him Redmond.' Like a ghost from my past, he had returned and I'd been haunted by what I'd done, ever shaking off my shame and I still felt an excruciating gnawing of guilt inside which always surprised me how strong it still was.

She turned around. 'You know him?'

'Yes. Not for years though. He went to America. San Francisco.'

'And where did he get the name from?'

'John Redmond. The Nationalist hero. His family was pretty political.'

'He's come home, so,' said Mary.

I nodded, eyes slightly blurry with shock and tried to focus on the words. *He will join the school until the end of the school year and dependent on performance and your feedback, a longer term of employment can be decided upon... we are, however, sure that Mr Power will be a good fit for Star of the Sea...*

He sounds just what we are looking for,' Mary called over from the kettle area.

Perhaps there was another Redmond Power? I sat heavily onto the edge of the desk. But another Redmond Power, a teacher? Unlikely. It *was* Red, it had to be. Back in Ireland after... what was it? After eighteen years. A lifetime. The letter was still in my slightly trembling hands. I bent my head over it, as though I was reading it, studying it intelligently, but inside I was all over the place, excitement, terror, elation and fear jostled for prominence.

'You can't throw a cat in this country without it landing on some fella you know. We're like toast crumbs, us Irish. We get everywhere. He sounds just the ticket. Fig roll?' Mary placed a mug of tea on the desk in front of me. 'I think today is a three-biscuit kind of day.'

'Does he know it's me?' I said, 'Does he know the name of the school principal here?'

'We can presume so... the department would have given him all the information.' Mary looked at me, puzzled, studying my reaction. 'Nice is he?'

I was being ridiculous. Yes it was a shock but it was such a long time ago, us, the whole thing. We'd both moved on. He was probably married, an array of children. And obviously I had Michael. I'd just have to get on with it.

Redmond Power was real, he *existed*. Not just a figment of my imagination, he was *alive*. The love of my life. Memories flashed into my mind, and I could see him again. I thought I'd forgotten everything, but it was all still there. I had remembered everything.

'Yes, he was nice. The nicest.'

BEFORE

The night before he left for San Francisco, Red was waiting for me on the steps of the bandstand on Dun Laoghaire pier. For a moment, I stood, watching him, as he looked out to sea, deep in thought. Muscular and tanned, his dark black hair cut short, his thick eyebrows, his beautiful brown eyes. I didn't want the world to keep turning, I just wanted to stay like this forever, looking at Redmond Power, with this glorious feeling inside me, my world in blossom. And then he looked up and saw me, his face breaking into the happiest of smiles and the two of us just grinned at each other, and then I began to run towards him, knowing the next thing I would know would be the feel of his chest, the pull of his arms and the sound of his voice. His arms pulling me into him, his kisses. 'I love you,' he would say. 'I love you, Tabitha Thomas.'

3

Behind Mary was the shape of a man coming into focus. 'Mr Power to see you, Tabitha.' Green cotton jacket, smart jeans. I'd read his CV that the department had sent over as though it held secrets or a code to something and then after all these years of not knowing anything and there it was, in black and white, jobs, experiences, volunteering, interests. A whole life. He'd put down Irish poetry and drama and climbing as his interests. The latter must have been a Californian thing. He mentioned some places I'd only half heard of – Yosemite, Sequoia and Joshua Tree. But climbing? I'd tried to imagine this new Red, this climbing Californian Red.

Over the years, it had become increasingly difficult to remember anything, even the colour of his eyes, the shape of his face or his height. But now here he was. Indisputably, unmistakeably Red. I would have recognised him anywhere. Hair greyer, but face the same, though more tanned, slightly lined, but the look in his eyes, the shape of the mouth, his ears! - hadn't changed. More handsome, if that was possible. Being older suited him.

'Hello Tab.'

He was taking me in as much as I was absorbing him, as though we were looking for clues to see what was left of each of us, the selves we had left behind.

His accent a little changed by all those years in America, but the way he said my name. *Tab*. The way he lingered on the 'a', resting on the 'b'. No one else said it like that, they rushed through it.

And more than anything, I found I wanted to touch him, to make sure he was real, if his arms felt as strong as they used to... And to hear him say my name again. *Tab*. In my ear. Just for me. *Tab*.

'Red, great to see you!' I held out my hand, smiling broadly. 'So, you're back...'

He shook my hand, briefly. 'Actually I've been back for six months now,' he said, sounding as nervous as me, which was almost a relief, that he wasn't totally immune to the past, that I wasn't *nothing*.

'Dad... my father's been ill so I came home and... well, decided to stay on for a while.'

His father had practically adopted me as a long-lost daughter 'Christy? How is he?'

'A stroke. He was trying to pretend that he was grand that I needn't come home. He's recovering though. Hobbling around, still doing too much. Organising meetings, shouting at the news, writing his poetry. His usual vices.' And then he smiled at me for the first time. 'On the mend, in other words. I've been bringing him for walks down the pier. Well, *shuffles* along the pier. Takes us an hour just to get to the bandstand.'

For a moment our eyes locked. We used to meet at the bandstand and then walk along the pier, arms wrapped around each other, deep happiness passing back and forth, only needing the other to ignite and spark. He looked away.

'That's good to hear, that he's on the mend.'

'If he stops giving out to the television, it'll do him and his heart the world of good.'

'Just keep him away from politics,' I said. 'Let him watch *Home And Away*...' I paused. 'Is that still on?'

Red smiled. 'I have no idea. It should be, that's all I will say.'

'It's probably gone. Like all my old favourites... Dynasty, Dallas, Dukes of Hazard...' We had immediately fallen back into the way we used to talk to each other. The one thing I had forgotten entirely. We never used to shut up.

'Anything not beginning with D?'

'Falcon Crest?'

He laughed. 'You were never a soap addict.'

'Well, maybe Christy and I should get together and become one. Save both of us.'

He was looking at me, curiously. Was he as surprised as I was? I had imagined far more awkwardness, unresolved anger.

'Would you like to sit down and we... we can go through things?' In a moment, I had changed the mood to polite formality again. Red pulled out the chair in front of my desk, hands folded on his lap. No ring, I noticed. *Not* that it was any of my business. And yet... and yet.

'The department have already interviewed you,' I said. 'So, we don't need to go through your CV...'

'Ten years teaching in elementary school in the US,' he said. 'Drama and English. Once I got my papers, that is. Before then, it was a few years of bar work. There were the obligatory painting and decorating years.' He smiled at me. 'Most of us Irish have those. And the year spent cooking in an Irish bar. Definitely put me off fried breakfasts.'

'What kind of school did you teach in?' I wanted to know everything. Where did he live, did he like it there, was he ever homesick, had Ireland changed much... had he ever thought of us?

'It was in East Bay,' he said. 'Amazing school. I learned more from the pupils than I think I ever taught them.'

'Like what?'

'Life lessons really,' he said. 'About how education is more than just learning, it's about arming yourself for the battle you are going to face when you have no one rooting for you. Nothing we were taught in teaching college.'

'And I thought it was just all about getting the children to be quiet.'

He smiled. 'I learned just how selfless and devoted and determined some mothers are to make sure their kids get to school every single day,' he went on, energised. 'I learned that I had no idea about the world, that living in Ireland had not equipped me for what life is like for all those who scrape by, who are treated as though they don't matter.' He blushed, a little, embarrassed by his enthusiasm.

'Well, I hope Star of the Sea is as rewarding...'

'Thank you.'

Red was looking at the picture of Rosie on my desk. 'Your daughter?'

I nodded. 'That's Rosie.'

'She looks just like you... Like you were... you know...' His words trailed off.

I stood up. 'I think that's everything. Mary has the class list of where they are at, what they've been working on, the names of the girls. Maybe you could have a look at that on the weekend and be ready to start on Monday?'

He nodded. 'Bright and early.' He got to his feet and held out his hand and smiled, as though we'd just concluded any normal meeting. 'Thank you...'

We smiled at each other, as we shook hands briefly.

'It's good to see you,' he said. 'I always wondered...'

For a moment, I couldn't find the words. My throat was dry. Me too, I wanted to say. I always wondered too. 'It's good to see you, Red.'

His hand felt warm and soft and strong and then he dropped mine and was gone.

BEFORE

The two of us, on a trip to the Blasket Islands, off the coast of Kerry. Camping on the mainland and then taking a small boat out, clambering up the rocks. Red shouting out a line by Patrick Kavanagh, one that we'd all learned for the Leaving Cert and all knew by heart. 'O I loved too much and by such and such is happiness thrown away.'

* * *

'You're right, he's very nice.' Mary poked her head round my office door, interrupting my daydream. 'Lovely so he is. We had a great old chat before I brought him in. Such a nice fella. Told me all about living in San Francisco. But you probably heard all the same. That story of being in the White House! Tripping up the steps. Calling Michelle *Michelle* instead of *Mrs* Obama. But naturally she didn't mind.'

'We actually didn't really have time for too much personal chat,' I said. 'You know, all business.'

'Well, time enough for a catch-up,' she said. 'Now, I've just had your mother on the phone.'

'My mother? Why didn't she call me?'

'She said you weren't answering...'

'Phone's on silent, that's why.' I'd turned it off when Red had come in and had forgotten to turn it back on.

'Wants to know about the sale of the Copse. Asked me if it was true.'

'Oh for goodness sake, I had a feeling she knew about it. She shouted something about trees the other morning. There's no secret she won't sniff out. MI5 should employ her.'

'*Secret* isn't in the Dalkey dictionary,' Mary said. 'Anyway, I told her that I'd pass on her message.'

Behind me, Mary's phone beeped. 'Excuse me,' she said, after quickly checking it. 'I have to make a quick call.'

From my window, beyond the hockey pitch, I could see the Copse. The trees were looking lovely at this time of year, all green leaves and squirrels. It would be a shame to see it go but this part of Dublin was pretty leafy. It wasn't as though we were depriving a concrete jungle of its only trees and it wasn't as it if we even used it.

'Tabitha...' Mary had returned. 'Is it all right if I leave early today? Now, if that's all right? I need to get into town. Molesworth Street. The office closes at 3.30 p.m.'

'Yes, of course.' I looked at her, interest piqued. 'That's the passport office, isn't it? Are you going anywhere?'

She didn't say anything for a moment, which was most unlike Mary. 'I'm not sure,' she said, finally. 'But I like to have it ready, you know. Just in case.'

'In case what?'

'In case... in case I have to go away.'

I laughed. 'Mary, you sound very mysterious.' But something in her face made me stop. 'Is everything all right Mary? Nothing's wrong, is it?' If there was a secret, she didn't want to divulge. And teasing wasn't appropriate.

'Nothing... nothing at all. Thank you, Tabitha. I'll see you tomorrow.'

4

In the window of my mother's house – my old home where I'd grown up – there was a sticker. Rather faded now, the yellow and red sticker said, *Atom-kraft? Nein Danke.*

She loved a cause did Nora. There had been the Dunnes Stores Apartheid bananas, the Mullaghmore sit-in, the Dun Laoghaire seafront. But her main place of activism had been a Peace Camp, hours and hours away in West Cork. The Government of the time wanted to build a nuclear fuel reprocessing site in this out-of-the-way beauty spot, a place of heather and gorse and stony fields and breath-taking views. But even though the plans were hastily shelved, the camp took on a different meaning, a nexus for the differently minded, those who weren't interested in following the herd. Nora began taking longer and longer leave from her job, eventually taking an open-ended sabbatical until she was down there pretty much permanently for four or so years. I did go and visit her there once. It was Rosaleen's suggestion. Anyway, I was fresh from my leaving Cert trauma, and at a loose end.

When I eventually got down to Mizen Head, after sixteen hours of travelling, I found it was a long way from the Shangri-La Nora had described in rapturous detail. Cold and muddy, it was far from any kind of romantic reverie. Toddlers and children ran riot, vats of lentils stew bubbled in giant cauldrons, the site hung with washing lines and Buddhist prayer flags. Everything was damp.

But there was singing and blazing bonfires. Nora stood giving a rousing rendition of 'We Shall Overcome', her long hair making her look as though she herself was aflame, her boyfriend Finty's arm slung around her shoulder, ruining the song with his tuneless growl. I never forgot about how my mother looked standing there, in the light of the bonfire. I finally understood what kept her there. She felt alive.

I put my key in the door and pushed my way inside. 'Mum!'

'In here...' Her voice from the front room, her swimsuit drying on the hall radiator. 'Just to warn you,' she said, 'I'm in a comprising position.'

She was on the floor, in some kind of contortion, right leg bent in front of her, the other stretching out behind.

'What on earth are you doing?'

'The pigeon,' she said. 'Or it could be the crow. I can't remember. For my back. Nellie was telling me about it earlier. Gave me a demonstration this morning. Said it has helped hers no end. Swimming is the only thing that loosens it out. But I can't exactly spend my life in the sea.'

'Very impressive. Your penguin. Or whatever it is.'

'*Crow*,' she said, rolling onto her back and hoisting herself up using the sofa as ballast. 'Pigeon. Whatever.'

'You're still pretty limber, Mum,' I said. 'I don't think I would be able to do that.'

'Swimming and cycling,' she said. 'And don't sit down.'

'You're sitting down now.'

'Always on the move, that's me.' She stood up and I followed her into the kitchen. 'Apart from the *brief* moments I sit down.' She turned and gave me a look. 'The sea was like a lake this morning, when I was down there. Nellie Noonan came down. You remember Nellie?'

I nodded.

'We had a good chat... about a few things.' Nora had a funny expression on her face, one I had seen before but couldn't quite place.

'Swimming is like meditating. Without the sitting down.'

'All right, all right, I get it. You're amazing and the rest of us who actually like sitting down and spend entire months on the sofa deserve all the aches and pains we get.'

'It would be good for you, that's all,' she said, 'wash away the cobwebs.'

'That's what Rosaleen used to say.' The two of us instinctively glanced at the framed photograph of Rosaleen on the dresser. 'Anyway, leave my cobwebs alone.'

'Now, how is Rosie getting on? I hope she isn't getting herself into too much of a twist about the exams. I hope you are not telling her they are the be all and end all. I mean, look at me. Not a single qualification to my name. Has it stopped me?'

'I don't think we should hold you up as any kind of trailblazer.'

'Well, you tell her that as soon as those exams are over, I want to take her away. West Cork, I was thinking. My old stomping ground.'

'Stomping?' I laughed. 'Still stomping are you?'

'Ah, you'd be surprised.' And there was that look again. The gleam in her eye.

'How would you get down there?'

'You could drive us?' She smiled sweetly.

'I don't think so... I still have nightmares after the last time I drove you somewhere. You made us listen to Paul Simon all the way down and all the way back. Every time I hear *Me And Julio* I start to feel claustrophobic.'

She wasn't listening but was rooting around in her cupboard. 'Now, you'll be wanting tea, I expect.' She opened a tin. 'I've run out of Barry's but I do have fennel and liquorice. Highly recommended by the lady in the health food shop. Well, until they asked me not to go in anymore...'

'What for?'

'Said I was putting off customers. But it's their fault for using Israeli chick peas. Anyway, let's see... We have Rooibos somewhere...'

'I'll drink whatever.' I had learned not to be too fussy in Nora's house.

Her voice muffled from the dark and dusty recesses of the food cupboard. 'Ah, here it is.' She stood up, holding onto the work surface to help herself up and squinted at the jar, reading the label. 'It's still in date. Just,' she said, filling the kettle. 'I think. Not that I can see a thing, anyway.'

'Put the light on then.'

'No, it's not as simple as that. Although that helps. It's just I'm going a bit blind, that's all,' she said. 'My eyes are getting bad. Can't see as much as I used to. Have to get right in there to get anything. I'm already on the large print books in the library with the pensioners!'

'Mum, you *are* a pensioner,' I reminded her.

'I asked if it was okay to keep cycling and Dr Jones said as long as I don't enter the Tour de France I should be fine.'

'But what is it?'

'They're thinking cataracts. Nothing to worry about. All very operable, they say. If it comes to that.'

'Oh Mum, why didn't you tell me?' It was horrible seeing her get old. In school, when we had been taught about Grace O'Malley, the sixteenth-century pirate queen who sailed the Mayo coast, ruling the waves, I had thought of Nora. *That was it*, I remember thinking, *she's a pirate queen*. And now even Nora was fading, her power slipping away. And I didn't like it.

'Anyway, enough about that, there *is* something I want to talk to you about.' Her eyes had suddenly taken on a gleam. So much for being half-blind, she suddenly looked excited and wholly alive. Now I knew where I'd seen that look before, that sense of purpose. And I knew exactly what she was thinking of. The trees.

'Mum,' I said quickly. 'It's none of your business.'

'Of course it's my business. It's everyone's business. Trees belong to everyone. You know when I was a little girl, we used to play there. And you played there. Remember? And I still know where all the paths are and where the blackberries are and where that itching powder plant is.'

'It's all overgrown now... there's nothing there. Just brambles and nettles. It's of no use to anyone.'

'Nature *belongs* to everyone.'

'We just need a small injection of cash and we have exhausted every other avenue. This seems like an obvious solution. Anyway, who told you?'

'Nellie.'

'And how on earth does she know?'

'She keeps an ear out. You know Nellie...'

'Mum,' I said. 'There's nothing to worry about, okay?'

'So it is true then? You are going to sell it?'

'I told you, nothing's decided. And when it is, you and Nellie will be the first to know. Brian Crowley from the board of governors is coming in to school this week. He says he's found a buyer.'

'Now, I've heard a few things about him...' she started.

'Mum, it's just because he wears a shirt and tie.' Nora was always too quick to judge. She only liked men who wore cardigans, preferably hand-knitted. By themselves. 'Listen, whatever happens, just trust me that it's for the right reasons. And whatever happens is going to be appropriate and sensitive. There's not going to be a housing estate or an industrial park. What would you say if the proposal was for a community centre? You'd like that wouldn't you?'

'I'd prefer the trees,' she said, looking utterly unconvinced.

* * *

That evening, I was foraging in the fridge for dinner. Thank God for eggs, I thought.

'Hi, sweetheart,' I said, hearing Rosie come into the kitchen. 'You're in luck. Banquet time. Oh yes.' I held up the eggs. 'Omelettes!'

'Omelettes!' She looked aghast. 'There's nothing else, is there? You haven't been shopping again. Other mothers are cooking and making everything nice for their daughters doing exams and you, you don't bother...'

'Well...'

'Anyway, I don't like omelettes.' She sounded on the verge of tears.

'Ro, don't tell me you're crying over an *omelette*?' I almost laughed, thinking she might join in and all would be well. But instead, she burst into sobs. 'Rosie,' I said, rushing to her, 'Rosie, what's wrong, sweetheart?' She pushed me away. 'It's an omelette. Only an omelette.'

She tried to speak. 'All the other mums are cooking proper meals,' she said. 'They're all cooking things like spaghetti bolognaise and shepherd's pie.'

'What?' This was becoming a little too dramatic, I thought. Rosie wasn't usually this emotional about food. She had always been relaxed about it, even when she became a vegetarian and, we all got over that shock, it was all pretty easy. We just upped the eggs and the tins of beans.

'And Maeve's mum is working through the Jamie Oliver cookbook for her,' she went on, increasingly agitated. 'They had *koftas* the other night.'

'Koftas? I wished we lived with Maeve's mum. Maybe she could move in with us.' I tried to make her laugh, but she looked away, furious.

'But we don't, do we?' she said, tearfully. 'We don't live with Maeve's mum. We aren't eating koftas. We're having omelettes again because you can't be bothered.'

'Rosie, come on, sweetheart. This is ridiculous. Anyway, you're a *vegetarian*. Koftas are made from lamb. Or chicken,' I said, suddenly doubting myself. 'Or whatever.'

'That's not the point!' And she started to cry again.

'Come here.' For a moment, she stood there, not quite knowing what to do and then she walked towards me and let me put my arms around her and cried into my shoulder. I could feel the tears soaking through my shirt. 'What is it? What's wrong?'

'Nothing. Sorry, Mum.' She lifted her head and wiped her eyes with the heels of her hands.

'It's all right,' I said gently. 'You don't have anything to be sorry about. You're under pressure, that's all, working for your exams.' As soon as I said the word, her faced changed, as though a great shadow passed over her, making her sink further into herself. 'Listen, I know they're awful, but you'll get through them, I know you will. Everything will be fine.'

'Mum... I'm not feeling well.'

'What do you mean?'

'I know I'm not ill, it's not that kind of not feeling well. It's something else. Like my heart is racing or I feel all fluttery inside like there's nothing left of me. Like I'm just empty. Like permanently hungry but nothing makes me feel better.'

'And do you feel like this all the time?' It was just exam stress, I reasoned. Normal exam stress. And it would be over soon. Not long to go. Rosie unpeeled herself from me and went to sit at the kitchen table.

'No, forget I said anything. I'm fine. Just not getting enough sleep. That's all.' Her feet were up on the chair, her knees tucked up against her chest, arms wrapped tightly around them. 'It's just that... it's just...' She rested her head on her knees for a moment, as though exhausted.

'What? Tell me.' I went and sat on the chair next to her and took her hand.

'It wasn't really anything,' she said, lifting her head. Let's just forget it. I just need some sugar. That's all. A Mars bar or something!' She tried to smile. 'And a good night's sleep. That's what you always say, isn't it? I think I'll get an early night tonight. And, Mum?'

'Yes?' I knew what that panic felt like, when you believed you teetered on the brink of annihilation. But you always got through it. And Rosie would too.

'I would love an omelette, if that's okay.'

'After your Mars bar or before?'

'At the same time. Melted on top?'

5

My closest friend, Clodagh Cassidy, is a newsreader and is practically the most famous person in the country. So well-known, that she once forgot her photo ID while taking a Ryanair flight to Paris and they let her on. *I know.*

After dinner, I sat down to watch the news. 'If you were watching last night,' Clodagh was saying on screen, 'then you will have seen our goodbye to Cathal O'Callaghan, who, after thirty-five stalwart years of weather reporting has retired to pursue his other passion, stargazing in Kerry. Well, tonight we welcome Bridget O'Flaherty, who is stepping into Cathal's shoes.'

The camera pulled into a wide shot and a tall woman, long red hair cascading down her back wearing an emerald green body-con dress came on screen. Smiling, Bridget gave a little wave of just her fingers. We hadn't seen the like on Irish television since Riverdance, when everything went a little bit sexy and no one knew what to do with themselves. Except this wasn't a little. This was a lot.

Bridget was now perching herself on the front of Clodagh's desk. 'I'm not literally filling Cathal's shoes!' She laughed. 'I don't do lace-ups. As you can see.' She waggled a sky-scraper patent platform seductively. I detected a slight eye flicker from Clodagh to beyond the camera.

'So, let's get going, shall we?' said Bridget.

The camera went to a close shot of Bridget as she began vaguely gesturing to a blue screen map of the country, but instead of the usual cloud or rain symbols, Ireland was dotted with emojis. Donegal had a thumbs-down on top of it. Galway had a wavy hand. Cork a thumbs-up and Dublin a crying with laughter face.

'So,' she said, 'you all will be wondering if ye'll need jackets tomorrow.' A jacket emoji popped up on screen. 'Well, in Donegal, bring your umbrellas...' Umbrella emoji. '...in Cork pack a jumper...' Jumper. '*And* the sun screen.' Sunglasses sun. Bridget laughed. 'And in Dublin, it's looking to be another gorgeous day!' She smiled for the camera, her head slightly cocked, looking right down the lens. 'So, that's it for this evening,' ended Bridget. 'I'll be back tomorrow.' And she winked.

* * *

By 7.30 p.m., Clodagh was on my doorstep, still in TV make-up, looking like an impossibly glamorous, a hyperreal version of herself. I'd just come down from upstairs after taking Rosie up a cup of herbal tea, which was supposed to be relaxing. And a chocolate biscuit. I suspected that they would count each other out, but Rosie had looked quite pleased with both offerings. 'You didn't *tell* me?' I knew exactly what she was referring to. Red. We'd all been friends at college.

'I've just run into him. In the newsagents. I almost died. He recognised me, despite the fact I have my TV face on. It took me ages to realise who it was. "Red Power," I said. "I thought you were dead."'

'Well, he's not,' I said breezily. 'And he's working in my school.' Just reminding myself of it made it seem strange. As though a unicorn had taken up residence in the garden. 'Are you coming in or just standing there on the doorstep.'

'I'm coming in,' she said, following me into the kitchen. 'You need to tell me everything. For a moment I thought that perhaps he was one of my farmer fans. Come to stalk me.' She sat down at the table and looked at me. 'Jesus Christ, Tab. How could you have not *told* me? How are you *coping*? Are you all right? Have you talked?'

'He only came in today. Starting on Monday...'

'God, *that* must be weird. Is it weird? I mean, on a scale of one to ten, how weird is it?'

'Eleven.'

'You should have told him about it years ago,' she said. 'You should have explained properly. I always said it. And then it wouldn't be weird. It might be nice. Meeting an old boyfriend. Reminisce gently, laugh a little and then move on, slightly nostalgic for the old days but relieved that you didn't end up together.'

'Will you stop projecting? That happened to you, didn't it? Which one was it?'

'Kevin Higgins,' she admitted. 'Met him last week. He should never have carried on playing rugby. His nose has been broken so many times, it's like he's had a potato transplanted on his face.'

'Clodes. Red and I are slightly different to you and Kev.'

'What are you going to do?'

'Nothing. He's only with us until the end of term and then he goes. Wherever. It's a stop gap. It's all fine. Don't panic. Anyway, it was all such a long time ago, wasn't it...? And I have Rosie now to worry about. And Michael.' Even though I hadn't seen him all week.

'Since when have you worried about Michael?'

'Can we change the subject?' I said. 'What about Bridget... she's a breath of fresh air.'

Clodagh rolled her eyes. 'That's the party line, anyway,' she said, gloomily. 'Breath of fresh fecking air. Ten years I've been presenting that programme. Ten years! There was a text surge, whatever that is. Twitter set itself on fire. I mean, we've had no streakers, no protestors, and no on-air nervous breakdown. Apart from my imminent one. Nothing. Until this. A mad woman doing the weather. She's like Dana's deranged lunatic aunt on some kind of sex drug.'

'She'll certainly get people talking,' I said, getting up to fill the kettle. 'Although I imagine that's entirely the point.'

'I mean, for feck's sake,' Clodagh went on, adrenaline taking longer than normal to dissipate. 'Did you see how she was *deliberately* upstaging me? Those shoes. I am surprised that she was able to walk in them.'

'You sound like her mother.'

'Her mother! *She* was sitting beside the camera, the entire time. She's her agent. Apparently, Bridget's an Irish dancer, toured the world with Riverdance...'

'I knew it!'

'Knew what?'

'She looks like a Riverdancer, that's all.'

6

Celia, my mother-in-law, was very much a hostess in the old-school style. She'd been giving dos and dinners since she and Michael Sr were newly-weds and he was an up-and-coming politician. I wasn't particularly looking forward to the pineapple and cheese on sticks or the mushroom vol-au-vents, but she had rung yesterday to make sure we were all still coming and checking that Rosie would be there and that Michael had arrived back from Brussels and he wouldn't be dashing off for some vote or problem, like he always did.

'I *know* politicians,' she reminded me. 'I know what they are like. Michael Sr was exactly the same. He was married to his constituents first and Michael Jr and I second. Oh, I know I go on about the old days,' she said, 'but I think you met a better class of person back then. People showed respect to Michael Sr. Tipping hats, calling him sir. *Listening* to what he had to say. I heard Michael Jr on the radio this morning and I was shocked to hear how disgracefully he was treated. The interviewer – if you can call him that – the interrupter, we shall say, well the interrupter just went on and on, not giving Michael a chance to talk about the Standards in Public Life directive. Which I must say, is a simply wonderful idea. If my Michael can't bring a bit of order to Europe, which is going to the dogs, then I don't know who can. You will be here for 2 p.m., won't you? Now, don't be late. I know timekeeping isn't your strong point, Tabitha.' She sighed as though it was only one in a long list of shortcomings. 'But please make an exception for my sake, will you. People want to see Michael, you know.' And she was gone.

My timekeeping wasn't what I would call an issue, in fact it was me who was standing in the hall today at 1.40 p.m. waiting for Rosie and Michael and looking at the framed photograph of me, Rosaleen and Nora on the hall table. Taken on a long ago trip to West Cork when I was Rosie's age and we're standing in front of Rosaleen's cherry tree in the garden of her family home outside Schull. The tree was her secret spot to get away from the world, she used to tell us, and there was a branch wide enough for her to crawl along and she'd look up into this cherry blossom world. Rosie and Rosaleen would have really liked each other, I thought, not for the first time. They would have got on so well. Rosaleen with her no-nonsense nurturing and Rosie with her lovely sense of humour. Well, her sense of humour that seemed to have disappeared.

'Rosie,' I called up the stairs, 'are you ready?' There was no answer. 'Rosie!' I called again. 'Come on!'

Michael had been in town all morning working – wearing what he deemed his casual clothes, of which there was little discernible difference from his weekday clothes – it was just a suit without a tie.

'Cufflinks!' said Michael. 'I need my cufflinks. You know the ones, my EU flags. People will want to see them.' He stopped for a moment. 'Everyone's always so interested in what goes on in Brussels. It's all anyone wants to talk about. Mammy's made me promise to talk to every- one. I'd better stay off the champers just in case I get some policy wrong and it's in all the papers!' He looked delighted at the thought of being mobbed by Celia's friends, all panting for the ins and outs of the European Parliament. 'Now, I need those cufflinks. People will *expect* them.'

A knock on the front door. 'Lucy!' Michael said, swinging open the door. 'Perfectly on time, as always. It's... exactly... seventeen minutes to two. Just as you said... to the dot!'

'I hope you don't mind, Tabitha,' she said, slightly embarrassed.

'Not at all, Lucy,' I said, 'the more the merrier.' I didn't care if Noel and

Liam Gallagher came along and had a proper fist-fight in the middle of the living room rug, as long as they made the afternoon slip by faster.

'Mammy has been in such a twizzle about the party,' said Michael, 'that she has been on the phone to me and to Lucy about it for weeks. The least Lucy deserves is an invitation.'

'Surely the least she deserves is a day off?' I said.

'What was that?'

'Nothing.

'Well, I bought her something,' said Lucy. 'I hope she'll like it.' She dragged a large present from outside which was beautifully wrapped in flowery paper and adorned with a giant pink bow. 'It's a crystal carriage clock. But Mary said that crystal carriage clocks are straight out of the 1970s.' She looked slightly crest-fallen.

'Lucy, thinking about Celia's décor and the food she serves, I am confident the 1970s is her favourite decade.' I hoped Lucy was going to be luckier buying presents for Celia than I had been over the years. Every posh scented candle, silk scarf, cashmere cardigan, designer *objet*, every single trinket I had ever bought her was usually re-gifted to someone else. One year, she even re-gifted me a rather nice blue cardigan the following Christmas. Hopefully Waterford crystal would be the breakthrough present.

'I do hope so!' said Lucy. 'Mary's always going to Ikea these days, buying trendy bits and bobs. But some people still like the more traditional things. My Mammy does for one. And...' she dropped her voice. 'It's a *second*. It's has a flaw, apparently, in the crystal. But you'd never know. Cost *half* what it should. I do like a bargain and it's *unnoticeable*.'

'She'll love it,' I said. 'And you don't have to tell her it's a second.'

'Have *you* seen my cufflinks?' said Michael to Lucy. 'I had them this week and now...' He began patting himself down in an increasingly frenzied way. 'The ones with the EU flag on. My special ones...'

'Inner pocket of your Louis Copeland?' she said immediately. 'You had them on Thursday when we had the SIPL meeting. With your blue shirt with the thin stripe.'

'Smart girl!' he said, charging up the stairs, meeting Rosie on the way down.

'At last!' I said. 'Come on, sweetheart, what on earth have you been doing up there?' But she looked pale and washed out. 'Are you okay? Are you feeling all right?'

'Yeah,' she said, huffily. 'Can you please stop going on?'

'Stop your fussing, Mammy,' said Michael, drumming down the stairs, twisting in his cufflinks. 'Fuss, fuss, fuss!'

* * *

When I met Michael, for some reason, intentionally or not, he made me laugh. He was earnest and sweet. And well-meaning. And I admired him. A young man standing up for what he believed in and I'd been brought up to value principles and conviction and, although he wasn't like Nora who thought nothing of camping out on a pavement to make a point, in his own way, he was putting himself out there. And more than anything, I wanted to have a baby.

Michael was equally in a hurry to settle down because for a man with serious political ambitions, a wife was an entirely necessary appendage. We weren't much of a success as a couple, even before Rosie arrived, but I hoped I had guaranteed Rosie extra years of happiness by giving her what I had thought was a proper family. But maybe it was perfectly okay to have two parents who were flatmates rather than passionate teammates. I wanted Rosie to have what I didn't. A Dad. A Father. Someone who would love her completely and utterly. I wanted her life to be wonderful. I had thought by staying with Michael, I couldn't fail. But now as I sat in the ministerial car beside my silent daughter, listening to my husband and his secretary chat about meetings and strategies – and all about the powers of milk – as if I wasn't there, I was beginning to wonder. Had it really been the best thing?

* * *

Michael had grown up in the house but for some reason – which I had never quite fathomed – he was never given a key and the four of us, clutching our gifts, smiles plastered to face, stood outside, waiting for Celia.

But it was Imelda Goggins, Celia's best pal, who let us in. School friends and maids of honour at each other's weddings, Celia and Imelda had lived in each other's pockets for the last half a century.

'Michael! How are you?' Imelda pressed her big, powdery face, close to his, kissing him hard on the cheek. 'Oh now, look what I've done.' She wiped her lipstick off his face with her thumb. 'There,' she pronounced. 'Good as new. Now, who do I hand him back to?' She looked enquiringly at me and then at Lucy. 'The wife or the secretary? Who is the power behind the throne? Well, that's what it was like with my Frank. His secretary, long dead now – good riddance – was a battle axe. Wouldn't allow him to do any actual work, waved him off to the golf course every day so she could just get on with things. I was petrified to ring the office for anything because she was always so busy. Frank was simply terrified of her. Just said, yes Enid. No Enid. Is it time for lunch yet? He got all the credit, though.' She then mouthed the next sentence, making no sound at all. 'And the salary.'

And just in time, there was Celia, elbow-barging Imelda out of the way, in a puff of Chanel No 5 and a haze of lilac, arms outstretched. She and Michael embraced in their curiously unaffectionate way, never quite making enough bodily contact for the hug to mean anything.

'And Rosie, darling...' And now it was my turn to be elbowed out of the way as she grabbed her granddaughter and briefly embraced her. 'How are you getting on, hmmm? Working hard? Hmmm? No hard work, no Trinity!'

Rosie opened her mouth to speak but Celia ploughed on.

'Tabitha...' She embraced me, stiffly, entirely without warmth. It was like trying to hug a lamppost. 'You are looking... your usual self. Gardening again?'

'No...' For a moment, I wondered what she meant. 'No, well I was last week... oh...' And then I realised that I was wearing my tweed jacket, which I had thought quite stylish.

'And Lucy,' she said, smoothly turning her attention to Lucy. 'You look marvellous. Such a pretty colour on you.'

'Thank you,' said Lucy, looking a little apologetically at me as the recipient of such obvious favouritism.

'Now... I can see you have your hands full... Imelda, maybe you can help everyone with their packages?' That was our signal to hand them over.

'Happy birthday, Celia.' I passed her the handmade and very expensive leather gloves I had bought from Michael, Rosie and me.

'Well, let's see what this is...' She pulled off the ribbon, opened the slim box and peeled open the tissue. 'Gloves?'

'Italian leather,' I said. 'Feel them.' I'd tried them on in the shop and they felt beautiful to wear. But it looked like I'd failed again.

'Gloves are what my mother always gave the staff for Christmas,' she said, nose wrinkling as she handed the box to Imelda.

Michael bristled beside me. 'But grandmother didn't have staff,' he said. 'She had a cleaning lady if that is what you are referring to?'

It was now all down to Lucy and her Waterford crystal. 'I have a little something,' said Lucy, passing the box to Celia. 'Happy birthday.'

'Oh you darling girl,' she said to Lucy. 'You shouldn't have.'

She really shouldn't have, I thought. But we waited, breath-bated, to see if this was the present which would make Celia happy. She handed the torn paper to Imelda and lifted up the box. 'Waterford Crystal?' she said curiously. 'A carriage clock?' We all waited to hear the result. It was like waiting for Simon Cowell to give his verdict. She pulled it out of the box, examining it with the eye of an expert on the Antiques Roadshow. 'What's this?' she said. 'A flaw. A scratch, here at the bottom.' We all tried to see what she was pointing at. 'Oh my poor dear, they've sold you a flawed piece of crystal. You'll have to take it back.' She passed it to Lucy who was green around the gills. Another failure. Michael gave Lucy a sympathetic look.

'Now, come along. Quickly. My other guests were told to be here for 1.45pm... I always give an early off when I'm giving a little gathering. Little tip for you there Lucy when hosting. Now give me your arm, and you Rosie. And Michael, you must talk to *everyone*. They're all been simply desperate to talk to you about Europe. So many questions! I said I can't possibly answer them all, but Michael will be only too pleased. There's a few policy points that need clarifying, there's the free-range pigs bill. And also, we need to hear all about SIPL... it's such a wonderful initiative. And you mentioned milk on the radio the other morning. The interviewer on *Morning Ireland* was positively cruel not to let you speak. I wrote to the director general. He knows who I am and I told him exactly what I thought about that excuse for a journalist. There are just no standards left anywhere. In public or *private* life.'

* * *

The room was full of Celia's people, friends from her Bridge group, from her previous political life, and neighbours. Moving in a huddle, we entered the living room and although the house was mock-Tudor on the outside, within it was mock-Versailles, all Aubusson rugs and gilt.

'Michael's here!' announced Celia. 'He flew in from Brussels especially!' She beamed at everyone in the room. 'Now, I know you are simply on the edge of your seats, dying to talk to him but no mobbing. We can't have Michaelmania. He is used to soirees in Brussels, so I hope my own, humbler one, does not disappoint.' She smiled, entirely confident that hers wouldn't, *couldn't*. 'Is it a soiree if it's the afternoon?' she went on. 'Hmm, I shall call it my après-midi-ee-ee.' Not sure where to stop, her sentence continued for far longer than it should. 'Is that right, Imelda? You're our Francophile... what with your house in the Languedoc.'

Imelda pushed her way through out little group. 'I think, Celia,' she said, 'that we might call it *un petit rassemblement*. We have friends, neighbours, in France. English they are, but his French is *magnifique*. Retired, but they are great for *parlez*-ing with *les locales*. He – Roger – *Ro-zhay* – likes to have a *rassemblement*. Always invites us he does, says we always make the party. He says it's because we're Irish, but I think it might be something to do with the fact that we always bring *une bouteille* of the finest *Bollinger*.' She pronounced it Boll-ah-zhay.

'Have you brought one today, Imelda?' asked Celia.

'I've bought a case of something else,' said Imelda. 'Just as good!'

'Oh, Imelda,' said Celia, softening, looking touched. 'Six bottles of champagne! You shouldn't have. What is it? Cristal? You know I love Cristal.'

'Oh no, not champagne,' said Imelda. 'I always think it should be drunk in France. It doesn't travel, you see. Just like Guinness. We've brought six bottles of sauvignon *blonh*. From Lidl. It's just so *good* for wine. Or *bon*, as we might say. *Assez remarkable*.' She handed the bottle to Celia. 'Frank's just opened a bottle. Here.'

'Oh so kind.' Celia's smile remained fixed as she took the glass. 'So, so kind. But *you* must drink that, I couldn't bear to think that you would be deprived of the ever-so-special wine that you have brought. You drink your...' She paused, nose wrinkled. 'Your *Lidl* wine.'

Imelda sniffed it as though she was a professional, swirled it around the glass and then sipped, closing her eyes with orgasmic ecstasy as it slipped down her throat. 'Delicious,' she murmured, determinedly smiling at Celia before Celia walked away, ready to introduce Michael and Lucy to European parliament groupies.

Imelda engaged me and Rosie in conversation. 'Celia's just furious that my Frank is still alive,' she said. 'She would prefer it if he was as dead as a doornail just like Michael Sr. Always so jealous.' How this friendship had survived five decades of sniping and snippiness, I had no idea. 'It was Frank's idea to buy in France and it's *assez bon* and everything, very *French*, but it's not home, is it? The weather's too good for one thing and tea doesn't taste the same. It's either the milk or the water, I can't work it out. But Frank likes the supermarkets over there. Wouldn't be caught dead in one here. But in France, it's a different story. Spends hours in the wine departments. His happy place, he says.'

I wondered whether I should start drinking copiously. 'Now, Rosie,' Imelda went on, 'how are you getting on with the Leaving? Your grandmother says you're on your way to Trinity. Now, that takes hard work. Ask my granddaughter Pippa. Such a clever girl. Was all set to do medicine in Trinity. Takes after my side of the family. Daddy was a doctor, you see. And then at the last moment changed her mind. There was nothing we could do to dissuade her. We all tried. Journalism, she wanted to do. Heart set on it. Decided that she took after her mother's side of the family. The grandfather was a newsagent, would you know?' She wrinkled her nose. 'A newsagent! Anyway, must dash, Frank has an empty glass and that can really upset him.'

I felt Frank's pain, I really did.

* * *

Michael had either been cornered by or had cornered a guest, his voice carrying across the room. 'Well, it's very interesting the way they do it,' he said. 'Everyone has their own pair of headphones...'

'Would you like another drink Rosie?' I said. 'More squash? Orange barley water?' We had spent the previous hour chatting to various guests, most of which were actually very nice, and we'd found each other again beside the buffet. 'Smoked salmon pinwheel thing? Cheese and pineapple on a stick?'

'Mum, I really want to go home.'

'I don't think Celia would let us,' I said. 'There's a special lock on the front door and the whole house is charged with electricity, that if you try to leave then you will be tasered into submission...' I had stayed off the wine, part from one glass of Imelda delicious wine.

'Mum, please...'

'Is it because everyone is talking to you about the exams? People are so awful, aren't they? I really wish there was another topic of conversation...

But Rosie just stood there, staring at the carpet.

'You two!' Lucy joined us, a glass of white wine in her hand. 'Isn't this party lovely?'

'Really lovely!' I lied.

'How are you getting on with the Leaving?' asked Lucy, turning to Rosie. 'Michael, I mean Mr Fogarty, your father, says you have your nose in your books all the time.'

Rosie didn't even smile.

'It's a terror all right,' went on Lucy, undeterred. 'I don't think I've ever been so stressed in all my life. Well, apart from that time that Mammy went to Lourdes and left me in charge and we had that leak and... well, let's just say, she wasn't best pleased. And the other time, I dented her new Punto. But the Leaving... I don't think I saw sunlight for six months what with all the revising.'

'Were you always interested in politics, Lucy?' I said, in an attempt to get her off Leaving Cert horror stories – which any Irish person, given half a chance, was only too willing to share, the trauma was so deeply rooted. Rosie slipped away from us.

'Always,' said Lucy. 'I managed to get myself a job with our local politician... well, he was just a local councillor then. I went off to college and he got elected to parliament and four years later he asked me if I wanted a permanent job. Mammy wasn't keen. It had been hard enough to persuade her to let me live in Dublin during term time and not take the bus every day.'

'But you're from Cavan.'

'Mammy said it would give me time to study...'

'Your boyfriend, Lucy, where is he based?' I was desperate to get the subject off exams and grasped at something, anything. Lucy looked blank. 'Your boyfriend? Michael said you had a boyfriend...'

'Oh him! Well, he's... well, it's hard to say. He's so busy.'

'What's his name?'

'Whose?'

'Your boyfriend's?'

'Septimus,' she said quickly.

'Septimus?'

'Yes...' She hesitated slightly. 'It's a... it's a lovely name, isn't it, a *really* lovely name?'

My nod was inconclusive. 'So where does... *Septimus* work?'

'Brussels. Yes, Brussels. He's just like me, one of the parliamentary secretaries for the EU. Agriculture. That's it. He tries to fly home to Ireland on a Friday night but he can't always make it.'

'And do you... do you live together?' I was beginning to have my doubts that this Septimus existed. Surely she wasn't making it up? Maybe... no. Surely not. Could she and Michael? No. He was too straight. But... I shook the idea out of my mind. He was all about standards. The standards in public life. He just *wouldn't* have an affair.

Lucy was chatting away, warming to her theme of this (fictitious?) boyfriend. 'Oh, we don't live together. Mammy'd have a fit! He, I mean, *Septimus*, has his own flat and I have mine. But then I am often away on the weekend, doing... my own work. We are both married to our jobs. Anyway, I should stay off this...' She waggled her wine glass. 'The flight is at 8 a.m.'

'Flight?'

'Vancouver,' she said, looking surprised. 'Didn't Michael tell you? It's a week-long trade mission.'

'Great.' I fixed a smile on my face. Michael never told me anything. He used to bother, out of courtesy, saying where he was and when he would be back. 'Canada should be lovely,' I said. 'How lucky you are.'

'Oh, but it's not a holiday,' she said. 'It's work, just thousands of miles away. We don't stop. It's just a quick sandwich if we are lucky. No sightseeing. You see, when the taxpayer is footing the bill, you have to be transparent.'

'Ethics, I suppose. You don't want to be caught out. What with the standards in public life thing.'

Across the room, we tuned into Michael's voice. 'Milk,' he was saying to one of Celia's bridge group, who was looking as interested as possible. 'Milk is my next thing. I think I've spotted something in milk...'

The woman drained her glass of wine.

On our side of the room, I turned back to Lucy. 'By the way,' she said. 'I was going to ask if you thought there was anything strange going on with Mary?'

There was actually. 'Why?'

'Well, we think, well, her Mammy and my Mammy think she is hiding something. The last few times she's been up, according to my mammy who heard from hers, she wasn't at all herself, at all, at all, according to Mammy. All distracted she was. Spent ages on the phone apparently. Had to go up the back field to get a signal. And then came back and her hands were shaking and she was all quiet. Spilt her tea on her saucer. And during *Winning Streak*, she didn't seem in the bit involved. Didn't shout out the answers or anything. Like she was in another world.'

'Does she usually?' I'd noticed that certain distractedness in Mary. Nothing hugely of note but enough. She seemed to drift off into her own thoughts far more than I'd ever noticed before. Staring into space and then having to force herself back into the present.

'Oh yes. Mary's the brainbox of the family. She was all A's in her Leaving, I can tell you. Could have done anything with her life. Well, her mammy wanted her to be a nun, thought then she could go and teach, you know? A good life, she said. You never had to worry about where to live or... or *men* or anything like that. But that's exactly what did happen, you see. She got herself involved with some man, you know, *before*. This is years ago now. I was still in school, thirteen or so, and Mary maybe she was eighteen or nineteen. But anyway, she was all set to join the Sisters of Charity, you know because her mammy had sent off for the application and Mary had gone to the orientation day and everything. But! At the very last minute, just when her bag was packed and in the hall by the front door, rosary beads bought, she ran off to London. Just like that. With a *man*.'

'A man!' Despite my feelings of terrible betrayal by gossiping about Mary, I was listening intently. 'But she's gay.'

'I know. But then, she wasn't. That came later.' She lowered her voice. 'He could have been *anyone*. So she disappeared and then a couple of weeks later, a postcard from Kentish Town. Her own mother was fit to be tied. Had to have a nip of whiskey before she was able to speak again.'

'Thank God she didn't join the nuns,' I said. '*That* was a lucky escape.'

'But instead,' picked up Lucy, 'she turned out to be... gay. Not that there is anything wrong with that but it took some getting used to. Her mother says nothing could surprise her about Mary. If she came home next with her head shaved and the Pope himself on her arm, she says she wouldn't be shocked. Far more understanding than my mammy would be, I can tell you.'

Behind me Rosie was tugging at my shirt.

'Mum...' There were tears in her eyes, all the colour had drained out of her face. 'Mum... I can't breathe...'

'Rosie?' Grabbing her by her arms, as though I thought she was going to collapse, I looked into her eyes. Panic. Fear. She desperately heaving and wheezing. 'Breathe in and breathe out, that's it, okay, that's it. Breathe in. Out.'

Michael was beside us, his hand on Rosie's back, he looked scared. 'What's going on?'

Behind him, the party had ground to a halt, Celia's face was a mixture of interest and irritation.

'Panic attack,' I said. 'I think. Now, Rosie, that's it, sweetheart.' For a moment I wasn't sure if she would start to breathe again normally, she was gasping and struggling for breath, my thoughts spiralling into visions of ambulances and hospitals. *Come on, Rosie.* But then she took a big gulp of air, and then another and then another and then a deeper one. Her eyes were filled with tears.

'Oh Mum,' she said, her hands to her face.

'It's okay, it's okay...' I soothed. 'We're going to go home, all right.'

'There!' said Michael. 'Back to normal. Everything's fine! Sorry about that, folks,' he said to the upturned faces. 'Just exam stress! We all know how it is.'

There were nods and knowing smiles, but I glared at him. This wasn't exam stress. People didn't have full-on panic attacks because of stress. Maybe it was the heat of the room, the incessant small talk, the cheese and pineapple on sticks... or maybe this was something far more serious.

'Rosie.' Her eyes were closed, she was folded into herself, arms around her knees. 'Rosie.' I tucked her hair behind her ear.

'I'm all right.' Her voice was tiny. 'I'm all right.' Her breathing was back to normal.

Michael was busy taking charge. 'Lucy! Call a taxi. Imelda, get Rosie's jacket'

Celia was aghast. 'Michael,' she said, 'I really don't think such a fuss needs to be made. A glass of water, a turn in the garden... surely...'

Michael ignored her and turned to me. 'I'll come home too. So will Lucy.'

'No, it's fine,' I said, firmly, knowing it would be much easier to care for Rosie on my own. 'I'll call you in an hour and let you know how Rosie is.'

'You stay, Dad,' said Rosie. 'You stay. Please. I'll be fine, I promise. And I am so sorry for spoiling the party...'

'You didn't,' said Michael and I at exactly the same time and we half-smiled at each other. He wasn't a great husband or life partner, that was true, but he wasn't a bad father. He loved Rosie, in his own way, and that was all you could ask, really.

'Are you sure, Rosie?' He patted her on the shoulder. 'You will call me, won't you?'

Rosie and I nodded, both anxious to get out of there with as little continuing fuss as possible. 'A taxi might be quicker than the car,' he said. 'I'd better stop Lucy from calling Terry. He'll be having his lunch.' He darted off just as Celia bent down.

'Rosie, my dear girl,' she said. 'What on earth was all that about? It looked like histrionics to me and it's important to regulate one's emotions. You're not that kind of girl, Rosie. You've never been one for crying and attention grabbing.'

'Celia!' I said, furiously. 'Can you just be sympathetic for one moment, please?'

'But I am!' Celia looked offended. 'I am giving Rosie some life advice. Always important to learn from any situation.'

'Mum, it's fine,' said Rosie. 'Grandma was just, you know, doing her best.'

'Exactly,' said Celia, giving me a look. 'Now, you know I don't see any point, whatsoever, in not speaking clearly and communicating one's thoughts and I do think it is important that my granddaughter learns when and how to have histrionics. I mean,' she glanced to see if her son was nearby, 'when I first heard that Michael Sr was *carrying on*, I did the same as Rosie. It didn't get me anywhere. Just added to my upset. Losing control is a complete waste of time. As my granddaughter, Rosie is made of strong stuff. Isn't that right, Rosie?'

'Yes, Grandma.'

'But...' I began but Rosie gave me a quick look and I let it go. For her sake.

'Rosie just needs a lie-down,' said Celia. 'Just a rest in a darkened room, aren't I right, dear? And a good night's sleep. Early to bed. Not staying up, gassing to your pals on the phone. I will call you later to see how you're getting on. And remember. Emotions. Keep them in check.'

'Thanks, Grandma. I will, Grandma.'

Michael called from across the room. 'Taxi's arrived.' Thank Christ, I thought. Any longer and I would have strangled Celia and shown her exactly what I looked like when my emotions were let loose.

Michael and I jostled with each other as we both tried to help Rosie on with her coat and be the one she leaned on as we walked to the car.

'Mum, Dad, I'm fine,' she insisted, trying to wriggle free.

'I know you are,' I said, equally firmly, but refused to let go.

Lucy pressed something into Rosie's hand. 'Rescue Remedy,' she said. 'It really works. I swear by it. Always helps with nerves and stress.'

'Thanks Lucy,' I said, thinking it would take more than a titchy bottle of something to sort out whatever was going on.

* * *

Back at home, Rosie put her head in her hands. 'Oh my God. I'm *so* embarrassed.'

'Has that happened to you before?'

'No,' she said quickly. 'Anyway, it was nothing.'

'Nothing? That wasn't nothing.'

She shrugged. 'Mum, people get stressed all the time. I've never had one of *those* before and I'm not going to have one again. Anyway, I just felt like I couldn't breathe for, like, a second. Maybe I'm allergic to pineapple. People are you know.'

'But Rosie... that looked like a panic attack.'

'It was just the exam talk. That's all anyone wants to talk to me about these days. It's as though for this entire year, that's all I'm defined by. Everyone else is hysterical about it, and I'm the one doing it. As though the Leaving Cert is a spectator sport for people.'

'Rosie, not everyone is having panic attacks. Yes, exams are stressful but this isn't quite normal...'

'Thanks a lot! Now I'm not normal. Thanks for your sympathy. Grandma was nicer to me. She was practical at least. But you're just saying I'm not normal! Why can't you just be nice? And stop trying to take control of everything. That's your problem, you don't like it when people don't do what you say...'

I was silent for a moment, wondering how to respond. 'I was just trying to say, you are not alone. I'm here. And I promise to be nice and not controlling. And you are normal. But panic attacks aren't. You are. But they're not. Do you see?'

'But I am alone,' she said, quietly. 'Mum, can we not talk about it? I'm fine. I just made a total fool of myself, that's all. I'll call Grandma and say sorry. Again.' She gave me one of her beautiful smiles. 'Mum, honestly. It's fine. Stop fussing, will you. There's *nothing* wrong! Now, I'm going to bed to get a good night's sleep, just like Grandma suggested. Now *good* night!'

She left me believing that this wasn't the end of the matter. And however much she wanted to brush things under the carpet, there was something seriously wrong. But I couldn't work out what. She was studying. She was bright. She would be okay. And she would be in college by September. What was wrong?

7

The drama and worry were such that I'd actually forgotten that Red was starting on the Monday morning but as I drove towards school, I saw him, ahead on the pavement, it all came back to me. Red was starting today.

I had drawn level with him and, for a moment, my foot hovered on the accelerator pedal. I could just drive off, pretend not to have seen him. And shaken these feelings out of me. Maybe I was feeling unsettled because of Rosie. I was worried, that was all. And my period was probably on its way. I just needed a bar of Dairy Milk and all would be well. Rosie *would* be okay. She was a bright, capable girl. Just sensitive. And what lovely, young seventeen-year-old wasn't? But as I glanced at him, he looked up and saw me, hand lifted in acknowledgment and I had no choice but to stop. Heart pumping, I rolled down the window and arranged my face into pleasant neutrality.

'No car?' I called out.

He shook his head. 'Not this morning, no,' he said, leaning into the window, smiling. 'The walk is doing me good.'

Oh Red, I thought. *Just get in the car and I'll tell you everything. Everything. And you might forgive me. You might not. I just want to tell you why I didn't get on that plane. And why I didn't answer your calls or explain anything to Christy when you sent him to talk to me.*

'Fresh air?' I asked.

So many times, I wondered what would have happened had I got on that flight, explained everything.

'Headspace,' he said. 'I'm feeling nervous.' He grinned. He didn't look particularly nervous. Red was always so supremely confident. The one thing, which made me feel better back then, was that Red was strong. He'd be all right.

'What on earth for?'

'You know, new school, new pupils to impress. New teachers to talk to in the staff room,' he said. 'That kind of thing. Like will my new colleagues find my break-time banter annoying or amusing? Will my briefcase be an object of ridicule?'

'Object of ridicule,' I said. 'Definitely.' He laughed and I watched his face for a moment and wondered what he really thought of me. Was he being polite? Had he decided to just pretend nothing had happened? How did he feel about me? Did he feel anything? 'And the staff are going to love you. Only man and everything. They are going to be delighted with you.'

'I need a beard,' he said. 'I was shaving this morning and I thought, there is something missing. I don't look teachery enough. What was it? A cord jacket? A cocktail of chalk dust and dandruff on my shoulders. No! A beard. I need a beard.'

'Look at me!' I said. 'I look like I'm going to a fancy dress party as a teacher. I couldn't be more of a cliché. Smart, poly-mix, inoffensive pastel-coloured jacket. Enough unnatural fibres to withstand a nuclear attack or, at least, life in a school.' I was enjoying myself. Too much. *Drive on, Tabitha*, I ordered myself, sensibly. *Drive on and stop thinking about him. This won't come to anything and the last thing you need is to start pining for your long lost love and a rekindled romance. You are a grown-up*, my inner voice said. *Act like one.* But it was almost like a physical pain, a longing. A visceral need, an ache that would only be soothed and quenched by being right there, like I used to be, pressed up against him. It was a physical force. Was it seeing him walking that had triggered this? Before I had only felt awkwardness, but seeing him with his hair curling over his collar, his sleeves rolled to his elbows. And how happy he looked. I wanted it. I wanted to be part of his world and I wanted him to be part of mine.

'Would you like a lift?' That was me, out loud.

'No,' he said, pulling back a little. 'No thanks.' 'I'll keep walking.'

'Yes, yes of course. Well, see you in school, Red. Goodbye.' And primly, like the good head teacher I was, I drove away. A great crush of disappointment, like I'd embarrassed myself, dared to imagine, to fantasise, hanging over me. I felt like a fool.

BEFORE

It was the morning of Rosaleen's funeral and I went down at dawn for a swim in the Forty Foot. I hadn't slept at all, not really, and had just been waiting for the light to creep into the world before grabbing my towel and cycling down.

It was so early I was the only person there and the sky was still grey and cold and I shivered as I slipped off my dress and jumper and took off my shoes and stepped into the freezing water.

Rosaleen. Rosaleen. I still couldn't believe that she was gone after those weeks of illness. I had thought every single day that this was the day she would get better, start getting her energy back, but when they told me that she had cancer and that there was nothing they could do about it, I still couldn't grasp it.

Red had phoned the night before from a public phone box.

'I wish I could be there with you,' he said. 'I can't believe you are going through it on your own.' He told me that his dad was going to come to the funeral. But the cost of a flight for Red was utterly prohibitive. Not when I was going to see him a mere three weeks later.

'I'll be waiting for you,' he said.

'I can't wait to see you,' I said. 'I just want to get away. And anyway, there's something I want to tell you...' The pips were going. We had seconds left. 'I love you,' I said.

'I love you too.'

The water was around my ankles and I could see my feet all blurry below the water. And then in I plunged, swimming down towards the bottom and then slowly, gracefully, resurfacing. I flipped over onto my back and looked at the sky, my secret inside me.

8

'Not too early I hope!' A booming voice and figure filled my office.

'Hello, Brian,' I said, shaking his hand. It felt strangely small compared to the usual male handshakes I was used to – the bone-crushers, the power-shake double-hand. With him it was like shaking the hand of a small child. Strangely disproportionate, the voluminous body and the petite hand. 'Not at all.' He was five minutes early. 'Won't you sit down?'

His face was rather fleshy, bulbous really. And he was permanently flushed. He sat down and leant back on the chair, his striped shirt slightly straining over his well-fed paunch. His tiny, beady eyes were following me intently. But he began with pleasantries. 'Do you golf, Ms Thomas?'

'Golf?' I almost laughed.

'I thought all you ladies golfed these days.'

Over the months, I'd learned that all conversations with Brian were a bit surreal. Nothing was simple with him and had realised, for sanity saving purposes, that the only thing to do was run with it. 'Oh no. I don't *sport* actually. I walk the pier, but I suspect that does not qualify as activity. And what about you Brian, do you *golf*?'

'Rugby's my game,' he said. 'Played for my school, was quite the effective front half, if I may say so myself. Scored a few tries that made the old man proud. Was on the school's team, you know. The '81 team.

We won the schools cup that year.' He shrugged modestly. 'That's the downside of having a daughter. Petula shows no interest in rugby, despite my best efforts. She's more interested in horses. Obsessed with them she is. Can't see the appeal myself. No, I stick to Rugby. A rather vocal spectator. Got myself a nice little ten-year ticket. Don't miss a game. Home or away.'

'Yes, the locations of the away matches would almost make me go,' I said. 'Rome. Paris... Cardiff...'

'Does your husband follow the rugby?' he asked. 'I've never seen him at any of the corporate events. Most of the local politicians are there, but maybe soccer's his game?'

'Michael's sport is scrabble,' I said. 'He was pretty good at it. Captained the school scrabble team and I think they even made it to the Leinster finals.'

Brian looked puzzled. '*Scrabble?* As in the word game?'

'Or was it Rummikub? I never can remember. Now, to business. Shall we get down to it?'

He smiled at me, showing his teeth, again, tiny little things, making him look like a crocodile eyeing a pelican. 'Now I really believe that what we are hoping to achieve with the land is something quite remarkable.'

'In what way?'

'Well, it's a mutually beneficial transaction. I liked what Sister... Sister... Whatshername... Kevin?'

'Kennedy.'

'I liked what Sister *Kennedy* called it. A Good Samaritan. As I said on the phone, I have found one. Him. A corporate Good Samaritan...'

'Is that not oxymoronic?' I said, smiling.

'There is nothing moronic about this plan, nothing at all,' he said, defensively. 'Are you...?' He eyed me carefully. 'Are you familiar with the corporate world, Ms Thomas?'

'Not particularly,' I said. 'I'm mean I'm aware it *exists*.'

'Well,' he smiled indulgently at me, 'it's about deals. The art of the deal, heard of that?'

I nodded. 'Vaguely.'

'So, he gives the school – us – the money and we give him a tiny little piece of land. It's worthless really. Hard to develop. He may or may not be able to build on it. But the point is, he wants to give back.'

'Well, you don't just give money for nothing. Take the opera for example. Say I'm a bank. Do I just give money to some piddling little opera company and get nothing back? Or do I give some cash to the aforementioned piddling operatics in exchange for something?'

'Ummm....'

'Exactly! I get something back. Tickets, nice seats for Beethoven or what have you. Or the bank's name on the programme. There's always something in return. And it's nice to have a box at the opera or your name saying how generous you are. It creates good feeling. Are you with me?'

'I think so.'

'What if you are a charity... do I just give you money no questions asked because I am a good and kind and nice bank?'

'You might...'

'No... I won't. Because I'll need something back for the taxman. I need a thank you. My name in the paper saying I gave x amount of yo-yos. Catch my drift?'

'Not really.'

'Say you're a school,' he was now speaking with exaggerated slowness.

'We are.'

'Great! Perfect. Well, I'm a developer and I want to give you money because I'm a good person. Do I just give you the money?'

'Yes?'

'No! I give you the money, but you give me something in exchange.'

'Like a plot of land?'

'Like a worthless, rocky, brambly plot of land.'

'Brian, if he was to build on it, would we have a say how the land was to be used? A community centre, I was thinking... or perhaps an elderly person's drop-in place...'

'Well, I am sure our GS, as I like to think of him, would be open to suggestions like that.'

Was this all BS rather than GS, I wondered. But land did get sold. In fact, years ago, some of the school was sold to developers and a housing estate, where many of our pupils lived, was built. There was precedence.

'Tabitha, I think we should call another meeting of the board of governors and we can then take a vote. I have a feeling that it might make sense to *them*,' he said, implying it was my lack or intelligence that was leading to my slightly muted reaction.

'Who is this man?'

'Our Good Samaritan? Freddie Boyle is his name. I've been looking into his background and asking a few of my contacts, and he's entirely kosher. Made a mint and now wants to give back. Make sure St Paul waves him through when it comes to his turn. Or maybe he's just got a heart of gold. He's going to give us 20,000 notes, no questions asked. The land is worth half, if that.'

'I think I might just get some advice... Ask an estate agent to come round.'

Brian looked hurt, crestfallen even. 'An estate agent... but...' His bottom lip stuck out. 'I thought I was looking after this for the school... I wanted to do this for the Star of the Sea, for Dalkey. I really believe with this project that we are giving back, you know? I'm all about the giving back. Anyway, it's not about selling the land for the highest price, we probably could get a better price. Some fool estate agent would convince you that it was worth ten times the price, but they'd be wrong. There's so much granite in there and it's such an awkward site. So that's why this Freddie is such a good fit for us...'

'Maybe...' I tried to think clearly. 'Would there be a contract that we could sign, stating all this.'

'Think, Tabitha,' he commanded. 'Think of the smiling faces of the little children glowing in the collective light of 100 iPads. Think of all that learning that is contained in a tiny computer. Like a million books all folded up and squashed inside, all ready for the pupils of Star of the Sea to read. Rest your mind on that image, Tabitha. And we'll see what Sister... Sister Thingy and the other ones have to say.'

'Sister Kennedy,' I reminded him. 'And Noleen Norris and Brendan Doherty,'

'Indeed.' The crocodile smile again. 'But personally, I think it is the best action for the school going forward and I am delighted, in my humble way, to be part of it.' He stood up and saluted me, his little child's hand flicked his forehead. 'Roger and out.'

'Roger,' I found myself repeating. But just then, there was a noise from outside, a chanting from somewhere.

'Oi, teacher, leave those trees alone!'

From my window I could see a small group of people were holding placards: Save Our Trees, Squatters Rights For Squirrels and Developers Deliver Doom. A scraggly, ragtag band of people, they were. I peered closer. Ah! There was Nellie Noonan, Nora's friend from swimming; there was a youngish man with dreadlocks and an old fleece; an older, bearded chap, with tiny glasses, wizened in stature and dressed professorially in a shabby brown suit; and a young woman dressed in a flowery dress, an old man's cardigan and a shaved head. And finally, there was an older woman with long hair and a scraggly Barbour. My mother.

'Oi teacher, leave those trees alone... Oi teacher, leave those trees alone.'

What fresh hell was this?

* * *

My mother. My mother!

I marched out, furious. They all turned to watch me storming over and their chanting petered out and then Nora began again and they picked up their shout.

'Oi, teacher...'

I fumed, as I speed-walked towards them. Was there *nothing* my mother wouldn't do? I'd told her to keep her nose out. And there she was, eyes gleaming. She had scented something. A protest. Her favourite thing in the world. A couple of picnic chairs had been set out and there was a small blue gas stove where a kettle was boiling away. They looked like they were settling in for the long haul.

Hands on my hips, I stood in front of them, as they looked at me expectantly, pleasantly even.

'What the hell do you think you are doing?' I hissed at Nora. 'This is just another of your protests... whales, salmon, nuclear weapons. All your various bandwagons. And now this! A tiny plot of land which is of no value to anyone. Except us. We might be able to get something from this. Something for the school. How could you? How could you embarrass me like this?'

She smiled at me. 'Tabitha,' she said, patiently. 'It's not personal. But we have a moral obligation to protest.'

'Who's we?'

'Us.' She nodded at the group. 'The Dalkey Wildlife Defenders.'

They all nodded, one or two gave me a little wave.

'Nellie and I played in the Copse as children and this is a matter we can't let go. It's not against you and your decisions. It's about trees being in peril and when they are, we have to act. It's what we do.' She smiled at me as though that was all that needed to be said, and I would walk away fully accepting her need to protest.

Oh no. Oh no, she wouldn't do this to me. She had spent her life, swanning about saving the habitats of geese or snails in sand dunes or on that bloody peace camp. She wasn't going to do this here. And now. With me.

'Mum, there is no peril,' I insisted, vaguely considering the alternative nostril breathing technique that Clodagh had demonstrated to keep calm. 'We are going to have a say in how the land is used, going forwards. I have suggested a community centre and they will take our considerations fully into the plans.'

Nora just looked at me. 'That's what they all say,' she said, turning to the older, bearded man. 'Don't they, Arthur?'

He nodded. 'We don't tend to believe the word of developers,' he said, politely. 'As a rule. Telling the truth is not in their interests.'

'Now, please. All of you. Go home. There is nothing to protest about and you are all, frankly, wasting your time.'

'Kettle's boiled!' said a voice behind Nora. All this time, Nellie had been blithely making a pot of tea in an old enamel teapot. 'Hello Tabitha,' she said cheerily as if this was nothing more than an enjoyable picnic. 'Join us for a brew? I've got some nice fruit cake.'

The older man, Arthur, cleared his throat and stepped forward. 'With respect, Ms Thomas, we are going to protest until the land remains under the protectorate of the school. As it has, for the last 300 years. And I hope you don't mind,' he went on politely, 'we're going to exercise our democratic right to protest. We won't be in your way, but we'll just be here until we can be sure that the safety and future of Dalkey greenery is assured. One felled tree is one too many.'

From the yard, I heard the bell go for break time and the immediate hysteria of children's voices racing out into the sunshine.

'Mum...' I said, fixing her with my beadiest eye. 'Go home.'

'We are here in support of the trees and wildlife.' Her fellow protestors all nodded in agreement. 'Nature has no voice that we can hear, so the Dalkey Wildlife Defenders will remain here until the Copse is safe from the developers. Now, let me introduce you to everyone. You know Nellie.' Nellie waved her tin cup at me. 'And this is Arthur. A veteran of these protests, just like me and Nellie.'

'Arthur Fitzgerald,' he said, holding out his hand, which I had no choice but to take. 'Doctor of Geology. University College Dublin. Retired. But not retired activist... this is something you never retire from.'

'The fire never goes out,' agreed Nora. 'And this is Robbo Cunningham.' She gestured towards the dreadlocked man who nimbly stepped over the kettle on the gas stove to shake my hand.

'Pleased to meet you,' he said, politely. 'I may not have been at Mizen Head or Mullaghmore, but I like to think I play my part in the good fight. Fracking is my thing but anything environmental, really.'

'And last,' said Nora, 'but not least is Leaf.'

'Just Leaf,' said the young woman in the man's cardigan, shaking my hand. 'I don't do surnames. Leaf is not my given name, though,' she explained. 'That's Sinead. I think I'm more a Leaf than a Sinead, don't you? I never felt right being Sinead, you know, like I was born with the wrong name. But as soon as I decided I was a Leaf, I felt totally different about myself. Like I had found *me*.'

Arthur had piped up and we all turned to listen. 'I remember when we were at Mullaghmore, the ancient stones of the Burren in the county of Clare,' he said. 'Nora, you were there, and Nellie. Well, it was over twenty years ago now and the council wanted to build a huge coach park right beside the stones. Well, that couldn't be right, not at all. And as they wouldn't give in or come to some agreement after the letters I wrote... well, we had to dig in.' He gave a chuckle. 'Well, we didn't actually dig in. That's what the council wanted to do. The digging was what we wanted to avoid. Isn't that right, Nora?'

'How could I forget, Arthur? You facing down the bulldozer. Nellie sitting on top of the stones.'

Nellie nodded happily. 'I nearly fell off,' she said. 'Several times. But there was no way that bulldozer was coming anywhere near us. We were younger then...'

'Okay,' I said, keen to put an end to this trip down memory lane and get back to the matter at hand, i.e., moving the protestors on. 'What if we ran a school-wide project on the trees and wildlife as a learning experience for the children? I just know how much they would gain from that. We will also promise to plant more trees on the school grounds. Recreate the Copse. And anyway, we may not even sell it. The board might not pass it. So, why don't you go home and I will keep you all fully informed about the situation.' I looked at them. 'Okay?'

But no one seemed to be listening particularly. Arthur was nodding away pleasantly. Nora was fiddling with her coat buttons. Nellie was digging through her handbag on the ground next to her. Leaf was stretching her neck out and it was only Robbo who seemed to paying any real attention.

'We're not going,' he said. 'I'm so sorry, Ms Thomas. We don't want to inconvenience you or the children. But we can't go.'

'Why not?'

'We can't abandon the trees to an unknown fate, Tabitha,' joined in Arthur, patiently. 'They've all been here longer than we have. They are wiser and stronger than anyone of us, yet they are defenceless against the chainsaw.'

'We're staying,' said Nora. 'Aren't we, Nellie?'

'Oh yes,' said Nellie. 'I've got my hot water bottle just in case it turns a bit nippy. We're used to a sit-in.'

'So, we're not going anywhere,' Nora reiterated.

'Right...' I stood there, not knowing what to do. 'But I would really like it if you would.'

They all shook their heads. 'Sorry,' said Robbo. 'We can't. Even if we wanted to.'

'We are beholden to stay,' explained Leaf. 'It's what we have signed up for. Saving the natural world from evil.'

'Evil is slightly strong...' I looked at them all. 'Please?'

'Sorry, Tabitha. We'll be here for as long as it takes.'

And there was nothing more I could do except walk away, leaving my mother and her posse of protestors behind.

9

Back in my office, I thought I would just lay my head on my desk and stay there, motionless. Maybe forever. What with Rosie, *and* Red's return, the protest was a confusion too far.

A knock on my door. 'Still here?' It was Red.

I'd spent eighteen years wondering about him and now he was here, I wished he would go back to California again. We could neither be colleagues or friends, however much we tried to pretend otherwise. It was just too awkward, the weight of our history clouding everything.

'Red...' I forced a smile. 'How's it going?'

'Well, despite the fact that I don't have a beard,' he said, 'it's been surprisingly good.'

'There's still time.' I smiled weakly. 'Between now and the end of term to grow one.'

'I could,' he said. 'I still have every chance of looking like a proper teacher.' He smiled. 'Listen, I wanted to ask about setting up a drama club with the girls. It could be a lunchtime thing, if we can get access to the hall. I asked them today if they were interested and they were all excited by the idea. It's something I always did in the States: a lunchtime drama group, and I thought that we could get something together here. It's what they need at this age. Something non-competitive, that's not based on academic work. And they get to play. Something girls forget to do after a certain age. Or rather they are not encouraged to do.'

Red had always been enthused about teaching, ever since we first trained together. He loved working with young people and it was heartening to see that he hadn't lost his spark. 'That sounds like a great idea,' I said, smiling. 'We just have to get permission from parents and work out the logistics. Will you talk to Mary about it in the morning?'

'Okay... thanks Tab.' I waited for him to go, but instead he lingered, as though there was something else.

'Tab, I was wondering...I hope you don't mind me asking but I've just seen your mother... protesting. What's going on?'

'Oh that?' I said airily. 'Nothing really.'

'But it is your mother...?' Any other brand-new teacher wouldn't be quizzing me, I thought, feeling irritated at this liberty Red was taking. But then, why shouldn't he take it? He wasn't just a brand-new teacher. He was Red.

'Yes it's her all right.' I sighed. 'It's about a plan to sell a very small slice of land, nothing that anyone should get energised about, but they are merely exercising their democratic right to protest.' It wasn't just Michael who had the monopoly on pomposity, I thought, as I spouted forth. But I didn't want Red to see that I wasn't in perfect control of my life. He had to see I had made a real success of everything.

'Why sell the land?'

'It's a way of bringing a much-needed cash injection into the school,' I went on, loftily. 'It's actually a very good plan. We are really short of money to do things in the school such as fix a roof, buy some chairs... a few iPads...'

'Really?'

'Look, nothing has been decided. I said I would give this my full consideration. And I will. It has to go in front of the board first and then I get the final say.'

'But you're not going to do it, are you?' he said. 'You can't sell the land... not for a few bits of plastic...'

'Red, we need money. The school exists on handouts from our parents. Every week we have some kind of money-making ploy, whether it's dress-up day, or a book sale. We are scrabbling for money all the time. We can't afford to resurface the playground or replace any broken desks or... invest in technology.'

'Right... Tabitha, I know it's not my place...'

I let that one hang there, hoping my silence would be enough of an answer.

'But,' he went on, oblivious to my annoyance, 'really? Trees for technology. I didn't think *you* would do that.'

'Well, Red, you don't know me that well, do you? And you shouldn't suggest that you do...'

Ignoring my rebuke, he pressed on, 'and now you've got a protest outside. How long are they going to be there for? They look like they are quite happy already. You don't need this. And the kids don't need a protest on their doorstep. It's not good for anyone. Come on, we'll find another way of raising the money. A sponsored football match. Anything.'

'It's fine,' I said, with a patronising smile. 'I am totally in control of the situation. And anyway, Red, you've just joined the school. It's hardly your concern.'

'You're right. I'm being presumptuous.'

'And, it's nothing,' I said. 'Just a little protest. My mother loves a protest, as you might remember. I think she was getting bored because she hadn't had a good fight on her hands since last year's save the lesser spotted earwig campaign. She's been banned from her local health food shop because she complained so often about them using Israeli chickpeas in their hummus...'

'But...'

'This is what she's like Red,' I reminded him. 'She likes a cause. Gives her a purpose in life.' I could feel my face going red with frustration and embarrassment. After all these years, Red had come back and instead of me showing him how together my life was, what a success I had made of things, the cracks, the reality, was already appearing.

'Ah, a purpose. We all need one of those. I must get one, one of these days.' He was helping me out, I knew that. He'd noticed how I was shifting awkwardly. 'Look, I'm sorry, asking all those questions. It's just that... I don't know.'

'It's all right.' I didn't know where the lines were either.

'Whatever happened to that man your mum used to go out with? What was his name?'

'Finty. Finty Somethingorother. O'Brien. Finty O'Brien.'

'Finty! That was him. Tattoo of some woman's name.'

'Bernadette. It looked as though it had been inked by someone with delirium tremens.'

Red laughed and I found my mouth twitching into a smile too.

'I asked him who Bernadette was once,' I said. 'She was a dog apparently.'

Red's loud guffaw echoed around the room. For a moment I wondered what it would be like if I brought him home for dinner, introduced him to Rosie. Could we be friends? It would be nice, I thought, having a new friend. A new old friend, someone who made me laugh. I wondered what his hand would feel like if I took it, if we went for a walk on the pier in Dun Laoghaire, where we always used to go. I wondered what life would have been like if only I hadn't gone swimming that day. If only...

BEFORE

Four in the morning and I had just hitched all the way from West Cork after leaving Nora and her boyfriend, Finty, at the Peace Camp on Mizen Head. Calling Red from a petrol station by the Red Cow Inn. And twenty minutes later, there he was. It was dark and cold and I had never been so tired. I had zigzagged my way up from the arse end of nowhere, thumbing lifts and waiting hours and hours. When I saw the old Nissan pulling into the forecourt, I burst into tears and then Red's arms around me, the smell of his old jacket, the light stubble on his face. Him kissing me, in the grey light of the dawn.

10

I was hoping that my mother and the other protestors would have had the good sense to pack up and not return but every day for the following week, they turned up in the morning before the first bell and packed up to go home at 4pm, to return the following morning.

On Friday, when I drove into school, there they were getting themselves sorted and giving me cheery waves. Robbo was pulling open a few picnic chairs and setting them at the stove where Nellie was already at the kettle, brewing up. Leaf had made what looked like a dandelion chain and was stringing it over her placards. It was as though they were settling in for Glastonbury.

And there was Nora, mug of tea in her hand, in the glow of the gas stove, looking radiant. The pirate queen.

I stopped the car and she walked over and peered in through my window.

'Mum, I think you should go now,' I said through the glass.

'Go where?' she said, innocently.

'Home.'

'Put your window down,' she ordered. 'That's better. Now, we can't leave, Tabitha. We explained it all to you. Not until that land remains part of the school.'

'Mum... please.'

'Sorry, Tab. Think of the trees.'

'Think of me! I've got enough going on with everything. Rosie's exams...' I didn't tell her about Rosie's panic attack because I didn't want to worry her. You see, that was typical. We all tiptoed around Nora, worrying about her feelings, but she never worried about any of us. Principles came first.

'I know,' she said, sweetly. 'I know you do and it's most unfortunate, but we don't have the gift of time. The end of term is nigh,' she went on. 'By the way, tell Rosie to call me. I haven't heard from her for ages.'

'She's finding it very tough,' I admitted. 'A lot of pressure.'

'It's too much,' said Nora. 'Too much for anyone, never mind a young girl.'

'But how else is she going to get to college?'

'There's more to life than college,' she answered. 'You know that. I never went and neither did your grandmother. And look at us.'

'Yes, look at you. Standing in a street protesting at some development. Trying to save trees that are probably riddled with some kind of disease and should for the good of their health be euthanised.' My pomposity, I noticed, was coming along brilliantly. 'Or chopped down, I suppose you could also say.'

'Aha! You said development! Which is why, Tabitha, we are here. Vigilance at all times. You always have to be alert where people can smell money.'

'Are you accusing me of being interested in money?' I said, aghast. 'My motives are purely for the benefits of the pupils.'

'No, you're not an avaricious person, Tabitha, I know that. But what about the other people involved. Be careful. Be suspicious. Always ask questions and never believe what you are told. That's what I've learned in my fifty years as an activist.'

'This is the modern world, Mum. You need to catch up.' I was so annoyed that I revved off too quickly and thought for one terrible moment that I had run over her foot. I had to look in the rear-view mirror to check, but thankfully she was walking back to the others without a limp, and then, horribly, I wished I *had* run over her foot.

* * *

The children were my biggest concern. It wasn't fair on them to have to walk past a protest everyday – however friendly the faces of the protestors – and not know what was going on. I needed to explain that whatever the school was planning was in their interests. And so I turned to the locus of any well-run school, the place where we gather as a community. I called a Special Assembly.

Standing at the front of the hall, the children cross-legged in front of me, the teachers, including Red, in a row at the back, I waited for silence.

I looked around at the school. Eighty bright little faces looked back. God, it felt good to be a teacher. You felt such a weight of responsibility, such trust. It was the most rewarding job in the world and although I wasn't in the classroom as much as I would have liked, my days consumed with the logistics of running a school, I still took great pride in our pupils.

'Now, to the reason why we've called this Special Assembly.' I smiled at them all and took my time, speaking slowly, to let them hear my words. There was pin-drop hush and I felt like a great actor on the stage, my audience in the palm of my hand. Now, Red could see how together my life was. What a success I was. How good I was at my job.

'I am sure,' I said, 'that many of you are asking questions about the group of people who've been standing outside the school all week. Does anyone know what it's about?'

They were an intelligent bunch and we would be able to have an interesting discussion, I was sure, explaining both sides of the argument and why it was so important that people were allowed to protest in this day and age. And I could explain what we would gain if we were to sell the land. I was feeling pretty confident, as I stood looking down at all the innocent faces, that they would see it from my point of view. Yes, we appreciated the Dalkey Wildlife Defenders point of view, and could even have a week looking at different forms of democratic protest. Projects. Outings. All sorts of things. This could be extremely beneficial to the school. This could be A Learning Experience. But more than anything, selling the land was A Very Good Thing for the school. One girl put up her hand.

'Yes, Molly?'

'They had a sign about saving squirrels. But why, what's going to happen to the squirrels?'

'Thank you, Molly,' I smiled indulgently. 'Yes, that's what they say, they do want to save squirrels...'

'Are you killing squirrels?' Her eyes were wide with horror. 'I love squirrels. We have some in our garden. We leave nuts out for them.'

'No,' I said firmly. 'No Molly. We are definitely not killing squirrels. I love them too. Everyone loves squirrels, don't they? It's about where squirrels live. Can anyone tell me where squirrels live?'

Hands shot up.

'Charlotte?'

'Houses?' Some of our pupils had other gifts rather than purely academic ones.

'No, not quite... well, maybe to them they are houses, so perhaps, technically, you are right, Charlotte, but there's another word I'm looking for. Trees. We all love trees don't we.'

'Are you killing trees as well?'

'No Molly. There won't be any tree killing.' I really hoped this promise did not turn out to be an empty one.

For a moment I looked up and made eye contact with Red. But he gave me nothing, no sense of quite how well or badly this was going, but there was a palpable atmosphere that this special assembly was special for all the wrong reasons as everyone stopped breathing for a moment and waited to hear how I would defend myself from accusations of squirrelicide and tree felling.

'Well, we are thinking of selling a section of land. The Copse. The overgrown bit, the nettley area full of brambles.

'The nature area?' one girl called out.

'Where we go and watch the butterflies,' said another.

'Yeah, we love the Copse,' said another voice.

'The adventure area!'

'What's that, Abigail?' I said.

'It's the best place in the school,' said Abigail, who was sitting at the side of the room. 'We are allowed to play there sometimes and it's magic. Like anything could happen.'

'Like what? Do you mean tripping up or having some kind of accident?' I'd had no idea that the children were even particularly aware of the Copse or that it had become imbued with magical properties but I was definitely aware that my little chat wasn't going to plan.

'No. Like you can have an adventure.'

All the girls began nodding and voices began chattering, the sound in the room was filled with happy memories about being in the Copse.

Another hand up. 'Poppy?'

'Is it in trouble? Are we going to save it like the people outside?'

'Not quite... well, yes it's in trouble and no we are not going to save it... I mean...'

A sea of shocked tiny faces.

'Whose side are we on?' said Poppy.

'It's not about sides,' I said. 'But we're not on the side of the protestors. You all want computers, don't you? You all want to be like the children in Willow Grove, isn't that right? With your own iPads. You would prefer that, wouldn't you?' My God, I thought, I've transitioned into Cruella De Vil. I used to think of myself as a kindly child-loving teacher. Now, I had become practically evil.

I looked around at all the faces of the children. Some were shaking their heads, and others began to cry. They held each other's hands for moral and emotional support. Oh dear God. This was not meant to happen. Even Mary, standing at the side door, beside me, had panic on her face. What would happen next? Would social services arrive to drag me away? Red, at the back of the hall, looked completely bemused, as though he was witnessing the breakdown of a previously well-respected figure, like seeing your favourite television presenter suddenly turn on you when you innocently asked for their autograph. And the children would go home and tell their parents that Ms Thomas wanted to kill trees and squirrels.

'Children, children!' I was screeching now, rising panic squeezing my vocal chords. 'Are you saying to me you don't want computers? But I thought you'd be delighted...'

Poppy managed to raise her hand, her eyes moist with tears. 'We'd much prefer to have our own squirrel, Ms Thomas. And our own butterfly.'

Alice in Sixth class raised her hand. 'And an adventure, Miss.'

* * *

'Well, that went well.'

Red had joined me as the girls walked out, line by line, some with their shoulders shaking as tears streamed down their faces, arms draped around each other, others looking at me as though I was suddenly not who they had once thought. I had hoped to run to the sanctuary of my office, but Red was probably delighted to see me implode.

'Well, it wasn't the unqualified success I had hoped.' I felt like a politician who has just lost an election. 'I don't think I quite communicated my point.' He thought me a fool, he must do. 'I think,' I admitted, realising that there was nowhere to hide, 'I just might have made everything worse. There's a bunch of pensioners outside the school who are convinced I am some kind of environmental vandal. Like an Irish, female Donald Trump. And I've just made half the school cry.'

'It's not that bad,' he said. 'If you believe that selling the land is the best thing to do, then you just have to carry on in the face of adversity. Even if your adversaries are children and pensioners. Neither of whom, by the way, should ever be underestimated. Courage in your convictions.' I had ghosted him. That was the phrase. Where someone just disappears from your life. Doesn't contact you, they have ghosted you. A horrible, cruel thing to do. Unforgiveable. Yet here he was acting as though he had forgiven me.

'My daughter is... struggling,' I said suddenly. He was the first person I had told. I had spent the last few weeks full to the brim with worry for her. And I didn't know what to do. 'She's doing her Leaving Cert.'

He was listening. 'She's finding it tough?'

I nodded. 'She hasn't come out of her room for months. We barely see her and when she did, like this weekend, we went to a family thing, she had a...' I stopped.

'A what?' he asked with genuine concern.

'A kind of panic attack. Or that's what it looked like. We had to come home. She says she's all right and that's normal... but... I just don't know.' My voice wobbled a little and I could feel emotion rush to the surface. Why was I telling Red this? I'd missed him, I realised. He'd always been so easy to talk to, such a good listener, gave such wise counsel. I could feel myself plugging back into him, opening up. It was so easy. As long as we didn't talk about the past, then maybe we could be friends. Of a sort. And it was only a month to the end of term. We could be friends for a month.

'What are you going to do?'

'I don't know,' I admitted. 'I don't know. But she's nearly there.' *We're all nearly there*, I thought. And real life could resume. Whatever real life was. Normality, then. But I wasn't sure I liked my reality, my normality too much. At least my mother was actually doing something. For a moment, I wished I was the protestor, the one with the Barbour jacket. Or Rosie heading off to college, a life awaiting.

'So you're both just hanging on,' said Red. 'Until the exams are over?'

I nodded. 'Isn't that what you do,' I said. 'With everything. Just hang on. Isn't that all any of us ever do? Just wait for things to pass?'

'No!' He laughed. 'That's what you might call a passive approach to life. Haven't you ever heard of grabbing the proverbial bull's horns?'

'I think you might have lived in California for too long. Here in Ireland we don't go round grabbing bull's horns. We like a nice quiet life. Complain about it, obviously, but wait for time to move on. It always does.'

I remembered this feeling, Red making everything all right.

He laughed again. 'Time has that habit of moving, doesn't it? Funny that.' He smiled at me. 'Look, I've got to get back to class. But let me know if you need to talk. I promise to keep the Californian on the down-low.' He began to turn away. 'Good to talk to you, Tab.'

* * *

Things, as they often do, got worse.

Every day the protestors made themselves even more at home. I thought that protesting was meant to be, by its very nature, an uncomfortable experience. You were meant to be sleeping in trees or lying on cold ground incurring piles or dysentery, often both. Leaf spent all day strumming a guitar, Arthur and Robbo were bent over an old radio, both with extra-long screwdrivers in their hands.

Others – neighbours from close to the school – would join them for a little sit in the sun and a cup of Nellie's special brew (the tea kind). It was looking rather amiable out there, sort of a new wave peace camp with Nora sitting in the middle of them all, looking delighted with herself, conscience fully intact.

I knew I was doing it for the best of intentions. At the end of term, the school would have a cheque for €20,000. We could make another Copse, we could plant trees. By September, all this would be forgotten about.

At the end of the school day, once all the children had streamed out in their screaming hoards, I spied on the protestors from the library window. Robbo stringing some bunting from the corner of the van, the other end was tied to the school railings. Arthur was on his mobile phone. What was he doing? Not reinforcements? Surely we wouldn't have every activist from Mizen to Malin Head descend on Dalkey? It wouldn't become a new Peace Camp, surely? And now Robbo was chalking on the road in huge letters. I couldn't quite make out what it was, but I'd come back with a hose, that night if I had to.

'We had a fella like that at home.' Mary joined me at the window.

'Like Robbo?'

'No, Brian Crowley. Would tell you what you wanted to hear and promise you the sun, moon and stars. And deliver nothing. Or nothing that you wanted or expected.'

'What happened?'

'Mammy wanted to do something with the old cow shed. Thought it might make a nice house for Granny to live in. They weren't getting on, stuck in the same house all day, so as Mammy wasn't going to move out, she decided that Granny should. Called in this fella, Mickey-John was his name. And he said he'd make the loveliest palace for Granny. And so we were all excited and the money was handed over, and Granny began making curtains and Mammy made plans to turn Granny's old bedroom into a room for her Daniel O'Donnell memorabilia. She's president of the Cavan chapter, you see. She's got boxes and boxes of Daniel-related... I was going to say *tat* but Mammy'd kill me. We'll call it knick-knacks – mugs, key rings, holy water bottles, T-shirts, teapots and what have you. Her pride and joy is her crocheted Daniel doll. I don't get the appeal at all. But it keeps her happy. So, all going well until the big unveiling.'

'What was it like?'

'A cow shed.'

'But it *was* a cow shed.'

'And thus it remained.'

'So the moral of the story is, once a cow shed always a cow shed?'

'Exactly. Or what I would say, beware of men promising gifts. They are always in the wrong size or not what you want.'

'Mary, what are you going on about?'

'Just promise me,' she said. 'Promise me that you have the final say.'

'I promise.'

'And you won't do anything hasty?'

There was a rap on the open door.

'Tab?' It was Fidelma Fahy, the teacher of Second class. 'Just to let you know that there is a reporter outside. From the news. And a cameraman. They're talking to the protestors now.'

'Oh God...' This was all I needed. The squirrel savers on the evening news, looking all brave and valiant, the David to my Goliath.

* * *

'Barry Whelan.' The reporter held out his hand. He looked younger than Rosie. When did news reporters get to be so young?

'Barry,' I said, smiling as though I was delighted to see him and was welcoming him to the school sports day or some other happy occasion. 'You're very welcome to Star of the Sea school.'

He didn't smile back, just nodded as though he wanted to get on with it. Or back to the satellite van for a smoke, I thought. 'Could we talk to you on camera?' he said. 'Just a few questions about what exactly the situation is here.'

'Well, everything's fine,' I said. 'I don't know why you've come all the way here. This is a small dispute. In fact, no it's not a dispute. It's *definitely* not a dispute. Please don't write that down. It's not even a misunderstanding. It's an ongoing conversation between the school community and concerned citizens, that's all.'

The camera was already on me, I realised, so I smiled again, the face and voice of reason and rationality. Mary was standing close by and gave me an encouraging thumbs-up.

'But *why* are they concerned?' Barry held the microphone near my mouth as I began to talk, words just falling from my mouth, hopefully in some kind of coherent order, but I wasn't entirely sure. Jesus Christ. Why hadn't I put on more make-up this morning? And I was wearing my black jacket. Shouldn't you never wear black on television, if you wanted to win people over? Isn't that what they advised politicians. I desperately tried to think what Michael had said about it once, but I hadn't really listened. Or maybe black *was* the right colour to wear, showing dignified, restrained power. Jesus, what was he saying now?

'Apparently, one of the protestors is your mother.'

'Well... I'm not sure I understand the question...'

'It's a simple one.' He raised an eyebrow, looking all of his twelve years. 'And you're a teacher so you shouldn't find it too difficult to answer.' What a smart-arse. 'Is she,' he went on, 'or is she not, your mother?'

'Yes,' I said weakly. 'Yes she is.' I looked over desperately at Mary, whose lip-biting and worried expression did nothing to reassure me.

'It must be an issue that she feels very strongly about for her to protest at her daughter's place of work.'

'She's a very principled woman,' I said, diplomatically. Or annoying. And frustrating and bloody minded. I smiled at Barry.

'And you're not.'

'Principled? No I am. I really am. It's just that we just have different principles.'

'Hers is to save the environment and yours is to destroy it. Yes?'

'No! I love the environment. I *love* trees. Who doesn't love trees? I mean, I even have a wood-burning stove at home.'

'So you like to burn *dead* trees but not enjoy them in their living state.'

'No... I...' God, this Barry was good. He was twisting everything to ensure he got a splash from this.

'So how are you going to resolve this issue?'

'I am not sure yet,' I said, 'but it will be. You see, Barry,' I said, trying to summon up some wisdom. Something moving, something that would make him and the viewers at home see that at times difficult decisions had to made but that things would work out. Trust and love. Bravery and... having the courage in your convictions. That was it. Right, something profound... 'You see, Barry, I believe the children are our future.' What was I saying? It came from deep within me. Words I had heard once and had never forgotten. It wasn't... it wasn't Whitney Houston was it? 'Teach them well and let *them* lead the way.' It *was* Whitney. Barry was looking at me, utterly bewildered, all his smart-arsery gone. 'What? Let the *pupils* make the decision?' He obviously was not a Whitney fan. More fool him, I thought. But I knew Red was fully familiar with her oeuvre and I saw his mouth was twitching from behind Barry, trying not to laugh. This day was not going well.

'No, I meant, I just... oh I don't know.'

Shrugging, shaking his head, he turned to the camera. 'Barry Whelan, for the Six O'clock News, at the environmental stand-off at the Star of the Sea school in Dalkey.'

The Dalkey Wildlife Defenders were huddled in a little group and obviously delighted at their success. Arthur was pouring something from a saucepan into mugs and handing them around and they were clinking them. Robbo gave me a thumbs up a big smile and what looked suspiciously liked a Heinz tomato soup moustache. Nora shouted something.

'What?' I shouted back.

'No hard feelings!' she called.

Round one to them.

Red and Mary joined me, Mary's face said it all, her mouth a wobble of uncertainty.

'What do you think?' I said to the two of them. 'Have I just made a complete mess of it all?'

'You did really well,' Mary lied. 'He was unnecessarily personal, I thought.'

I glanced at Red who pushed his hands through his hair, his face inscrutable.

'They might not show it,' went on Mary. 'There'll probably be a bigger story that will go instead. Like a fire. Or a robbery. We've just got to pray for bigger news.'

'Red?' I was desperate to know what he thought. He must think I'm a total fool. A proper idiot.

'I think you are doing brilliantly,' he said, 'under very difficult circumstances.'

'But Red, I made children cry. And now I've quoted Whitney Houston on national television.'

He laughed then. 'That was my favourite bit, it has to be said.'

I looked at Mary who was desperately trying to stop her mouth from smiling.

'I don't know why you didn't go the whole hog and quote Johnny Logan...' He began speaking in an actor's voice, *'don't, don't close your heart to how you feel. Dream, and don't be afraid the dream's not real... close your eyes, pretend it's just the two of us again... make believe this moment's here to stay...'*

Mary was laughing outwardly now.

'It's too soon for humour,' I tried to say. 'I'm not ready.'

But the two of them began singing loudly, together... *'Hold me now... don't cry. Don't say a word, just hold me now and I will know though we're apart, we'll always be together, forever in love...'*

Red had his arm around Mary and they swayed side to side, laughing and singing lustily. But they weren't quite finished, *'what do you say when words are not enough...'*

When the performance was finally over, I said. 'I never had you down as a Johnny Logan fan, Mary. I thought you were better than that?'

'Never!' he said, grinning. 'Eurovision 1987. What a year! When Ireland couldn't lose the damn thing!'

'Johnny Forever!' said Mary. 'Well that's what I had scribbled on all my school books. I was going to get it tattooed. But then I realised it wasn't Johnny I fancied but Linda Martyn.'

Red turned to Mary. 'We should do karaoke sometime. You can be Linda Martin. I'll be Johnny.'

'I'll hold you to that, Redmond!' she said, as we watched him run off back into school. 'Lifts the spirits he does.'

* * *

Mary's hopes that we might get knocked off the news by a flood or an armed robbery didn't come to pass. It was, unfortunately a slow news day. Clodagh texted just before 6pm:

Watch the Six, you've made it. Fame at last. Just remember I am a puppet in the hands of evil producer Lucinda.

It was such an occasion that Rosie left her bedroom to come and watch that night's news. I wasn't sure if I wanted her to see me being bamboozled by a child journalist.

She was looking better. Maybe it *had* just been a lack of breakfast and a sleepless night that had caused her panic attack at Celia's party. She was even chatty and had brought down her varnish to paint her nails while watching TV, I noted with approval. She used to do that kind of thing all the time. Whatever stress she had been under had passed, I was sure of it.

On screen, Clodagh was, as always, dressed impeccably in a crisp white shirt and statement necklace, hair smoothed into a perfect bob, as she went through all the news, the national, the international, effortlessly inter-viewing trade unionists and politicians. Then we had sport, long and detailed accounts of big matches and small.

'They've put you at the end,' said Rosie. 'You're the And Finally.'

'That's a good thing,' I decided. 'They won't give much time to it, then. If they do it at all.' I was still hopeful.

'The things is, Mum,' she said. 'You're not going to win this.'

'What do you mean I'm not going to win this? I don't want to win. I don't see it as a competition.' But it was, and I wanted to win. As, I supposed my mother did too.

'I know that,' she said. 'But from an outside perspective, you represent the corporate fat cats, the developers. Granny is standing up for trees.'

'Really? That's what people would think?' Nobody liked fat cats, that was for sure. 'I'm just trying to do the right thing for the pupils,' I insisted. 'Anyway, just because she's for the trees doesn't mean she's right.'

'I'm not saying that,' she said, 'but it's about the popular vote, isn't it? She's going to win that easily.' See, a politician's child always thinks about things like this.

'Sometimes you have to make difficult decisions,' I said. 'It would be much easier to spend one's life at protests and saying no to everything. Try doing a nine-to-five job and have two hundred parents breathing down your neck every day. I know I'm the Dalkey equivalent of Amazonian loggers destroying the rainforest. I wouldn't be surprised if your grandmother invited Sting down to sing about trees and squirrels.'

Rosie laughed.

'You're on *her* side,' I teased, pleased to hear her lovely laugh again. 'Oh, I see where your loyalties lie.'

'I'm on yours, obviously,' she insisted. 'But I can also see Granny's point.'

I thought back to Red and Mary's duet earlier. 'Or Johnny Logan. He might be cheaper than Sting. Although I don't think Johnny sings much about tree felling and environmental destruction.'

'Johnny who? What are you going on about?'

'Nothing.' But I smiled, thinking of the two of them. Red always brought out the best in people. Long ago, I would have been singing along with him, not being the pursed-lip buzzkill.

'The problem is,' I said, 'but don't tell anyone, okay, but I see her point too. But it's bloody infuriating that she's doing this. I need to make the decision about whether to sell the land or not without the pressure of a protest outside the school gates. It might be a very good idea to sell it. We can create another wildlife area. But she's not giving me the space to make this decision.'

'They won't be there much longer,' she assured me. 'They'll find something else to protest against.'

'Shhh... there's Bridget.' I waved a hand to shush her.

'Thanks, Clodagh, a-may-zing.' Bridget was looking particularly sexy this evening, wearing a dress which was skin-tight with one long zip from the top to the bottom which she had pulled tantalisingly low around her cleavage. 'So, how's it going with you, everyone?' She looked straight down the camera. 'Hope you're all nice and comfortable, I know I am. Let's see what the weather was like around the country...'

We watched as she spoke about rain in Donegal, strong winds on the Aran Islands, scorching sun in Co Kerry and intermittent showers on the

East Coast. Just another day of perplexing Irish weather. 'And now back to Clodagh... over to you Clodes!'

'Thank you... er, Bridget. And finally,' said Clodagh, her face a mask of professionalism, 'a local County Dublin school has found itself embroiled in an interesting domestic drama. Head teacher Tabitha Thomas of Star of the Sea primary in Dalkey, Co Dublin, had to confront a group of protestors who have vowed to protect a plot of land which the school wishes to sell to raise money. The protestors claim that the plot contains ancient oak trees, as well as being the habitat of birds and squirrels. And one of the protestors is the mother of the head teacher, Tabitha Thomas, herself. Our reporter Barry Whelan headed down to Dalkey to find out what was behind this unusual mother-daughter scrap...'

And there was Nora, speaking brilliantly about the importance of standing up for those things that would otherwise remain undefended. She was sorry that I was involved, but she was compelled to act in this case. Nellie, Arthur, Robbo and Leaf, all had their turn and were entirely sympathetic and convincing. And then there was me, at a weird angle, looking as though I was looming at the camera. My eyes kept flickering to one side (towards Mary), which made me appear slightly shifty and untrustworthy.

'Not one of my best professional moments,' I said to Rosie after we had both sat there in stunned silence for a few moments.

Dun Laoghaire has two piers which reach into the sea in two curves forming an almost complete circle. And it's along their limestone flags, either on the West or the East pier, most of south county Dublin stretch their legs. And it was where I went when I needed to clear my head. The sale of the Copse was bothering me, the money seeming less and less important as different issues clouded what I had once thought an obvious and simple issue.

The pier was full that summer evening, dog walkers, couples, small children on trikes weaving precariously close to the edge as we made our way to the lighthouse and back again. But just as I reached the bandstand, halfway along, I saw Red with his dad; the two of them, like everyone else, taking an evening stroll in the pink-tinged dusk.

For a moment, I panicked. It was one thing dealing with Red every day; we'd transcended awkwardness and were easing into a grey area of not friends but not acquaintances. But Christy was different. I'd let him down as well, rejecting him when I ghosted Red. I'd managed to avoid Christy all these years, our paths and worlds never colliding. Until now.

I thought I might get away with pretending I hadn't noticed them, but Red saw me and said something to Christy, who looked up, bright-eyed, like an elderly meerkat. And I had no choice but to lift my hand in a wave and they both waved back. There was nothing for it but to go over. I felt a burning shame at my cowardice but also a loss for these two good men. My life, I realised, had been poorer without them.

'Hello Tab,' said Red. 'Lovely evening.'

'Yes it is,' I said and leaned towards Christy and kissed him on the cheek.

'Well, well, well,' he said. 'Where have you been hiding, Tabitha?' He peered at me, wonderingly, as though I was some great unsolved mystery. 'Now you're a sight for my old eyes. We haven't seen you in some years. And you're looking all the better for it. Red told me he was teaching in your school.'

'Hello Christy,' I said, 'nice to see you too. After all this time... and Red, lovely evening.' I smiled at them both without actually making eye contact.

'Red insisted we came down,' said Christy, the same eyes as Red, I remembered, and the same smile. 'Says I've been stuck inside so much, twiddling the old thumbs. I don't come down to the pier. I like to shuffle about the town instead.'

'How are you feeling? Red told me you'd been ill.'

'Still kicking. It'll take more than a stroke to knock me over. Like an ancient oak, I am. But then this fella here turns up...' he nodded at Red, '... as though I'm on my way out. So I says to him there was no need, no need at all, but he insists on sticking around.' He looked at Red affectionately. 'Who'd have thought it?' went on Christy. 'You two in the same school.'

'I know, small world, isn't it?'

'It's only to the end of term, though,' said Red, as though he didn't want to give Christy any ideas of a great reunion. 'It's been... nice seeing Tab again.'

'Well, it must be!' said Christy. 'Lovely girl like Tabitha. Head teacher at the school. I've been following your progress, young lady. And married. To Michael Fogarty. Well, I didn't see that coming... but maybe there's more to him than the stuffed shirt.'

For a moment, I wanted to laugh. Trust Christy to cut straight through the awkwardness and put everything out there. But Red looked annoyed.

'Dad...' he warned.

'What? Statement of fact, is it not. Tabitha, statement of fact?'

I nodded. 'No, that is true.' But I wanted to tell them both that it had been a mistake, that to the outside world, it must seem as though Michael and I were happy. After all, we were still together. I wanted to explain why I hadn't left, or why I'd married him in the first place. 'And a daughter,' I said instead. 'Rosie.'

'Ah! The rose of summer. Lovely,' said Christy, smiling, oblivious to Red's shifting from foot to foot, itching to get going again and away from me and all I represented. It was one thing being polite to me in school but he obviously didn't want to socialise with me and chatting on the pier would definitely qualify as socialising.

'Now, the school,' went on Christy. 'I saw on the news. The protest. Nice to see some of the old faces again. I recognised Arthur Fitzgerald. Haven't seen him for years now. And your mam, of course. Might have a wander down myself and say hello.'

'Dad,' said Red. 'Please don't *you* join the protest? It's enough that one parent of the teaching faculty is involved. Another would be a parent too far.' He smiled at me, apologetically, shaking his head.

'They look like they are in for the long haul,' continued Christy, ignoring him. 'You'll find it hard to shift that type, you know, the ones with the Primus stove and the camping chairs. They'll be there next Christmas with the oil barrel fire, the tents.'

'It'll be fine,' I told Christy. 'I'm sure of it. There's no way this'll still be going until Christmas. We have to make a decision one way or the other.'

'And which way are ye leaning? Trees or no trees?'

'Dad, you make it sound like a game show,' said Red. 'Ignore him Tab. Dad, it's a difficult decision. Tabitha is already going through enough without anyone poking and prodding.'

'I'm only asking,' he said, innocently. 'Anyway, Tabitha here doesn't mind, do you, loveen? She's not the type to take umbrage and offence... She's one of us.' He smiled at me, confident in his pronouncement. But there was a slight puzzlement in his eyes as if to say, she was one of us but something happened and now... now she's married to a Progressive Conservative.

'I haven't made a decision yet, Christy.' I managed to keep my voice steady. 'But when I do, you will be the first to know.'

He nodded. 'Listen,' he said. 'I want to see you sometime. Come over to the house. Cup of tea and a chinwag. We haven't had one of those in quite a few years. Time to stop being a stranger.'

For a moment, I didn't think I was going to be able to get the words out. For years, I thought that they both hated me and I would never be forgiven and here he was being so lovely. 'I'll call in,' I managed.

'Promise me?' He caught my hand in his two big warm rough hands and held it tightly. 'What about tomorrow?'

'I'll come, I promise.' I felt nervous, as though I was putting on an old coat and wasn't sure it was going to fit. But I wanted to be that person who wore that old coat so much. I hadn't realised I still could.

We said our goodbyes and I walked into the darkening sky, towards the red lighthouse at the end of the pier. It hadn't been just Red I'd missed, it was Christy too. And it was the person I used to be. I missed all of it and wanted it back.

* * *

There was no doorbell on the door, just the old lion head knocker, so I rapped, loudly, and stood back, holding a yucca plant. Christy was always growing things. Or he used to. There were always spider plants rooting in little plastic cups of soil or plants trailing up the pipes in the kitchen. The house was exactly as I remembered it. Large, Victorian and in one of the wrought-ironed railed squares in Dun Laoghaire, but shabbier and more run-down than its neighbours.

And then, something, a noise, a figure, materialising through the glass.

'Just in time,' said Christy. He always used to say that to us when we'd come home, me and Red. 'In time for what?' we'd say and he'd answer, 'whatever you want.'

'In time for what?' I said.

'Whatever you want,' he said, making me smile.

'These are for you,' I said, handing over some biscuits and the plant. 'I don't know if you still...'

'Still eat shortbread?' he said. 'You bet I do. Whatever the doctors tell me.'

'And still green-fingered?'

He nodded. 'I feel like a matron on a ward sometimes, tending all my little plants, nursing them to bloom or to sprout. And this plant is a beauty. Like a tiny slice of jungle. You shouldn't have. Now, tea. Come downstairs will you? I've just had my writers' group and there's some fruit cake left over. I always say, if you're going to have to listen to bad poetry – mainly mine, it has to be said – then fruit cake helps the situation enormously. Or we can open these fancy biscuits. You've missed Red, he's gone for a walk.'

'That's okay,' I said, following him into the large hall; with the staircase that led upstairs, the coving and ceiling roses, and I noticed that nothing had changed: same paper, same paint on the walls, same tangle of vine twisting around the banister. 'I came to see you.' But I hadn't realised how much I wanted to see Red until I knew he wasn't going to be there and felt disappointment curl around my insides.

'Red's on at me to get the house cleaned,' he said. 'He's starting one room at a time. Doesn't understand how I live like this. I don't see it, but he says the dust isn't good for me.' Christy leant heavily on the handrail as we descended into to the kitchen, his breath all wheezy. Maybe, I thought, Red had a point about the dust. 'He's done downstairs, so the kitchen is visitor-friendly.'

'So you're doing well, then,' I said. 'Apart from your son being on at you to dust more.'

He turned on the stairs. 'Well, I'm not doing too badly. Red is a one to worry... I'm not dead yet.'

BEFORE

Laughing and giggling. Red carrying me on his back down these stairs when I thought I'd broken a leg. I hadn't. I'd just sprained if after drinking too much cheap wine at a party. And then the next morning, Christy putting a fried breakfast in front of me, Red already tucking in.

'You need to get some fat on those bones,' he said, giving me a wink. 'Get that into ye.'

'Dad, enough of the personal remarks,' Red had said. 'You need to get some fat off yours.'

It was always such a comfort to be with the two of them in that lovely, quiet house.

'What are you up to today?' said Christy.

'I don't know,' said Red, glancing at me. 'What do you feel like doing?'

'The boat to Dalkey Island?' I said. 'I haven't been there since I was little. Mum took me.'

'Now, that's an island,' said Christy. 'It doesn't belong to people at all, just the goats.'

'How are we going to get there?' said Red.

'A boat.' I grinned at Red. 'Obviously. You can ask one of the fishermen to take you out. It might blow away our hangovers.'

'I think,' said Red, carefully. 'I think you might be on to something there.'

And we did. For a fiver, one of the boatmen dropped us off on the island and once we were landed, and our seasickness quelled, we explored: walking the full perimeter, exploring the old ruins and sitting for ages, Red lying down, hands behind his head, me cross-legged making daisy chains.

'You know, Tab?' he said, waking up. 'I think this is all I need in life. Us on an island. Where no one and nothing can reach us.'

* * *

'Sit yourself down there, Tabitha,' Christy said, pointing to his old armchair and faded cushion beside a wood burner. 'And I'll make the tea.'

'How is the writers' group going? How many are you?'

'There's the six of us now. The stalwarts. All the way from Peggy who's going on eighty-seven, down to Charles who's a mere stripling of 67. Poetry isn't bad at all. But you know something, Tabitha? I don't know what I'd do without my poetry. Writing my little verses keeps me sane. I seem to have become more prolific as I've got older. It's like I have to put everything down, make sense of everything, before I can't anymore. Don't stop, actually.'

He was wiping out two mugs with a tea towel and he unwrapped a large, almond-topped fruit cake, the kind of cake no one makes anymore. 'Peggy's this is,' he said. 'We get all the reading and critiquing over and done with and then we have our reward.'

He handed me a mug of tea and a slice of cake. If I closed my eyes I could be twenty all over again. Our last year at college, Red and I practically lived in the room upstairs.

'Now, there's something I've been wondering, and before Red gets back I had better get it off my chest. So, tell me this and tell me no more,' he said. 'Why did you marry someone like Michael Fogarty? I thought you were one of us. And well, they're the ones getting rid of the bowls club here in the town and cutting the winter fuel allowance. And a friend of mine, his daughter, well, she's living in a bed and breakfast, grotty place it is, with three children, because they've run out of council houses.'

'I know,' I said. 'But I'm still the same. I still vote the same way. Michael is...' Christy was exactly the same as he used to be but I was mortified he was asking about Michael. Michael who I'd married only a year after ending it with Red. Michael the father of my child. Christy never minded asking you the awkward questions if he needed to know something. He needed to fully understand everything about the world until he was satisfied.

'I couldn't believe it Tabitha,' said Christy, 'when I heard. Not one of *them*, I thought to meself. That right shower with their shiny cars and shiny heads and shiny suits, doing nothing for the working man or woman.'

'Michael isn't that bad,' I said, compelled to defend Michael. I didn't want him to think I had married some right-wing lunatic. Michael was a moderate. And a good person. 'Actually, he was against the bowls club closing.'

'I saw your mam at the protest,' he said, letting Michael go. 'She's a mighty woman, isn't she?'

I nodded. 'That's one way of putting it.'

'And your daughter? Rose of summer... what age is she now?'

'She's doing her Leaving. Working hard you know. A bit stressed but...'

'You were just the same, working hard, a good brain, all that,' he said, taking the lid off the teapot and pouring in more hot water from the kettle.

'Was I?' I couldn't remember being like that, but I was touched by how he remembered me. We chatted for a long time, about Christy's coming and goings, my life at the school. I told him about Rosie and about Nora. We talked about films we'd seen and books read. It was like the old days. And then, a noise upstairs.

'Dad?' Red's voice from above our heads caused beads of sweat to ping all over me, fear and excitement and delight at his imminence.

'Down here! With a special visitor.' Christy winked at me, indulgently.

'Oh yes?'

Footsteps coming down the steps into the kitchen ... and there was Red.

'Hello Tab,' he said, looking a little taken aback, as though he'd forgotten all about Christy's invitation to me. 'I thought Dad meant the writers' group. I was hoping to hear a bit of Heaney...'

'Well, maybe Tabitha will oblige,' said Christy. 'Tea Red?' He filled the kettle. 'What will you give us, Tabitha?'

'Oh God,' I said. 'You're not going to make me recite something...'

Christy had a terrible habit of forcing people to do things, be someone they didn't quite think they were. And when you'd done it, you realised that you were better for it. But today, with sweat prickling my back and my mouth dry, and brain gone, I knew I wouldn't be able to rise to the challenge. 'What about some Pam Ayres,' I said. '*O I Wish I'd Looked After Me Teeth?*'

Red laughed but Christy said, 'and what's so funny. Poetry is poetry. Don't tell me Redmond Power that you are a poetry snob. We don't allow them in this house, do we Tabitha?'

I shook my head and winked at Red. 'No, Christy, no we don't.' Red was smiling broadly. It was like the old days. 'It's just like the old days,' said Christy.

'I was just thinking that,' said Red, glancing at me. Me too. Me too, I thought. 'How are you feeling, Dad?' he said. 'Did the poetry group tire you out?'

'Not at all. Strong as an ox I am.'

'Dad, you had a stroke six months ago. You have to face your own...'

'Decrepitude.'

'No,' said Red, but he was smiling. 'Limitations. We all have them.'

'Limitations are all in the mind. So, I need a stick but that's not going to stop me. And if you have an active mind, you're more than half-way there.'

'I was asking Tabitha about the bowls club,' went on Christy. 'It was quite the blow for us oldies when it closed. But I know it hasn't got anything to do with her. But we still haven't found a place to convene. I suppose that's why we enjoy the writer's group so much. Oldies United.' He chuckled.

'The last thing Tab needs is you banging on about things. Anyway, it's not good for you, getting excited. And you should stop watching the news.' He turned to me, making proper eye contact for the first time. 'He just shouts at it. Thought he was going to have another stroke last night.'

'It's keeping me going,' said Christy. 'I'd go to an early grave watching *Cash in the Attic* or *Pointless*.'

I shouldn't have come, I thought, suddenly, a wave of nostalgia washing over me, and loss, loss for the person I once was. And by coming here I was trying to recapture. But it had been a mistake. You don't just drop in on your old life and you can't just be the person you once were.

'I'd better go,' I said, standing up. 'I'll be back in to see you, okay, Christy?'

'But you've just got here,' said Christy. 'Stay for some more of Peggy's cake. You can have an even bigger slice this time.'

'No, I've got to go. But I'll come back.'

'Promise?'

I nodded.

'Well, then, I'll see you out.' Christy began to stand up. 'And you'll take some of the cake, won't you? She'll be delighted when I tell her that a slice went to Michael Fogarty's home. She'll like that, she will.' He chuckled again. Peggy obviously wasn't someone Michael could rely on for her vote.

'Sorry,' mouthed Red as Christy wrapped up a large slice in greaseproof paper.

'Michael's more of a Mr Kipling man,' I said. 'He's suspicious of home-made.' We all laughed, and I thought how a receptive audience always made disloyalty easier.

'You haven't changed, Tabitha,' said Christy, passing me the package. 'Not one little bit. Still got that beautiful smile.'

'I'll see her out, Dad,' said Red. 'You stay there, you have enough going up and down as it is.'

As he followed me up the stairs, his body close behind mine, the closest we had been, physically, for years and I could feel this magnetic tug that in a moment I would turn around mid-step and we would touch as though some kind of bodily memory compelled me to. At the front door, I stood aside while he opened it.

'He's looking well,' I said.

'When I first got home, he wasn't his usual self. Tired, thin, that kind of thing. He was doing strange things. In hospital, I found him reading a copy of the *Daily Mail*.'

'That must have been quite a shock. Which was worse, hearing he'd had a stroke or seeing him reading the *Daily Mail*?'

'The *Daily Mail*, obviously. I mean for a life-long, actual card-carrying socialist, a man who writes poems about the unequal tax systems of this country and wrote an epic poem based on a night in an A&E department, to see him reading a right-wing paper was the far bigger scare.' And he grinned right at me. And for a moment there was Red again. *My* Red. 'But I think it did him the power of good. Like electric shock treatment. He had to get well. Put the world to rights again. Write his poems. Give out about things.'

'I hope he's onto more edifying newspapers these days.'

'Yes, it's grand. The doctor prescribed him a combination of the *Irish Times* and the *Guardian*, so he's on the road to making a full recovery.'

'Let me know if Christy wants a copy of the *New Statesman*. I hear it's like EPO for socialists.' I was rewarded with that grin again, the one that brought me right back to a different age. 'He must be happy you're back?'

He nodded. 'Yeah and I'm glad to be back. Didn't think I would be. But it's good to be home.'

'So, what did you miss?' I knew I was stalling, not wanting to say goodbye. 'When you were away?'

'Barry's tea. That was my number one. And proper chocolate. Irish Cadbury's. A nice quiet pub. With no television on and an auld fella at the bar.' He smiled. 'The usual expat longings. And having a laugh.'

'Have you not laughed in all the time you've been away?' I said, pretending to be shocked.

'There's a particular way of having fun that we Irish do. I missed it.' We made eye contact for a moment but he looked away, quickly.

'So...' I said. 'Nice seeing you both together.'

'And you, Tab. It's nice seeing you.'

I walked down the path to my car feeling a sense of emptiness that I hadn't felt in years.

BEFORE

Christy was standing there on the doorstep when I opened the door. 'Are ye all right? Red was waiting...' His face changed as he looked at me. 'What's wrong?' he said. 'We're all fierce worried about you.'

'Nothing's wrong,' I said. 'Nothing. I just want...' What did I want? Just to be on my own. It seemed like the only thing that might keep me going was if I just didn't see anyone. 'Tell Red I'm sorry,' I said. 'But I don't want to see him.'

Christy's eyes were full of empathy. 'Tabitha, I think...'

'Please, I don't want to,' I said. 'I don't want to see him again.'

Christy, bless him, tried again, more desperately this time, for Red's sake, I knew. But also for mine. He was such a good soul. 'Tabitha, you don't look well,' he said. 'Who's here? Is your Mam here? Who's looking after ye?'

'Everything's fine Christy. Everything's fine.' And I closed the door on him and after a few weeks, the phone stopped ringing and there were no more knocks on the door. And I got what I wanted, to be alone.

* * *

When Rosie was six, I left Michael and we moved into Nora's house, my old home, and Michael arrived home to find me pushing boxes into a car.

It was then or never. Any later and Rosie would have been too aware, the repercussions of divorce too hard for her to deal with. It was a miserable marriage, the loneliness of two people sharing a home and a daughter but nothing much to say to each other.

'Michael, I'm not happy,' I said. 'Let me go.'

'It's not a question of happiness,' he said, shaking his head at me, as though I hadn't grasped something fundamental, as though I was slightly stupid and he had to explain what life is all about. 'It's a question of just staying married. That's all people have to do. We don't have an awful marriage. We have a daughter. How bad is it, really?'

'I want to be loved. Taken care of...' My words sounded immature and stupid.

'Taken care of? Whatever do you mean? I thought you feminists didn't want that kind of nonsense. I thought you could stand on your own two feet.'

'I do and I can. That's not what I want...'Oh God, what did I want? I was beginning to lose confidence in everything. I didn't know what was the right thing to do? I had been so sure and now... now, it felt like I was the last person to make the right decisions as to my and my daughter's future happiness.

'So you don't want to be taken care of?' he said, shaking his head. 'I'm confused. I have no idea what you want or what you are even asking for. And you don't even know.'

'I just want you to bring me a cup of tea,' I said, lamely. 'I want you to know how I like it, how much milk I like in it and which is my favourite mug.' I felt tears welling up at the corners of my eyes.

'What?' He almost laughed. 'You're joking? But how would I know those things?' he went on, angry at me for crying, and my confusion and what he saw was weakness, 'You don't even know how I like mine.'

'I do!'

'How then?'

'Full-fat milk, in second, colour of dark toffee, served in your Royal Tara bone china mug.'

'Yes, well... but tea is just tea... it doesn't actually matter how you like it. You can't expect me to go to Mammy and tell her that you have ended our marriage because I didn't know how you liked your tea?'

'It's a metaphor! A symbol,' I said. 'A boiled-down microcosm of our marriage.'

He shook his head and spoke quietly, 'Mammy was right when she said I shouldn't marry you.'

And so, I picked up my case and I went and he didn't stop me. But Celia did. She knocked on the door.

'Tabitha,' she said icily.

'Hello, Celia.'

'I was wondering...' Her tone was icy, imperious, '...when you were going to return my granddaughter to her father?'

'I'm not.'

'But you can't do that,' she said, looking at me as though I was faintly disgusting. 'The child belongs with her father. All children need fathers, did you not know that? Well, it depends on the father but in this case, I think we can all agree that Michael is a good father, the best kind of father to a little girl like Rosie. You didn't have one so you don't understand how elemental they are. Do you want Rosie to grow up without a proper family, the two parents... a *normal,* loving home?'

'But we're not happy...'

'Correction,' she said. '*You're* not happy. Michael informs me that he is happy. He was perfectly happy with you and your life together. You've just got to get yourself happy and stop asking for too much. Life isn't about trying to be happy. It's about sacrifice, tenacity, keeping going. There will be moments of happiness and pleasure, yes. But that is it not daily life. And nor should it be. When will you see sense?' She looked around, worried in case any neighbours were nearby, listening. 'And we can't have this discussion on the doorstep,' she said, shoulder barging past me.

'Celia,' I said, 'we can't have this discussion at all. It's between me and Michael.'

'Yes,' she tried a softer approach, 'but he's incapable, you know that. But, Tabitha, he's not a bad man. Not a serial killer or murderer. He told me about the tea.'

'It's not about the tea...'

'And I understand,' she said, 'I really do. It's the little things. The thoughtful things. Michael Sr wasn't good in terms of affection, remembering my birthday that kind of thing. Michael is just like his father. But I realised that there was a bigger picture. And you should too.'

'Is everything all right, Tabitha?' Nora was hovering in the background.

'Yes, thanks, Mum.'

'Hello, Nora,' said Celia, trying to smile, 'how lovely to see you again. And you are looking... splendid. That cardigan. It has a hand-knitted quality that is very charming. I think I saw something very similar in Brown Thomas last week. Yves St Laurent perhaps?'

'Nearly,' said Nora. 'St Vincent De Paul.'

'It's all right, Mum,' I said. 'I just want to talk to Celia for a moment.' I gave Nora a reassuring smile. I could handle this.

'Tabitha,' Celia began again, 'he needs you. He can't become a politician, like his father, if he is divorced. No one would trust him. They'd all wonder why his wife left him and *no one* would believe it was because of the silly matter of a cup of tea...'

'It's not about the tea!' Why didn't these people just get it? It wasn't the tea, it was something deeper, something that said about how I wanted to be loved, deeply and properly for who I was. Not be in some working partnership. I wanted more.

'They'd imagine terrible things about him. That maybe he had, oh I don't know, predilections, peccadilloes, *partialities*. Perhaps, they might think he was homosexual...'

'I don't care what people think.'

'No, dear, you obviously don't. But I do. And Michael does. And that little girl who is going to grow up without a father, she does too. Think of Rosie, her needs. Her *rights*. And, Tabitha, marriage is not meant to be fun. You're not supposed to actually enjoy it. Hard slog is what it is. But worth it in the end. When you are standing by the graveside, dressed in black, and you look back on a long marriage, you will think it worth it.'

'I can't wait that long,' I said, wanting to laugh at the weird turn the conversation was taking. 'Celia, he calls me Mammy.'

'Tabitha, that's nothing. Michael Senior used to call me *Mrs Fogarty*. What is in a name?'

'But we just aren't compatible...'

'Now, you're just being silly. Think of it as a business, and Michael is your colleague. You don't expect compatibility and passion and superb tea-making skills from someone you work with, hmmm? That's just naïve.' She smiled at me, sensing victory. 'I was married to Michael Senior for thirty-five years. And all that mattered was the team. I mean, there were a few incidents I had to turn a blind eye to. There was one woman who wouldn't stop phoning the house. And then there was that columnist that developed quite the crush... but I ploughed on. Eyes on the prize.'

The prize being the widow at the graveside, I thought. The dowager political wife.

'Thank you, Celia,' I said, edging her back to the door and holding it open. 'I appreciate you coming round, I really do.' I felt resolve and determination falling away. They were right, she and Michael. I was young and immature. I was asking for something that didn't belong in real life. I had a daughter to think about. I had wanted marriage and I had got myself into this relationship. I couldn't bail out of 'us', crying about love and tea, just because it wasn't perfect.

'You need to think very clearly about what you want to do, Tabitha.' She was now standing on the doorstep. 'And be clever about your life. Don't just throw it away over a cup of tea.'

12

One day, the following week, during morning lessons, I walked down to the Copse. It was a beautiful place, this triangular patch – on one side the school playing field, the other side high garden fences and, on the third side, the sea - however much it would have been more convenient for it to be a place barren of charm was blindingly obvious. A pair of blue tits happily flittered about, dipping up and down, having the time of their lives, tangles of honeysuckle and brambles now dotted with white flowers would later be black with berries. And, there were the trees; oak and birches and larches and a holly. With the sounds of the birds, the view of the glittering, sparkling sea, the soothing and restorative quality was undeniable.

A bench, I thought, would be good in the clearing between the trees. A place where the children could come in their lunch hour to get away from the noise of the playground. A space to think. We all needed quiet time and often we forget that children need it just as much as adults. We keep them so busy, so occupied, barking orders and ferrying them from school to home to classes. And then in school, it doesn't stop. But here, down here, at the edge of the school, was the perfect place for quiet.

I wished there was another way to raise the money, I really did. We'd just have to create another place, just like this. Okay it might take a couple of years to mature. But the blue tits and butterflies would find their way back, surely.

Over at the other side of the playing field, the familiar two by two trickle of children singing a song, every one of them word perfect, caught my attention.

Let it go, let it go, don't hold it back any more...

And leading this merry band of girls was Red. I watched as he turned to face them, as they reached the brow of the curve, his hands in the air, conducting them, their voices soaring into the crescendo, they meant every word.

I don't care! What the people say!

They all paused, letting the sentiment infuse their spirits.

The cold never bothered me anyway!

They shouted it out, arms puncturing the air with emphasis, their tiny voices combined to carry into the wind and the world, their collective call to arms.

And there was Red singing it as hard and as passionately as the rest of them. He turned to check they were all still following behind, and then smiled at Grace and Jenny who were walking beside him as they shouted out the last line. For a moment, my heart stopped. And all my feelings about him being at the school stopped being so confused and became very clear indeed. He couldn't stay. He would have to leave. I couldn't feel like this and carry on and be normal and look after Rosie and deal with my mother and do my job and keep house for Michael. I realised I was in love with him. Always had been and always would. Nothing had changed. Nothing at all. I felt exactly as I did when he left for San Francisco. Deeply in love. I had just pretended I didn't love him but I'd never fallen out of love with him. I'd just gone in a different direction. But love for him had been waiting, patiently, like a coat ready to be slipped on again.

And then he looked up and saw me. And I couldn't smile or wave or even pull myself together for long enough to try and look pirate queenly or headmistressy. I felt a wretchedness spread through my body. He was a complication too far. He would have to go. I stood up and began to walk towards them, it was the only way back to the school.

'Good morning, Mr Power,' I said, stopping beside them. 'Good morning girls.'

'Good morning, Ms Thomas,' they chorused, with far less enthusiasm that they had mustered a moment ago when singing 'Let It Go'. They bustled around him, like a protective mob.

'Still in fine voice, I'm glad to hear, Mr Power. You're not teaching the girls songs from the 1980s?'

He grinned at me, blushing slightly. 'Ah, yes... I've really got to stop. Or go for singing lessons. And *Let It Go* is song we all know. I don't think Johnny Logan would go down well.' He smiled at me. 'Anyway, we thought we'd get out of the classroom and come down to the Copse...'

'While we still can,' said Molly.

'It's such a beautiful day,' he said, 'that I thought that we'd go and practise our story-telling outdoors. They were full of questions about the Copse and we thought it might be a nice idea to pay it a visit before... you know...' He looked at me, searchingly. 'If that's all right?' he added solicitously.

'All the girls are working on their memoirs,' he went on, 'the story of their lives and they have to then perform it to the class.'

'That sounds very interesting girls,' I smiled at them all, wishing I had the easy charm of Red who would never make a child cry.

'Find a place to sit down, girls,' he said, as they avoided the nettles and stretched out under trees, doing handstands, making daisy chains, plaiting grasses. He turned back to me just as a leaf blew into his hair and I watched it flutter there until he brushed it away.

'I'd better get back and let you go on with your lesson.' I thought that if I stayed for much longer, I wouldn't ever want to leave, and would sit down with the girls and gaze at Red as rapturously as they looked up at him.

'How's your daughter?' he said. 'How's Rosie?'

'Better,' I said. 'Much better. She seems really good at the moment.'

'That's good to hear,' he said.

I walked back to school, wishing I could have stayed and made daisy chains with them and sung songs and hung out with Red. And the Copse. How could I sell it? Would it be really worth it?

BEFORE

'I wish I was there with you.' Red's voice was faraway, the line crackly. Our old red phone had a dodgy plastic receiver that used to fall off and had been sellotaped back on. It made even local calls sound faraway and crackly. 'Can't be helped,' I said. 'We'll be fine.'

'How's Nora?'

'Slightly manic. She's cleaning the house from top to bottom... even polished the brass on the front door.'

He laughed, gently. 'Everyone copes in different ways.'

'She says Rosaleen wouldn't like everyone coming if the brass wasn't shiny. She's even taken down all the net curtains and washed them, putting them back up while they were still damp. The house smells of washing powder.'

'And, how are you?'

'Fine...' I put my hand on my stomach. 'I'll be fine,' I said. My flight was booked for a following week. My suitcase was already half-packed, had been for months. 'Anyway, I'll see you in a few days. Not long now.'

'I've got so much to show you,' he said. 'We can explore San Francisco together. Just you and me. I've been saving some things for you, so we can do them together...'

'Like what?'

'Alcatraz!' He laughed. 'Bet you can't wait for that one.'

I laughed with him. 'I'm sure I'll get my own back,' I said. 'Find something that you're going to hate.'

'I was thinking that we can take weekend trips, up to the Napa Valley.' He sounded excited, eager for me to come and join him. 'Apparently it's beautiful there and we could hire a car or take a train.'

'Sounds lovely.' And it did, it sounded like life was meant to sound for two young people, happy with each other, glad to have left Ireland. For a bit. Living abroad, exploring the world. 'I can't wait.'

At dawn, the next day, it was bright and sunny, a golden day stretching out across Ireland. Rosaleen would have loved a day like today, I thought, and she would have gone for her daily swim. She would never have missed it, not if the weather was as perfect as this.

As I pedalled through the quiet streets, grief hit me for the first time. Nora and I had spent the last few days scrubbing and cleaning and making phone calls and meeting with the funeral directors, and this was the first time, I had been left alone with my thoughts. Grief unfolded over me, a slow, seeping of a thing, like I was litmus paper dipped in loss.

Rosaleen is dead, I said to myself, Rosaleen is dead. And the words suddenly turned from just a meaningless collection of sounds into something real, something horrible. Rosaleen is dead.

At the Forty Foot, I changed into my swimsuit and stood for a moment at the side, the water like a pool, glistening in the early morning summer sun, lapping at my toes.

And then I dived in, just like I had done with Rosaleen all those times. From when she had first taught me to swim, me gripping onto her like a baby monkey to when I was grown and tall and she was older and needing my hand to lean on as she stepped down into the sea.

But I don't know if it was the sea – the shock of the cold or the force of it – but as I hit the water I felt a pain in my belly. A searing pain, like a cramp, a wrench. I'd never felt like this before and I immediately knew something bad had happened.

But then again I'd never been pregnant before.

13

'Scrambled all right for you?'

Michael frowned, as he whipped through the *Irish Times*, eyes darting up and down rows. He'd arrived home from Brussels or Belfast, I wasn't quite sure, at 7 a.m. and was experimenting with weekend casual. Not just the suit and no tie, this was a new departure. A chino. A V-neck sweater. A polo shirt. The slip-on trainer. I suspected the influence of Lucy the Marvel.

'Fried, thank you, Mammy,' he said, still expertly scanning the paper to see what might have been have said about him. Good or bad, he didn't mind. That was the thing about politicians; hides so thick, they would survive a nuclear holocaust. A low day would be when he hadn't been mentioned at all.

'Tea? Coffee?' I felt like a B&B lady. 'Tinned prunes? Rice Crispies? A supermarket scone passed off as homemade?'

'What?'

'Nothing. So, tea?'

'Milk, actually, Mammy. A fine, big glass of milk.'

'Coming up.' I poured it out. 'Would you like a straw? Some Nesquik. I could put it in a sippy cup?'

He looked up again. 'Sorry Mammy, did you say something?'

'Here's your milk.' I put his glass down beside him.

'Delicious.' He took a big gulp. 'I feel healthier already,' he said, eyes returned to the paper as I cracked an egg into the frying pan and stood for a moment watching it sizzle.

'Your friend Clodagh's in here,' he said. 'At the back. In the going-out pages...'

'The social column?' I looked over his shoulder at the paper and there indeed was Clodagh, standing with Max wearing a black tuxedo and not smiling. 'He looks his usual friendly self,' I said.

'What's that?' Michael didn't take his eyes off the paper.

'It's just that for some reason Clodagh is going out with a man who doesn't seem to like people. Or smiling.' I slid the egg from the pan onto his plate.

'Mmmhmmm.' Michael buttered more toast, and stared at Max for a moment.

'He needs milk,' he said.

'Who?'

'Clodagh's fella. He looks pasty. Pale. As though he's spent his life in a dark room. He needs a glass of milk. Put colour in his cheeks. Look at me.'

'What?'

'No, look at me. Actually look at me. See my cheeks. What colour are they?'

I peered at his face. I hadn't been so close to him in years or paid so much attention. 'You do look healthy,' I admitted. 'Definitely not pasty. A high colour, one might say.' Heightened by the white of the teeth, I thought.

'See!' he was triumphant. 'Now, I think that milk is what is wrong with Rosie. It's her vegetarianism. If she would just eat normally, then maybe she wouldn't be short of breath and feeling all light-headed.'

'You are prescribing a glass of milk.'

'That's right.' His eyes moved to another page.

'I wish I'd known this,' I said. 'I'm sure other people need to know the miraculous benefits of milk.'

'Well, now you do.' It was hard to believe now what a breath of fresh air Michael seemed when I met him. Exotic, really. A twenty-five-year-old suit-wearing, briefcase-swinging, young conservative. Couldn't have been more different to Red, which is exactly what I thought I needed. Even his need to keep his socks on when we slept together seemed endearing. Cold feet, I thought. Podophobia, perhaps. Athlete's foot? Strange but surmountable. Who, after all, didn't have strange habits, weird predilections?

'Do you think we should encourage her to take a year out after the exams? Not go straight to college. Take a breather?'

'A breather? I know, why don't we let her just lie around all day and watch daytime television? Maybe encourage her to take up smoking. Or rolling her own cigarettes and wearing tie-dye clothing? Perhaps develop a Jack Daniels habit? Hmmm?'

'Michael...'

'She doesn't need a year off. Okay, so it's a tough year but this is how you prove yourself to yourself. You get through things. It's something you wouldn't understand,' he said. 'You're not thinking straight. What with the protest and everything. Lucy has brought me up to speed. I can't say I'm not shocked that your mother is involved. Exactly the kind of thing she would do. Rabble-rousing. She'd protest about the closing of a door.' He paused. 'So, what stage are you at?'

'Just thinking about it. Trying to come to a decision. I can't think of another way we can raise money. The school is falling apart. But it's impossible to make clear-headed decisions when you have a group of well-meaning and extremely pleasant protestors outside.'

'Welcome to my world,' he said grimly.

'And one of them is your mother I don't want to give in just because they are there. I can't seem to decide. I don't feel that anyone is on my side... not even Mary...' Or Red, I thought. 'I feel quite alone...' I never unburdened myself to Michael. I had become used to just living in my own head and it felt good to let it out but when I looked up, Michael was concentrating hard on his phone.

'I downloaded this app,' he said. 'It's to see how well I sleep. I had eight and a half hours last night... isn't that good? Going to go for nine tonight. Good solid REM.'

'That sounds like a great ambition,' I said. 'Good luck with it.' He hadn't listened to a word I'd said.

'It's all about letting the body relax. You know I spend all day rushing

about, everyone wanting a piece of me and then it's so hard to switch off...
hot milk is the answer...'

'I am so delighted for you...'

'Jesus!' He looked up suddenly. 'What's the time?'

'Nine a.m.'

'Jayze, Terry's going to be here in a minute.'

Within moments we heard the sound of the horn of the ministerial car and Michael rushed out of the door, calling goodbye to Rosie upstairs. From the living room window, I saw Terry in the front of the car, facing front and, in the back, was Lucy the Marvel. They never stopping politicking.

14

'This year, weather girl. Next year president of the world.' Clodagh slapped down some magazines. 'She's taking over the planet. She's on the cover of four of these.'

'She gets away with leather trousers,' I said. For the cover of the *Irish Woman*, Bridget was in an Aran jumper, her hands around a hot chocolate. Strapline: 'Getting Cosy with TV's latest superstar'.

'TV's latest monster more like,' said Clodagh. 'Listen to this. *"Always take off your make-up. I never go to bed without making sure I'm cleansed and toned," said the red-haired beauty. "I drink three litres of water a day and it's muesli for breakfast. No Full Irishes for me!" the weather-girl laughed.'* Clodagh sighed and rolled her eyes. 'She sounds so bloody *nice*, doesn't she? Little do they know... She told me I was getting *old*. But in a *nice* way. Well-meaning.' Clodagh pulled a face.

'But you're not. You're forty-two.'

'Yes, in a rational, normal world, I am the proverbial spring chicken. But I was chatting to Jackie, the make-up artist, and we were talking about Botox, does it work, where the best place to go is.' She held up her hand. 'Before you say anything, I'm not doing it. We were just talking. Starving myself is one thing, being injected with an unknown substance is a step too far in the pursuit of youthful loveliness. Anyway, we didn't realise that Bridget, who I thought was on her phone, Snapchatting or whatever. Tindering probably. She's single and on the look-out, apparently. So Jackie is pretty militant about Botox, she says your choice is to have it or never go outside, stay in permanently darkened rooms.'

'You forgot ageing gracefully.'

'There's that. Or there's ageing disgracefully. Anyway, so we are chatting away and guess who pipes up? Got it in one. So Bridget says, *"The problem is, Clodagh, you got old. It happens to everyone. You've had your moment in the sun."* And then Jackie says it's the sun that's the problem and everything got a bit confused, but when I asked Bridget if she had meant to be so rude, she said she wasn't being and that she was so sorry if she hurt my feelings, but had I ever thought about buying a cat because they are great company when you are old.'

'She's just got a weird sense of humour.'

'Jackie and I were just looking at each other, shaking our heads, and all I could think about was that I *had* been thinking about getting a cat. I never liked them, but suddenly they seem like the perfect addition to my life. I mean, I used to like to buy new things. But now all I'm fantasising about is having a little cat to welcome me home at night. But obviously I didn't tell *her* that.' She sighed. 'And Max has given her an extra minute. Lucinda is *furious.*'

'Surely there's not enough actual weather?' Ireland was decidedly unexciting in its meteorological conditions. The whole country would become hysterical with excitement if it snowed for more than half an hour or if the sun came out and it was properly hot in the summer so that people left work early to clear the supermarket shelves of charcoal and sausages. Mainly, things were pretty boring weather-wise.

'She's so popular with the viewers, apparently, that they want less news and more weather. Well, more Bridget, really. *She* told me today, while I was still reeling from the getting old and cat comment and self-soothing with an apricot yogurt. Said she wondered why Max hadn't told me and thought I would have known. And then she said she hoped I wouldn't be too upset by it and she has admired me since she was tiny. When she was leaping around the living room learning her Irish dancing steps, I'd be on in the corner. I am the reason she got into broadcasting.' Clodagh let out a snort. 'Broadcasting! Ha! I wouldn't be surprised if she starts Irish dancing tomorrow. Riverdances onto the set, playing the tin whistle. And I've just got to roll with it.'

'What does Max say?'

'He won't talk about it with me. He says that his conversations with the talent...'

'The talent?'

'Those of us on air... he says they're private. Between him and their agents. In Bridget's case, her terrifying mother.'

'But Max must be on your side... surely he must be aware of how precarious you feel...'

'He is all about figures and ratings and approval panels and focus groups. He doesn't do emotions or feelings. He's all about the job. Which is why, supposedly, he's such a brilliant manager. And so terrible at showing empathy.'

I shook my head. 'What are you doing with all these lunatics, Clodagh? Why don't you give it all up, do a nice knitting course, get into basket weaving?' I didn't understand why she put up with this crazy world and with Max. But then, she didn't understand why I put up with Michael.

'You'll meet the lunatics at my party,' she said. 'Now...' she paused. 'I hope you don't mind, but Red's coming. I met him the other day and mentioned it. How are you two getting along?'

'Fine. It's weird but it's almost as though it would be so easy to slip back into something. Every time we talk, we find ourselves talking so normally, as though nothing ever happened, but then we both pull back as soon as we remember.'

Clodagh contemplated me for a moment.

'You still love him,' she said.

'Leave it Clodagh,' I said. 'Please. It's complicated, I won't deny that but...' She was right, though. I still loved him and there was nothing I could do.

'Mid-life crisis,' Clodagh deduced. 'Not to worry, I'm having one too.'

'Are women allowed to have them? I thought they were strictly the preserve of men.'

'What are we allowed to have then?' she said,

'Funny turns, hot flushes, menopausal meltdowns, mental breakdowns...'

'Well, whatever I'm having, it feels like I need to do something different.' She looked at me. 'We could get a flat together, like the old days. You move out. Rosie will be in college soon and we could hang out in our pyjamas, eat toast... just like we used to. Come on, what's stopping you? Think about it,' she persisted, 'you would never have to see Celia ever again.'

'Now I'm tempted. A life without my mother-in-law is something I would seriously contemplate.' I laughed. 'But really, there's nothing wrong. Michael and I rub along...'

'Rub along?' She raised an eyebrow. 'When was the last time you *rubbed* along?'

'Listen, there is nothing unusual about us. It's just your common or garden lacklustre marriage, nothing for *you* to worry about.' But I was thinking about Red when I spoke. What would he say if he knew things between me and Michael were cool to the point of freezing? Would he be pleased that my marriage hadn't quite worked out for me or would he be sorry that I threw him and us away for lack-lustre?

'And that's good enough for you?'

'It hasn't been that bad,' I insisted. 'Michael's a good person.'

'With good teeth,' said Clodagh. 'You forgot the teeth.'

'Blinding,' I agreed.

'His teeth alone would get you home on a dark night in a power cut,' she said.

'But what about you Clodagh? What's it been... six months? When is Maximus moving in? Or are you having cold feet?' I hoped she was. What if she married him out of sheer loneliness, shackled to him for the rest of his life. 'Are you hoping to be Mrs Max Pratt? Clodagh Pratt?'

'It doesn't go well, does it?' she grinned. 'But no. Not yet. Maybe never. Sometimes you need to be in a relationship to remember all the good things about being single.'

'Like what?'

'Like never compromising, not having to share your bed. Never explaining.' She sighed. 'I Miss that. And it means that I can eat yogurts for dinner and watch *Game of Thrones* and wear my old Waterboys' T-shirt and no one can judge.'

'And is there any one you would give your Waterboys' T-shirt up for?'

'Apart from Mike Scott himself,' she said, 'no. Anyway, I don't think Max has ever knowingly eaten a yogurt, or seen *Game of Thrones* or worn a T-shirt. He's on the uptight spectrum. Rarely smiles. The only thing that makes him happy is work.'

I laughed. 'You're joking. Tell me you're joking.'

'I can't work out if he has some kind of facial paralysis and actually can't, or doesn't find anything I say remotely amusing or, perhaps, never learned how to. Grew up with fundamentalists or whatever.' She stopped. 'Actually, do you have any yogurts?' she said. 'I'm starving. Haven't eaten since the morning. I know you have those nice ones. You always do.'

I stood up and fetched one and a spoon. 'You've got to eat more than a yogurt, you know. It's not good for you.'

'*Of course* it's not good for me! *Of course* this is wrong and terrible, but I can't remember the last time I derived any pleasure in any food that wasn't a yogurt since... since we were students and always stopped for a kebab on the way home. Do you remember? God, they were nice.'

'So buy a kebab.'

She shook her head at me. 'You think this is easy, don't you? You try being on television every night. You wouldn't believe the letters I get. From *women*! They hate my hair, or my blouse, or my earrings. Or I look like I've put on weight. Or my make-up was all weird. Or that blue is not my colour or my mouth is a funny shape. And, if you were subjected to that, you'd be starving yourself as well. *And* looking at your mouth in the mirror all the time to see if it was wonky.' She paused. 'It's not, is it?'

* * *

The sound of a key in the door. 'Yoo-hoo! Mammy!'

'Mammy?' she mouthed, shaking her head. 'When are you going to leave?'

I shrugged helplessly.

'There you are!' Michael opened the kitchen door. 'And Clodagh...' His smile died on his face. Unlike the farming community of Ireland, he was no fan of Clodagh. She was too brash for his liking, too loud. And she wasn't much of a sycophant. 'What a lovely surprise,' he said. 'Again.'

'Isn't it?' said Clodagh, pleasantly. 'And what brings you home,' she said. 'Brussels closed for business?'

'Well, Clodagh,' he said patiently, 'Brussels is a city and therefore can't technically shut. But if you are referring to the European Parliament then it is still open but I'm just not there. I have Dublin business to take care of.' He went over to the fridge and poured himself a glass of milk and drank it down in one. 'Now milk is a drink, wouldn't you say Clodagh?'

'Yes, it's a drink, you could say that Michael.'

'No, but it's a *drink*. It's the kind of drink that men don't drink.'

'Don't they?' Clodagh looked puzzled. 'Is there a law?'

'There should be,' said Michael, a faraway look taking over his face. 'There *could* be. In fact, I might do a focus grouping on the subject. I think if we made people – men – drink milk then it would be good for everyone. Good for farmers, good for bones, good for the Irish economy. It could be seen as a patriotic thing to do.'

'So you're going to make it a law?' said Clodagh. 'The new milk quotas?'

'Ha! That's a good one. Well, I just said it might be worth investigating. At the moment, men are bombarded with beer adverts. Drink this beer or that alcoholic beverage but no one says the same about milk. And why is that? Hmmm?'

We shook our heads. 'Not alcoholic?' I suggested.

'Unless you add vodka,' said Clodagh. 'Then it's a *drink* drink.'

'No, milk is a man's drink, only *I* seem be aware of that fact.'

'I don't think so,' said Clodagh. 'People have been drinking milk for millennia.'

'But not straight out of the carton,' said Michael. 'After a gym session. Or in a pub. And why not?'

'There's a conspiracy against cows?'

'No. Men!' Michael was triumphant. 'You hadn't thought about that had you? We are told to drink beer and wine and caffeine and all those things that are bad for you. But no one develops a campaign to encourage men to drink milk. Which is good for you. Which might keep you alive. So hence my new campaign. Once I've passed SIPL, I'll pass milk.'

Clodagh laughed. 'Sounds like you need a doctor.' She stood up to leave.

'There's something on your face, Michael,' I said. 'On your top lip. A milk moustache.'

'Aha!' he wiped it away with the back of his hand. 'I'll just have to bring that into the legislation. Milk moustaches are now cool. Hipsters have their beards. Real men have milk moustaches.' He laughed. 'That's my slogan. I can see it now. And dairy farmers are going to love me. I'm thinking a cabinet position by the next political term.'

He was incorrigible and unstoppable, undaunted by potential failure and possible ridicule, he was a proper politician and as I've said before, you had to admire them.

'Got a slogan for you,' he said. 'What about Milk Makes Men *Men*?'

At the door, we hugged goodbye. 'You with Mike the Milkman and me with Maximus Pratt. I don't know which of us has done better.'

'If we didn't laugh...'

'We'd cry. And laugh. At the same time.' She hugged me again, tighter this time. 'And thanks for allowing me to let off steam.'

* * *

Over the previous week, I had declined all Nora's calls to me and, studiously ignoring her when I drove into school, even though, out of the corner of my eye, I could see her getting up to come towards the car or trying to wave. But by the Friday afternoon, I had felt wretched about the whole thing. And she didn't look happy either, her face turning from eager enthusiasm at the sight of my car at the beginning of the week to resigned deflation by the end.

Eventually, after another sleepless night, I had to do something. Michael, I assumed, wherever he was, would have been sleeping soundly, his app registering his uninterrupted hours of deep sleep. It was ironic he could sleep so well, and always had done, even though he made decisions every day with directly affected people's lives, yet I couldn't sleep because I was worried about the sale of a few trees.

Just after 6 a.m., I got out of bed, pulled on my tracksuit bottoms. And I began to drive towards where I knew Nora would be. The Forty Foot.

It was going to be a beautiful day and as I rounded the corner at Sandy-cove, the sea was shimmering across the bay. A group of seagulls were stretching their wings on the wall by the beach, easing themselves into the morning and for one moment, I felt like undressing and slipping into the cool water, feeling it on my skin, the ripples of the waves against my face, the salt on my lips. But then, I remembered. The thought of the water, the darkness below, the seaweedy depths, the rocks, the unknown. I pulled my jacket around me, glad to be on dry land.

'Beautiful morning,' said a man, coming the other way, towel rolled under his arm, dressing gown on over his trunks. I stood at the edge of the rocks. Out there, somewhere, in the Irish Sea was my mother. I scanned the water. Nothing. But suddenly there she was, a tiny dot among the waves. Head sticking out of the water, as she swam around in a lazy, languorous, undulating breaststroke, her freckly arms propelling her gently through the water as she was lifted and bobbed over the gentle waves. And then she flipped over onto her back and floated there, looking up at the sky, seeming entirely at peace and utterly free.

And then, flipping back over, she began swimming back to shore, her slow stroke pulling her closer and closer to me. Slowly but surely, she began to appear. Not just a red-haired dot but a person, with a nose and a mouth.

Just before the seabed became too shallow and the rocks too close, she flipped over again, soaking her head and her face, allowing the water to penetrate her scalp, to wash over her face. A daily baptism. And with the grace of a seal, she found her footing and pulled herself up the steps.

'What are you doing here?' she said.

'Oh, you know, just doing my Christmas shopping.'

She grinned. 'And I thought you were looking for me. To say sorry for not taking my calls. For ignoring me. Rosie told me to give you time. So I am.' She waved to another swimmer. 'Morning, Mary... yes, beautiful...' She walked over to her towel, which was in a heap with her clothes and bag, and picked it up.

'You should be saying sorry to me!' God, she was infuriating. 'That's why I'm here.'

'For me to say sorry? But why? What for?' She began rubbing herself.

'The protest... listen...'

'Tabitha, I've explained everything. It's not personal. It's just something we have to do. We are compelled to do it. I don't know why we have to fall out about it. You know I don't believe in falling out with anyone...'

'But it feels personal, like you are targeting me. *And* it's embarrassing.'

'But that doesn't matter, does it? That kind of thing, worrying about what people think of you, doesn't matter. Not in the grand scheme of things.' She stood there, naked from the waist up while she found her bra and shirt.

'Well, what is the grand scheme of things?' It was so simple for Nora. Life was in black and white, us and them, capitalists and socialists, swimmers and non-swimmers. Rarely did other people's points of view entered her consciousness, which made her navigation of the world easier for her but far more complicated for those around her.

'The trees. The wildlife. The principle.'

'Principle?'

'Yes, if none of us had principles, then we'd be in a very sorry state.'

'Mum, just stop it will you? Stop the protest...'

'Will you stop the development?' She waved to someone else. 'Morning, Gordon... yes, so beautiful. We are lucky, are we not?' She turned back to me, expectantly. 'The school should retain control over that land. Our greatest resources are being used as collateral in an exchange for money. This is the kind of struggle that we indigenous people need to make a stand about. I shouldn't have to explain this to you. You are my daughter after all.'

'Indigenous?' I laughed. 'You're not a Native American.'

'Maybe not, but as a proud Irish woman I know how precious land can be taken from us. Trees and oxygen and wildlife and nature can't be measured and sold like a piece of silk. I think Dalkey deserves better than that. Have you not thought about other ways of using the land?'

I paused, thinking back to the day when Red and the children came down. That was good use of the land. But no, we needed the money. It would be better for the long-term gain of the school. Nora was just using emotion to win. 'Mum, I told you. It's full of nettles and brambles.'

'And what's wrong with them? Your grandmother used both of them. Nettle soup, do you remember. And bramble jelly.' She was pulling on her trousers now, buckling her belt.

She paused. 'Can we just forget about it? I'll carry on and you'll carry on and no hard feelings? Hello, Fiona, yes, lovely day.'

'Well, would *you* just stop? Nellie and Arthur and the others, they can carry on. But you, would you retire gracefully?'

'I can't, Tabitha,' she said, as we began to walk to my car. 'I wish I could, but I can't. I am an environmentalist. That's what I do, have always done. I can't give up now.'

'Why can't you?'

'Principle.' She shrugged. 'Bloody-mindedness.' She laughed. 'That's what Rosaleen used to say about me. She used to say I was my own woman. And I think she might say the same about you.' She smiled at me.

'Bloody-minded?' I tried to look outraged but I quite liked the idea that I was a little bit bloody-minded. She'd won me over, as she always did.

'Tell me about Rosie, the poor loveen. I phoned her yesterday, did she tell you?'

'I don't really know. She seems better.'

'I'll get her swimming again, that's what I'll do. It'll do her the power of good.' She looked at me. 'And we'll go to West Cork. I'll get the two of you down there if it's the last thing I do. It'll be fun. When was the last time you had fun?'

I tried to think.

'See!' she said triumphantly.

She looked at me as we stopped at the car. 'Tabitha...' Finally, she was going to say sorry.

'Yes?' I would be gracious and accept her apology, but I would also say how much she had hurt me and that it was not acceptable.

'Could you give me a lift home? Puncture. I had to walk this morning.'

She smiled at me. That was the problem with Nora, she was charm personified. She never let anyone be annoyed with her for too long.

'In you get.'

15

The next morning as I drove past the protestors, Nora waved at me to stop and when I slowed down, she leaned into my window. 'Come and say hello to Christy.'

'Christy Power?' I said. 'Red's dad Christy?'

She nodded. 'The very one. He's writing a poem, or a collection of poems. He's just read one out to us. "Nora's Last Stand". I told him there was no way it was going to be, but he said it flowed better this way.'

I parked the car and walked over to them. Christy was sitting on Nellie's flowery picnic chair, with his notebook, sucking on an old chewed pencil ruminatively.

'Well, young Tabitha,' he said, and began to try and get up.

'Hello Christy,' I said, easing him back down. 'What are you doing here?'

'I meant to come down weeks ago, swell the numbers a bit, but my legs haven't been so good.'

'There are new people here every day,' I said. 'It's turning into a day care for the retired.'

'You see, Tabitha,' he said. 'You never lose your passion. Eyesight, ability to sprint 100 metres, to cook a soufflé, but you never lose your principles.'

'Since when did you cook a soufflé, Christy?' said Nellie. 'I don't think it was on soufflés you were reared.'

'Bacon and cabbage,' he said, giving her a wink. 'Like we all were. But I wouldn't mind a soufflé. Just to see if they are as nice as they sound...'

He was right, I thought, as I listened along. They had created something, my mother and her pals, they had created a sense of community, a cause, a reason to be, out of passion and commitment. They had created a space for people to come down, have a chat, pass the time of day, hold placards and feel part of something greater than they were.

'So, you're never going to sell the land, are ye?' said Christy. 'It's a bit hare-brained, wouldn't you say. Have these fine people not convinced you yet? You are going to tell the developers where to go, aren't you?' He was smiling at me but Christy meant business. They all did. These were not pensioners who gave up. Christy had survived the death of his wife, bringing up a son on his own. He'd left school at fourteen and had worked his way up in the council to a nice, desk job. *And* he wrote poetry.

'I don't know,' I admitted. 'It's kind of hard to make a decision when you have protestors clouding your thoughts.'

'I know you'll do the right thing,' he said. 'Whatever the outcome. You've got a good heart, you have.'

'Tea, Christy?' said Robbo. 'Nice and hot?'

'Thank you, lad,' said Christy. 'I was just saying to your mother, how nice it was that you and Red were... you know, friendly again.'

Nora just gave me a shrug and a weird smile, as if she hadn't contributed to this particular part of the conversation.

'I'd better go,' I said. 'Are you here for the day, Christy?'

'I think so. If Robbo over there keeps the tea coming.' He gave Robbo a wink.

'The more the merrier,' said Nora. 'We need all the reinforcements we can get. Now, Tabitha, at this board meeting tonight, you're to tell this Brian Crowley, that you won't be selling.'

'But, Mum, it's not that simple,' I said, crossly. I admired the protestors and couldn't help but be impressed by the community they had created, a mini movement. It may not be of the magnitude of the Sheep's Head Peace

Camp but it was significant. But it still didn't take away from the fact that our school needed money.

'Well, whatever you decide,' said Christy, 'we all know your heart is in the right place. Decisions can be difficult.'

I flashed him a grateful smile, touched by his kindness.

'They don't have to be,' said Nora. 'This decision is wrong. Pure and simple.'

'Let me just write that down,' said Christy. 'It'll be good for the poem.'

* * *

Nora had been right, I thought. I didn't have fun anymore. The last time I had gone out was to Celia's soiree and that didn't count. But at Clodagh's party, there surely was an opportunity for fun and to prove to my mother that I too could have a laugh. Drinking, music... and Red. He didn't make me feel fun. Just awkward.

And then there was the not insignificant issue of what I was actually going to put on. I mean, what did people wear to parties these days? At Celia's, everyone was in various shades of taupe. But to a cool, media party?

Unless you counted my collection of sensible suits for school or my tracksuit bottoms and cashmere jumpers (all slightly bobbly, if truth be told), I had *nothing* to wear. And the thing was, I wanted to look sexy. Attractive. Still got it. That kind of thing. Things that I hadn't asked of myself in years. If Red was going to be there, I didn't want to turn up in my easy-care separates.

Jeans. Try the jeans. And my black top. Better perhaps than with the black trousers? What about my ballet flats? Hmmm. I assessed myself in the mirror. No. No way. I looked like a nun on a night-off. Maybe it was the way I was standing, slightly hunched? I pulled myself up, ballerina style.

'Mum! Oh my God!' Rosie was standing at the door, laughing. 'Oh my god what are you doing, you look ridiculous!' *She* looked effortlessly gorgeous as always, in her old tracksuit bottoms, long hair loosely tied. 'Mum... you haven't gone mad, have you?'

'I think I might have. I was just trying to look nice. It's Clodagh's party and it's going to be full of scary media folk. No one eats, apparently, and they all have personal trainers and dieticians and food coaches and...' I sounded pathetic, I knew that. 'I just want to up my game...'

'Up your game?'

'Just a bit. Not enough to win Wimbledon or anything, but enough not to embarrass myself by tripping over the balls or getting tangled in the net...' my metaphor drifted away, exhausted. 'Listen, I know it's stupid and it goes against everything I've ever taught you about being yourself and not trying to fit in. I know that it's not feminist or empowering, but for one night, just one night, I don't want to look like a principal of a suburban national school. I want to look like... like utterly unlike me. I want to look nice.' I didn't want to tell her about Red. How could I explain that one? That I wanted to look nice for a man that wasn't my husband and someone with whom I shared a secret past.

'You do look nice,' she said, loyally. 'You always look nice. But if you want to look a little bit more glamorous, then I'll help you.'

'But I don't want to take you away from your books.'

'I need a break,' she said. 'I'll just get you out of the house and then I'll go back to them.'

'Or go and see Alice and Meg?' I suggested. 'It is Friday night after all.'

'They'll be working too,' she said, quickly. 'Everyone is. Anyway, I'll give you a hand.'

'I don't even know what's fashionable anymore. I don't even know how to get dressed. I mean, are jeans still even a thing? Or is it something else entirely. Dungarees or spacesuits. I have no idea.'

'No, jeans are still a thing,' she reassured. 'But you can't wear them with that.' She eyed my blouse. 'Take it off...'

'But...'

'Off.' She scanned the contents of my wardrobe with the eye of a personal shopper. 'Right then...'

I felt almost giddy with delight, sharing this moment with her. I missed her, I had been so worried about her, yet here she was, bossing me about, being my daughter again, the one I loved with all my heart.

'What about this?' She held up a top on which I had spent a ridiculous amount of money and it had hung, reproachfully, in my wardrobe for three years. A daily reminder of my profligacy.

'It's not me. Too low-cut,' I said. 'And too tight. It might be okay if I was a yoga teacher, living in LA, existing on nettles. And had an entirely different personality. And face. And body. *Then*, then it would be gorgeous on me. But there's not enough time. I mean, I can't even touch my toes...'

'So? Try it on.'

I didn't argue and pulled it on.

'Now the jeans.'

I did as I was told, wriggling in. They were tight but not insurmountable or un-get-in-able.

'Good,' said Rosie, narrow-eyed, with an air of Henry Higgins, surveying and scrutinising. 'Now the shoes.'

'I thought I could wear my flats. They're comfortable and...'

'Comfort?' She looked at me as though I had suggested wearing a pair of novelty Garfield slippers. 'Oh no, tonight is not about comfort...'

'Who are you?' I said. 'What kind of creature have I raised? I thought high heels were a symbol of male oppression?'

'Mum,' she said. 'It's *one* night. Wearing high heels is not going to kill you. You wear those flat shoes every day. They're like slippers.'

'Which is why I wear them.'

'These.' She produced another vast waste of money. They weren't me, respectable teacher, mother and politician's wife. I had worn them only once and never again. '*These* are perfect.'

'They are ridiculous,' I insisted.

'Try them on.'

Wobbling fawn-like, I waited for Rosie's verdict. Her beautiful face frowning with concentration. How could I regret any decision I had ever made when I had Rosie to show for it?

'There's one thing missing,' she said. 'One moment!' She ran from the room and returned with a pair of hoop earrings which she had borrowed from me and never returned. 'And these.' She stepped back while I looped them through my ears. 'Right,' she said with triumph. 'You are perfect. Beautiful, actually.'

'Really?' I was pathetically grateful for the compliment.

She laughed. 'One hundred per cent yes. You look like my mum, but different.' She was the Rosie of a year ago, before this year of exam stress and the end of things with Jake. Smiling, delighted at her success in the fashion makeover.

'You remind me of Rosaleen,' I said. 'I called you after her, you know. Little rose, Rosaleen and Rosie.'

She came over and hugged me and, for a moment, we held each other, as though she was still my little girl and needed one of my long hugs.

'Rosie?' I said when we pulled away. 'Everything okay?'

She nodded. 'Have a good time, Mum. You won't be too late, will you?'

I shook my head. 'Are you worried about me?'

'No. I just... I just like you being at home, that's all.'

'I won't be late, I promise.'

And she smiled as I waved from the front door, those Rosaleen blue eyes.

* * *

'You look gorgeous.' Clodagh eyed me approvingly, swiping two glasses of champagne from a passing tray and handing one to me. 'I knew you were still in there, under the school-teacher exterior, the old Tabitha lurks.'

'Shut up, Clodes,' I said. 'It's easy for you. You don't have to try. Tonight, I am the product of my daughter. Rosie was my stylist.'

'Well, she did a wonderful job. What's this?' I had handed over her present. 'Oooh...' She tore off the paper. '*Pride and Prejudice*! Thank you!'

'It's a special edition. And read this...' I said, pulling out a card I'd made.

'*You are invited to a Jane Austen weekend in Bath with your best friend, Tabitha, who, by the way, is paying for everything. Just say the date! Really?*' she squealed. 'That is the best present ever. Are you sure?'

'Totally. I can't wait myself. I thought we could go to Bath for a posh weekend away and have treatments in the spa there and do all things Jane Austen.' At college, Clodagh was obsessed with Jane Austen and wrote her final dissertation on female empowerment in the novels of... etc. 'I mean,' I said, 'we can't not celebrate your *fortieth* birthday! Well, we did, two years ago and it was so good, we should do it all over again.' Thinking back, that was last time I had had fun.

She laughed. 'Tab, this is why you're my best friend. No one in the world knows me like you do. Thank you!' She clutched me hard. 'Let's go in the autumn. Deal?'

'Just say the date... my finger is hovering over the Ryanair confirm flights button.'

She smiled and dropped her voice. 'It's the perfect trip for two women in their mid-forties...'

'Mid? Early, surely!' I dropped my voice significantly. 'We're only forty-two.'

'Whatever, it's immaterial, really. Just remember, yesterday I was thirty-nine. Tonight I am a mere forty. It's magic.'

'Got it. Now, who's here? Anyone famous, glamorous. I am expecting top-notch celebrities. Some scandal that will end up in the tabloids in the morning.' I looked around and spotted a couple of famous faces. A few soap stars. A DJ was over in the corner playing music I had never heard before – it certainly wasn't Johnny Logan. 'Where's Max?'

'Somewhere over there,' she said, waving a hand vaguely. 'On his mobile probably. Or having a fag.' She rolled her eyes. 'No one is meant to know he's a smoker because I think he thinks it shows weakness. I mean, he is *obsessed* with his health. He's always drinking green slime and worrying about the lines on his face. He doesn't want people to know his fallibilities.'

I laughed. 'But he does *drink*, doesn't he?'

'Are you mad? You can't work in the media and be teetotal. You'd have your NUJ card taken off you.' She paused. 'He's a man of contrasts. But that's what makes him interesting.' She paused. 'Kind of.'

'Clodagh! Loveen!' In front of us was a vision of shimmering green. Long red hair cascading over her shoulders, voluptuous curves barely contained. Bridget O'Flaherty. She looked even more amazing in the flesh. Fleshier, really.

'Bridget!' Clodagh hugged her, air-kissing as though they were long-lost friends. 'So lovely that you came.'

'I would not have missed this for anything. I just love parties, especially ones like this. It's full of the old dinosaurs of Irish television. All those ones who you thought had popped their clogs years ago. I mean, I just saw Val Connolly. Who exhumed him?'

'Val?' said Clodagh. I could tell she was doing her best to hold on to her smile 'He runs his own production company now. Makes millions.' She turned to me and imperceptibly widened her eyes giving a tiny shake of her head.

'Well, not as disinteresting as I initially thought,' said Bridget. 'I always say, there are only two points to a man. One, if he's drop-dead gorgeous, or two, if he's loaded. Normally, I like both.'

Clodagh managed to mouth 'see what I mean' to me. 'Tab,' she said, 'I should have introduced you... this is Bridget O'Flaherty, our new weather...

'The new *meteorologist* and television personality,' said Bridget. 'Or that's what my agent wants me to call myself. It's meaningless, to me, but she *insists* on it. Absolutely insists. Says I'm not just a pretty face. Well, she says I'm that, but she would wouldn't she, being my mother and everything. Meteorologist and television personality, that's me! Anyway, pleased to meet you.' She shook my hand.

'Tabitha,' I said. 'Clodagh's friend. No media connections. Just here for the free champagne.'

'So, how old *are* you, Clodagh?' she said.

'Forty,' said Clodagh, quickly, eyes giving a flicker.

'Really?' Bridget raised a sceptical brow.

'Yes really! Goodness me, you don't think I am younger than that, do you?' went on Clodagh. 'You don't think I am pretending to be older than I actually am to lend myself a sense of gravitas?'

'Gravitas? Is that something to do with gravity?'

'No,' said Clodagh. 'It's to do with gravy. On your roast chicken.'

Bridget looked confused, but I was beginning to laugh, discreetly.

'We all like gravitas, Bridget,' Clodagh continued. 'Except some of us were born with it, some of us have gravitas thrust upon us and others don't even know what it is.'

'Oh do fuck off,' said Bridget, sweetly. 'All I'm saying is that you don't look forty...'

'Nor do you,' said Clodagh.

'But *obviously* I don't!' said Bridget.

'You look fifty!' Clodagh drained her glass of champagne. 'Oh, aren't you?'

'I'm fecking thirty-one,' said Bridget, rattled. 'It's just that I've been working – professionally – since I was five. It's really ageing, those late nights and having to get on the road again. Fecking Riverdance. Even now, if I walk into a shop and they are playing the music, I can feel my feet start to twitch, and my knees start to ache. I can hear the voice of our teacher shouting at us to keep on. I can't walk around Temple Bar or any of the tourist shops. It's all Mammy's fault. She put me on the stage, spotted my talent early. Her own dancing career was cruelly cut short by a terrible accident that involved a bullock at the St Patrick's Day parade when she was twelve. Never got over it and she put all her effort into me. When my knees packed in, she thought television was our only answer. She's over there, actually.' She pointed out a woman who looked like a slightly older version of Bridget, the same look entirely, but she was shorter and her hair an *un*natural shade of red.

Then Bridget suddenly shouted. 'Selfie!' And put both arms around us and held up her phone. 'This, ladies, is going on Twitter,' she said. 'I try and post every fifteen minutes. Everyone smile!'

And just as I was clinched in this media sandwich, I saw a face looking over at me. Red. He waved his hand, an indiscernible expression on his face, while I disentangled myself from Bridget's limbs.

Maybe it was the effect of the champagne, but all I wanted to do was put my two hands around his face and pull him towards me and kiss him. I wanted to remember what he tasted like, what it felt to feel his breath on mine, feel the heat of his skin on me.

* * *

Clodagh passed me another glass of Prosecco as soon as Bridget had gone to air-kiss and schmooze others. 'You look like you need this,' she said. 'I know I do. What do you think of her?'

'Who?'

'What's wrong with you? You're miles away.'

'She's...' I came back to the conversation. 'She's just like all you media types. Self-obsessed.'

She sank her wine. 'You're right,' she said. 'But who else would put them through this except for self-obsessed, masochistic narcissists.' She lowered her voice. 'Talking of another one.' And then, louder, 'Max! I thought you'd disappeared somewhere.'

And there was Max, shorter and plainer than I had remembered, wearing a black polo-neck, like a miniature James Bond, or at least someone trying to channel James Bond. And failing. He didn't smile. 'No, but I'm not going to stay much longer,' he said. 'I'm going to head off.' He nodded at me, ignoring Clodagh's obvious disappointment.

'Max, how's it going?' I said, while Clodagh began speaking.

'But, it's my party,' she said. 'It's only getting started.'

'Clodagh. I'm tired. I've been working all week. I am not fecking twenty-five any longer.'

'Excuse me a moment,' I said, wondering why Clodagh bothered her arse with this charmless excuse for a boyfriend. And she questioned why I had stayed with Michael! Yet there she was, with someone who, every time I met him, displayed as much charisma as a boiled turnip. He looked not unlike one too.

For a moment, I stood, not knowing what to do. I was aware of Red out of the corner of my eye, still in conversation with someone. I couldn't walk up to him. He'd waved. Was that enough. I mean, I'd see him again on Monday. We didn't need to talk to each other tonight, did we? But then, he was suddenly alone, the man he'd been talking to had gone. And Red looked directly at me. The two of us stood, watching each other, in the middle of the melee, the noise, the talking, the braying. Bridget was taking another selfie in the midst of a group. I recognised Lucinda, Clodagh's producer, who was trying not to be head locked into the group.

Without thinking, we moved towards each other and then we were standing in front of one another.

'Hi Red,' I said. 'How's it going?'

'Grand, you?'

'Lovely thanks. How's your dad? It was really nice to see him again,' I began gabbling. 'He's looking well, better than I thought he would, you know, after a stroke. And the house is the same. It was nice to see it again. And tell him that Michael didn't have any of Peggy's cake, but Rosie and I loved it...'

'She makes a good cake,' he said. 'I think she might put whiskey into it.'

'No wonder it was good. Maybe I shouldn't have given so much of it to Rosie. But it was good to see her eating something.'

He smiled. 'I remember once finishing off the sherry trifle for Christmas... I was eight. Oh my God. Mam had made me a separate one, in a tiny bowl, without sherry, but I polished off the adults' one. I've never had sherry since. Sick as a dog. I can still smell it now. There's that wine shop in Sandycove, and I can't even walk past because of the smell. It smells of being sick on Christmas night.'

'I don't think that is what they are going for,' I said, laughing. 'Anyway, you've never told me that!' I was behaving as though there hadn't been an eighteen year hiatus, as though we were still together.

'Tab,' he spoke carefully, reminding me that there was a yawning gap between us, 'there's a lot you don't know about me.'

'I know, I'm sorry.' Jesus, I was forgetting myself, slipping into a place, a feeling, I had no business being.

'Forget it. Okay?'

I nodded. *And breathe. And smile.* I thought.

'So,' he said, as though we were starting all over again. 'Having a good time?'

'Well, I just met Bridget O'Flaherty, weather supremo, meteorological tsar...so *that* was exciting.' I was working hard to keep things light, to stop myself from either slipping into our easy repartee which left me confused or to start crying and force him to confront what happened. Neither was going to help our current working situation but all I knew was, standing there with him, his body close to mine, bending to speak into each other's ears so we could hear each other above the music, I was happy. For the first time in years, I was happy. I could feel it, a warmth in my stomach, a fizzing in my synapses, and a lightness in my toes. Happiness. A strange and lovely feeling. Fun. I was in danger of actually having fun.

'*Tsarina.*'

'What?'

'Weather tsarina, surely?'

'Indeed, weather tsarina, sultana... princess of precipitation? Which do you prefer?'

'Sultana, definitely. I see no raisin not to.'

'Red!' I giggled. 'You can do better than that.'

'The problem is, I can't,' he said, making us both laugh again. 'So meeting this sultana then. Highlight of your life?'

'*The* highlight,' I said. 'Apart from the time I met Orville the duck at the stage door of the Gaiety after the panto.'

He laughed. 'You see, I did not know that about you. Mine was meeting Ray Houghton. I thought I was going to have a heart attack. I was eighteen,' he chuckled. 'Old enough to know better, but he was such a hero. Scoring that goal at Italia '90. But he was well used to idiot boys like me being goggle-eyed and slack-jawed. A real hero. You don't meet many of *them* every day.'

'A bit better than Orville,' I said. 'And there I was thinking that meeting a green puppet could be the greatest brush with fame and you go and trump me with your story of meeting a man who single-handedly improved the mental health of an entire nation.'

'Sorry about that,' he said, laughing again. From behind us we heard the sound of 'Happy Birthday' being sung. We watched as a huge cake was pushed on a trolley towards Clodagh and a surge of people followed, all singing. And then a chorus of 'For She's A Jolly Good Fellow', which someone changed to 'For She's A Jolly Good Newsreader' started up, whilst Clodagh attempted to blow out the candles. But for some reason, before she had even mustered enough breath, Bridget had swept over them, with the zeal of a firefighter determined to put out all flames, however miniature.

'Sorry!' she smiled at everyone. 'Instinct! I see birthday candles and I just have to blow them out!' She clutched Clodagh's arm. 'I hope you don't mind, Clodes?'

Clodagh looked as though she minded a great deal indeed. And as the cake began to be sliced up and handed around, she and Max were asked to pose for some photographer. But Bridget slipped in between them, holding a slice of cake in a paper napkin and as the shutter clicked, the cake totally obscured Clodagh's face. I thought of Clodagh's stricken expression whenever Max was around. Why did she bother with him? Why was such a cool and successful woman like Clodagh bothering her arse with Maximum Pratt?

'What the hell is happening to this country?' said Red. 'I leave and everything is normal and upstaging people is considered entirely un-Irish. I come back and we're all in competition with each other. It's dog eat dog.'

'If anyone blew out my birthday candles,' I said, 'I don't think I'd be too happy. It's one of those things that you just don't do. Like cancel the barbecue because it's raining or not watch *Christmas Top of the Pops*.' I'd decided somewhere between Orville and Ray Houghton that I was just going to give in to this. I wasn't going to run off. I wanted to be here, right now. Talking to an old friend. Okay, so we had history and it was slightly awkward and there was so much we weren't saying, but for now, at this level, it was glorious.

'Do people still do that?' he asked. 'Really?'

'I don't know if it's still on,' I admitted. 'But every Christmas, when I am sitting at my mother-in-law's dining table eating turkey, I wish I was at home, just me and Rosie, watching *Top of the Pops*.'

'We watched it,' he said. 'Do you remember? It was just us and we roasted a chicken. You made the worst gravy I have ever tasted.'

'And you insisted on making something from Delia Smith. Something involving asparagus. It didn't work. Mushy asparagus, if I remember rightly.' We'd had fun that day too. We'd had a lot of fun when we were together. We used to laugh a lot. And I'd stopped laughing over the years, and it was incredible to remember that I was still that person who laughed. Red seemed to be enjoying himself because he was laughing as much as I was.

'I was just trying to show off,' he said. 'Impress you. Obviously didn't work.'

'Well...' I wasn't quite sure what to say. *Yes, it did work. You did impress me. And I'm still impressed. More than impressed, actually.*

He was looking at me. 'You look... you look beautiful.'

'Sorry?' I said, frowning. *What* did he just say?

'You look beautiful,' he repeated. And he blushed. I could see it, the pink spreading from his neck to the top of his head. I'd forgotten that he used to blush but now it all came back to me. He blushed that time he asked me out for a drink, and the first time we kissed on the bandstand on the pier when it had begun to rain. How could I have forgotten? But if I had remembered it, I would have thought it was just a youthful affliction, not something a grown man, someone so assured, could do.

And I wanted to kiss him again just like that time on the bandstand. I wanted to be that twenty-two-year-old all over again.

'Red...' I began. 'Red... I...' I wanted to say that I was sorry. I wanted to explain why it had happened, my excuse, my reason. An answer for him.

He was looking at me, intently.

'Red, there's something I need to say...' But behind us we heard a voice. Bridget.

* * *

'There you are, Tabitha,' she said, as though we were old friends. 'I've been looking for you everywhere...' She turned to Red. 'Oh hello. Bridget O'Flaherty.' She held out her hand. 'And who are you?' She inched a shoulder in front of me, so that it was just her and Red talking and me hanging around. 'Don't tell me what you do,' she said. 'Production company? Managing director?'

'Nothing like that,' he said. 'I'm a school teacher. Red Power. Good to meet you.'

'Oh.' For a moment, Bridget was quiet, the only sound was her brain whirring, trying to work out if it was worth her while to be attracted to a teacher. 'When did teachers get to be so handsome?' She put her hand on the lapel of Red's jacket and stood so I was slightly obscured.

'You know,' she said. 'There's something I've always wondered... how teachers manage to keep control of a classroom? I mean, we were always so naughty. I just wondered what you might do if someone you were trying to teach was being bold.'

I could hear Red laugh but I couldn't see his face because Bridget had actually moved so she was blocking me off entirely. And then another group edged towards us so I was being cut off from them, Bridget's back right in my face. Clodagh came up to me and pulled me to the bar. 'I need a drink. A large one. Or a tiny but lethal one.'

'Not tequila?' I said, looking back at Red and Bridget. 'You know what dark powers tequila has over you.'

'Don't care,' she said, waving to the bar tender. Red had moved and was looking over at me but maybe, I thought, Bridget had done us a service. We couldn't stand there, having a good time. I was married. There was a whole lifetime behind us. We had grown up. If we tried to be friends, then it would very likely go wrong, leaving us worse off, perhaps, than before. And Red was a handsome and lovely man. He needed to find someone with whom he could settle down. I had to let him go a second time, wipe out any thoughts or feelings I might have for him.

'Two shots of tequila,' said Clodagh, mascara slightly smudged.

'Are you all right,' I said, focussing on her, forgetting Red. 'Have you been *crying*? At your own *party*?'

'Max,' she sighed heavily. 'Says he's going home, that *he's* tired. I said it was my birthday and he said I was like a spoilt child. So I told him that I'd had enough.'

'What?'

'I told him, that I didn't want to see him again.'

'Really? At your own birthday?'

'Yes, really. Me and Maximus Pratticus are no more.' She gave a half-smile. 'And now I'm single. Fucking *again*.'

'Clodagh... remember? You *like* being single,' I said, arranging my face into one of concern but inside I was relieved that Clodagh was no longer saddled with the man called Pratt. I glanced over at Red again, he and Bridget were now deep in conversation.

'Just give me time, that's all,' Clodagh was saying. 'A day or two and I'll remember. But for now, let me get a little bit maudlin.'

'Okay. Go ahead. You've got 48 hours starting now.'

'Right.' She sucked in air, and focussed her mind. 'It's really not fair. I've worked my arse off all these years, but here I am aged...' she dropped her voice to a rasp... 'forty-fecking-two... and what do I have to show for it? A career that is being threatened by a pneumatic weather girl with dodgy knees and a man who would rather spend his evenings at home than with me at my party. Surely I can do better than this?'

'You can do whatever you put your mind to...'

'I'm thinking of an ashram, in India.' Clodagh was warming to her theme. 'Or maybe running a nice little B & B in the foothills of somewhere. They always have to be foothills, don't they?'

'I don't even know what a foothill is,' I said.

'I think it involves a hill, anyway,' said Clodagh confidently. 'And a foot.' And we both laughed. But then she wiped away a tear. 'So my brief encounter is over,' she said. 'Appropriate, him being so short.'

'Clodes, don't cry... please don't cry.' This wasn't the glamourous 40th birthday party either of us has imagined, Clodagh in tears, me bewildered and bothered by Red.

'It's the champagne,' she said. 'I'm the only person in the world on whom it doesn't have an effervescent effect.'

'And the tequila,' I said. 'This is what it does. It makes people who aren't natural criers, who stay stony faced at *The Color Purple* or *It's A Wonderful Life*, into cry-babies.'

'I did cry at both those films,' she said. 'But Max is neither a smiler nor a crier. He didn't cry once at Dunkirk. The whole cinema was in floods and he was calm and collected. I think he might have been supporting the *other side*.'

I laughed.

'I'll have to carry on being nice to him,' she went on. 'My contract is up at the end of the month so I have to be professional and charming. When what I really want to do is set fire to his balls.'

'Are they flammable then?'

'When I finish with them, they will be. But what about Red. He looks cosy with old Bridget... are you okay with that? How are you? You never say anything!' she said. 'How awkward is it, really? And don't give me that everything's fine, it's not weird at all. Because it must be. And I shouldn't have invited him tonight. I'm sorry.'

We both looked over at Red and Bridget, still talking. Well, she was anyway. His back was to us.

'It's weird and awkward and... the same,' I admitted. 'I still feel the same.'

'Good God no! You mean that you still, you know... still love him?'

'Yeah,' I nodded, resigned. 'So it's horrible. Can't wait for the term to be over actually. And then I might never see him again except for brief encounters on the pier or whatever.'

'Oh Tab,' she said, hugging me. 'I'm so sorry.'

'I'm fine, I'm more worried about Rosie doing her exams, you know?'

'So, why aren't you crying?' she said. 'You're drinking it too. Maybe you need another shot. A pint! A pint of tequila.'

'I don't know,' I said. 'I should be. Because I'm not happy.'

'What do you mean?'

'I'm not happy. Not really. Okay, so you make me happy. And my job. And Rosie is the best thing ever, but I'm not happy, not really, not deeply. Something's missing.'

'Tell me about it.' Clodagh signalled for two more tequilas.

'It's like I'm living half a life,' I rambled. 'And I so desperately want all of me to be alive. Do you know what I'm saying?'

'I think so.'

'I hate being married to Michael.' On I droned, the tequila loosening my tongue. This was probably why I never had any fun. I turned into a self-pitying fool at the first whiff of alcohol. 'And I can't complain because he's all right, really. But he's not interested in me.' I was starting to slur. 'And I'm not interested in him.' I picked up my refreshed tequila. 'But do you know what the worst thing is?'

Clodagh was agog, with drink, I realised, and definitely *not* my fascinating story. 'What is it?' she whispered.

'I've been married to a man for seventeen years who calls me Mammy.'

'Maybe he doesn't know your name,' she said, 'and it's been so long and he's too embarrassed to ask you what it is.' And the two of us began to laugh.

She passed me another shot. 'Ready?'

We both launched the drinks down our throats, faces contorted with the sheer horror.

'You know,' she said, signalling for two more. 'If there's one thing I've learned it's that things can change just like that. It's happened to me so often that I've stopped taking anything for granted. I mean, look at madam over there, talking to Red. I've got a funny feeling that she's going to cause a few waves.'

I looked over at Red and Bridget but they had gone.

'You see,' said Clodagh, slurring. 'It's my theory that you never get everything you want at the same time. Keeps you persevering, you see. So all those things you want, nice relationships, happy career, children, a glass of rosé, that kind of thing. Basic needs in other words. You can't have all of them at the same time. Each has to take its turn. So, you have a child, your career suffers. If you meet someone nice...'

'You become allergic to rosé?'

'Exactly.' Clodagh looked as plastered as I felt.

'Clodagh, I think you and I just might have had too much to drink.'

'How very dare you!' she said. 'I haven't had half enough!' She held up her newly refilled shot glass. 'Tonight,' she declared. 'Tonight I drink tequila.' She tossed it back. 'God, that's disgusting,' she said. 'Disgustingly good.'

16

The next morning, I wondered if I was the only school principal in the world who was suffering from the effects of too much tequila. I suspected not. But my mood darkened and my head throbbed further when I remembered it was the morning of this term's cake sale.

I lay in bed for a moment, trying to focus and come to. The last thing I remembered was Clodagh promising to come to the cake sale.

'I wouldn't miss it for the world,' she had said. 'You have no idea, Tab. You have no idea how much I want my life to be normal, surrounded by normal people.'

'Normal? My life?' I was pretty drunk at this point in the evening, my head swimming, our conversation deep and engrossing. The world put to rights. 'I am surrounded by lunatics.'

Clodagh wouldn't accept it. 'There'z lunatics and there'z lunatics.' She was really indistinct now, her head and eyelids drooping. 'You don't know the lunacy I have to deal with. Day in, day out. And Max,' she said. 'He's so lunaticky that he won't wear underpants twice.'

'What do you mean? He washes them after every wear? That's normal.'

'No!' She put a finger to her lips. 'No! I mean, he doesn't wear them ever again. Don't tell a soul. He'd kill me.' She made a slicing action across her throat. 'He'd kill me.'

'He's mad,' I said. 'Mad Max!'

'Mad Max!' She was nodding and laughing.

'Mad Max!' I had hooted again. '*Mad* Max! Do you get it?'

And the two of us began laughing so much, we started to slide off our chairs. I remember Clodagh on her knees, trying to get up. And then a conga danced past us, famous and not so famous faces whizzing by. Bridget was there, I think I remember, but no Red. Sheer horror on Lucinda's face, as though she was running with the bulls in Pamplona and was terrified that she would be trampled. Clodagh was scooped up into the melee and I, sensibly, took it as my cue to leave.

Lying in bed, I put the pillow over my face. Oh Jesus. Why had I thought it was a good idea to do shots last night? Not that it was *ever* a good idea to do tequila shots.

What had happened to Red? Gone home, I had assumed. Not with Bridget, though. Which was a small consolation. But I was meant to be a grown woman. A *married* woman. And yet here I was, lying, hungover and sick to my very being, thinking about him.

* * *

My car was having its annual service in the garage but the walk would not only do me good but it would bring me past a very nice coffee place where I could get a takeaway.

Once I arrived in the school hall, there were Victoria sponges as far as the eye could see, teetering piles of brownies and biscuits. Angela Leahy, Fifth class teacher, was putting out paper cups in a regimented line, and Sarah Casey (Second class) was looking more than a little excited at being the one who was in charge of the tea urn.

Even some of the protestors were helping out, basically feeling members of the school's wider community. Maybe their plan was to buy enough cake that we would easily earn enough money and there would be no question of selling the Copse. Arthur was on the ground fixing a table and Nellie was unveiling an impressive looking pineapple upside cake and a chocolate-covered tray bake.

'Red was here earlier,' Mary said. 'Carrying things in. Setting up the tables, you know. He got the keys and set up at 8am. Spent a good two hours getting all the tables and chairs out of the storeroom. The place was in a state. He managed to find two of those big brooms and we got the place shipshape in no time.'

Red? I thought he'd be too hungover.'

'He said he was at Clodagh's party last night. Said he didn't stay long. Weren't you talking to him?'

'I was, for a bit,' I said, deflation mingling with my hungover brain. I didn't think he'd be at the cake sale at all, and now I'd heard he'd been and gone. 'Has he gone home?' Please say no, I thought.

'No, just off to get some breakfast,' she explained. 'Said he wouldn't be long.' She chuckled. 'You know, he's been such a great addition to the staff, I must say. We'll be sad if he has to leave us at the end of term. Can't do enough for any of us and always making us laugh in the staff room. You know he carries Ms Morrissey's bags in from her car every morning? The operation on her back was postponed. Again. He's become quite the pet of the staff. We say we don't know what the school will do without him. He's started a little lunch club on a Friday and each of us brings in things to eat. It's all very civilised.'

That did sound nice. Sometimes being head teacher meant you missed out on the craic, having instead to worry about leaks in the roof or raising money.

'I'm determined to beat last year's total of €260,' Mary went on, arranging lemon drizzles and fairy cakes on plates. 'We've upped the prices of these little cakes by 5c, and the big cakes by 50c.'

'You should be on *The Apprentice*,' I said. 'Lord Sugar would love you.'

My tequila headache was really beginning to kick in. 'I'm just going to take two painkillers,' I said. 'Thanks for saying that Mary, I'll be back in a moment.'

'Ah! Here he is!' she said. 'Mr Eurovision himself!'

Red was walking towards us, a coffee in one hand and a bagel in the other. 'Shhh!' he said to Mary, smiling. 'I don't want everyone to know about my double life.' He turned to me. 'Hi Tab. How's the head?'

'Not too bad,' I lied. 'How's yours?'

He shrugged. 'Didn't stay long,' he said. 'Home by midnight.' And then he was distracted by two golden tea bracks that Mary had just unwrapped. 'I'll buy one of those,' said Red. 'Look even better than the ones my mam used to make. Here's €10 to get us started.' He passed a note to Mary which she put in the ice cream tub. Put one aside for me? Dad will love it. And I'll head over to the tea stall. Apparently that's where I've been put. Not to be trusted with the cakes or I might eat them.'

'Knowing you, you will,' teased Mary. 'Go on, off with you!'

She turned to me and laughed. 'He's a divil,' she said, as soon as he'd gone.

'That's one way of putting it,' I said moderately, but thinking, a sexy divil at that. However, these adulterous musings were disturbed by a voice.

'I'll have that chocolate one.' It was Clodagh wearing dark glasses. 'I mean, I won't actually eat it, but I can sniff and study it for a while and imagine I am eating it'

I laughed, delighted and amazed to see her. 'Please. Just eat it. I'll *make* you eat it. Anyway, what are you doing here? I'm wrecked, you must be destroyed!'

'I think I'm still drunk, actually,' said Clodagh, in a low voice. 'But I said I'd come and – ta-dah! - here I am.' She groaned. 'God, that was a bit enthusiastic.'

Mary was bristling beside me, waiting to be introduced.

'Clodagh this is Mary Hooley, school secretary and the brains of the operation. Mary, this is my friend Clodagh Cassidy.'

'Indeed it is!' said Mary, giving Clodagh a hearty and prolonged handshake. 'And what a pleasure it is to have a celebrity here! You might help us sell even more cakes!'

'Thank you, Mary,' said Clodagh, taking off her glasses. 'Tabitha is always telling me about you, how she couldn't do a thing without you.'

Mary blushed. 'Well, you know, I do my best...'

'Why don't you put me to work and I will try and sell a few cakes for you?' Clodagh offered.

She came behind the table to us and I gave her an apron. 'How are you?' I asked out of the corner of my mouth.

'Like a terminally ill amoeba,' she said quietly, while smiling at everyone radiantly. 'It's all your fault for ordering that tequila.'

'You ordered it,' I reminded her. 'It's all your fault that we both feel like this.'

'That's why I'm here. Solidarity,' she said. 'Friends who do shots together, sell cakes together.'

'Thanks Clodes.'

'My pleasure. And sorry for the tequila.'

'Let's just never do it again. Next time afternoon tea. Anyway, have you heard from Max?'

She nodded. 'He called this morning,' she said. 'Said he was sorry.'

'Sorry?'

'For being tired. I think it was one of those apologies that aren't really meant.'

'Like, sorry for breathing.'

'For being alive.' She gave me a half-smile that almost broke my heart.

'Can we just sell some cakes?' she said. 'Before I eat them all. This room is either my greatest nightmare or the best dream ever. Cakes as far as the eye can see.' She stopped. 'Don't worry about me, Tab,' she said. 'So he's a bit of a prick. Maximus Prickus.' We both giggled immaturely for a moment. 'But I'll be all right, okay? Good riddance et cetera.'

'Oh my God, Bridget!'

'What?'

'Yo! Clodagh!' And now Bridget was making a beeline towards us, through the crowds of parents and pupils who had begun to arrive. She didn't look at all hung-over, she was as fresh as a daisy, flaunting her youthful ability to flash detoxify.

'Bridget?' said Clodagh. 'What are *you* doing here?'

'You told me all about it, said I had to come. Remember?' She scanned the room, looking for someone.

'Tequila-talk,' said Clodagh, under her breath. 'What *was* I thinking?'

'I only live down the road in Monkstown and I was up with my trainer anyway,' carried on Bridget. 'And I want to have another little chat with that gorgeous teacher guy, Redmond. He said he had to be up early to come to a cake sale, so here I am. Anyway, my *momager* says it's all about being with the people. Getting down to their level. Being approachable. Just like them. Without having to be *like* them.'

Clodagh rolled her eyes, but Mary, was delighted. 'Another celebrity!' she said. 'It'll be the best cake sale ever! We won't need to sell the Copse now, eh Tabitha?'

'So, where is he?'

'Tea urn,' I said, defeated by Bridget. This was how Clodagh must feel, I thought.

He felt the weight of our gaze and he looked up to find the four of us all staring at him. He managed a nod and carried on wrestling with a giant teapot.

'Well, if it isn't... yourself off the weather.' Brian Crowley was looking delighted at the sight of Bridget as he made his way over to us. 'Brian Crowley, board of governors...' He dug out his phone. 'May I?' He was panting slightly like a dog on heat.

'For fifty euro,' said Bridget, looking unruffled.

Brian hesitated. 'That's a bit steep,' he said.

'Go on then,' he said. 'They'll love this, the lads at the golf club. The Connemara Cracker, they call you. Brings a little spice to our day, you know what I mean?' He lunged at her face, phone aloft, going in for a killer kiss as Mary and I stood there, appalled. But Bridget moved her face the tiniest amount so his lips planted right on her cheek and she pulled away, smiling, hand out.

'Fifty euro please.'

He put his hand in his pocket and pulled out a large note. 'And just a word of advice.' She leaned into his ear, speaking quietly and slowly. 'If you ever put your hand on my arse again, you will be very sorry you ever thought you could get a cheap thrill from me.' Brian paled. 'Make it another fifty euro and I won't make a formal complaint to the Gardaí.'

With his porky hands, he pulled another large note out from his wallet and handed it over. Mary and I made eye contact, impressed. She was good. 'Thank you,' she said sweetly, and handed them straight to Mary. 'For the general coffers. I'll just pop over and say hello to Redmond,' she said, slipping away and strutting to the tea table. We watched with fascinated horror.

Clodagh rolled her eyes at me. 'Surely Red wouldn't go for someone like Bridget,' she said. 'Surely he's got more sense?'

I shrugged. 'Who knows?' I hoped not but what red blooded male wouldn't.

'I'm sure he'll be happy about it,' insisted Mary. 'Lovely girl like Bridget O'Flaherty showing an interest. He'll be very flattered.'

The three of us watched as Bridget chatted to him and then, next minute, she was behind the table and was standing very closely behind him as he showed her how to use the tea urn. She reached around him to grip the spout.

'It's like the scene from *Ghost*,' said Clodagh, with a shudder.

'Well, we should stop staring,' said Mary. 'And sell a few more cakes.'

'Yes,' I said. 'Yes, we should.' But I kept one eye on Bridget and Red, watching how she was pouring out tea for people, taking the money, flirting with everyone. Red glanced over at me and I looked away.

* * *

Finally, when everything was over, Mary was collecting all the various ice cream tubs full of coppers and change and we were sweeping and clearing up, Clodagh and Bridget were talking on the other side of the room, and Red joined me.

'That seems to have been a success,' he said. 'In my limited experience of cake sales.'

'They didn't have then in California, then?' I said.

'No, they are peculiarly Irish,' he replied. 'They were into sponsored sports, basketball tournaments, baseball games.' He smiled at me. 'Not that I want to give Mary any more money-spinning ideas.'

'What's that?' she said. 'Did someone say money-spinning?' She had five ice cream tubs balanced between her hands and her chin. 'Have you come up with another way of raising money, Red?'

'Not really,' he said. 'I think you are doing brilliantly well without me.'

'Maybe,' she said, teasing him, 'you could try your hand at some singing? A bit of Johnny Logan? Or do you have other Eurovision people you can take off?'

'That's it!' said Red laughing. 'Finally, someone has recognised my talent, finally you've seen me for who I really am. A man with the face and body of an ordinary person but with the heart of Johnny Logan.' He turned to Mary. 'Will you manage me Mary? Together we can be rich! Together, I can realise my full potential...'

'Deal,' said Mary. 'Now, what about *What's Another Year*? Give us a bit of that one...'

'But I don't have my white suit on,' he said. 'I won't be able to give it the full Johnny.'

'What would Johnny do?' I said.

'He'd just get on with it,' said Mary. 'So...'

'Get on with it.' The three of us were laughing as Red took a broom and began cradling it like a microphone and began crooning into the handle. '*I've been waiting for such a long time...* Come on, sing it with me Mary...' He put his arm around her shoulders and they sung together.

'*I've been waiting such a long time, looking out for you. But you're not here. What's another year?*'

I'd never actually felt the need to cry at a Johnny Logan song before but I actually felt a lump in my throat, my eyes misty. God, maybe it was a sign of age when you began being moved by Johnny Logan and Eurovision.

'*I've been waiting such a long time, reaching out for you. But you're not near.*'

They paused, locking eyes, swaying together.

'*What's another year?*'

'What?' I said when they had finished. 'Only two verses?'

'I think that's enough,' said Red. 'We might need to work on it.' He was smiling but I could see that he had noticed me welling up. 'What do you think Mary?' he said, 'do you think we have it?'

'No,' she said. 'We don't have it at all. But we can keep trying. Now, I meant to say about our film night tonight...'

But we'd been joined by Bridget, who tapped Red on the shoulder.

'What was that?' she said.

'What was what?'

'The singing?'

'Johnny Logan,' he said. 'Did you know recognise it. I know we don't actually do the great man any favours, do we Mary?'

She was laughing. 'No one could, Red,' she said. 'Only Johnny is Johnny.'

'Who's Johnny Logan?' said Bridget making the three of us jerk our heads to face her.

'Who's Johnny Logan?' Mary couldn't believe what she'd just heard.

'Yes,' said Bridget. 'Who's Johnny Logan?'

'Only Ireland's greatest *Eurovisioner...*' said Red and then turned to us. '*Eurovisionist?*'

We nodded. That sounded right.

'Won it two times,' explained Red. 'The man can't *lose* Eurovision. He's our best hope to reclaim our crown.'

Bridget was looking at us as though we were mad. 'I don't get it,' she said. 'I can't tell if you are joking or not.'

'Joking about Johnny?' said Red.

'The very idea!' said Mary.

'Whatever,' dismissed Bridget. 'Listen Red,' she said, all business-like. 'Can I have a word?' He nodded and she pulled him to one side, while Mary and I continued sweeping.

'I was wondering,' Bridget said, 'if you were doing anything interesting this evening?'

'I am actually.' He sounded surprised at her question. 'I'm going to the cinema with Mary,' he said. 'So...'

'So what?'

'So... no. Sorry Bridget.' He called over to Mary. 'We're going to see an old French film. Aren't we, Mary? Mary is educating me in the art of the French film. I'm a philistine, in her eyes.'

What was this? I wanted to go to see a French film with the two of them. It sounded lovely.

'That's right, Red,' Mary called and walked over to them. 'I mentioned that I was a fan of *Jean de Florette* and he's never seen it – can you imagine! – so, it's on and we're going. Unless...' She had noticed the daggers that Bridget was glaring at her. 'But, Red, if you have other ideas, we can go another time... it's not a problem.'

'We're going,' he said firmly. 'I need to do something about my general philistinism. Man cannot live by Johnny Logan alone.'

'But he can try,' said Mary. She scurried over to me and busied herself sorting out a huge pile of empty Tupperware, ready to be returned to their owners. Bridget moved so she and Red were hidden from our prying eyes.

Clodagh came up with Mary's tea brack, now wrapped in foil, for Red. As she was a few yards away from them, she realised that some kind of intimate discussion was going on and she did an abrupt about-turn and sidled to me, giving me a look. I nodded in return. She began picking up fluff and bits from the floor with her fingers, the two of us working in silence.

'But...' Bridget obviously was unused to men not falling at her feet. 'Would you like to do something else? Something with me, perhaps? Something that doesn't involve strange foreign films. I'm thinking cocktails, something to eat. Hang out in town.'

'God, I'm so sorry, Bridget,' he said quietly. 'But I am way too old for all that.' I kept sweeping the floor, pretending I wasn't listening to every word, thrilled he wasn't falling for Bridget's obvious charms.

'Sounds fun, though,' Red said politely, speaking quietly, 'I'm sure you know loads of people who would want to go.'

Bridget was looking utterly bewildered. 'Really?' she said.

He nodded. 'Really. People not old like me,' he said gently. 'I'm ancient...'

'But...'

He stood there with his massive pile of cartons and boxes like a contestant on an old kids' show, trying not to drop a thing.

'Right,' she said slowly. 'Okay. Let me know if you change your mind.'

'I will...' He glanced at me and saw me looking, widening his eyes a fraction.

'So, I'll be going.' She shook her head, slightly, as though she couldn't believe it. 'Red,' she said, 'I have to ask you something.'

'What?'

'Are you gay?' She was blinking at him, as though something just didn't compute. 'Because I can't think of another reason. I mean, you disappeared last night, you don't want to come out with me tonight. I just don't... I just don't understand. Normally... usually... this doesn't happen.'

Clodagh and I, eyes wide, looked at each other. I was worried that Red would drop everything in a huge cacophony of old containers. But he laughed. 'I'm not gay, Bridget,' he said, lowering his voice so low, my ear drums were on the point of bursting with the effort of trying to hear.

She hesitated for a moment. 'Let me know if you change your mind, okay?' And she walked out, without saying goodbye to anyone else. Life lesson, I told myself. Even Bridget has to face rejection at least once.

He nodded. 'I will. Thank you.' Now, he was able to put down everything he was carrying on the table by the door while Clodagh scurried over with the cake. 'Here's Mary's cake, Red' she said. 'She says it's yours.'

'Thank you, Clodagh,' he said calmly as though he hadn't just had a really unusual conversation, flattering and awkward and... weird. 'What are you taking?'

'A chocolate roulade,' she admitted. 'I'm going home to eat the whole thing with a cup of tea and an old film on the telly.'

'What an afternoon,' he laughed.

'Sometimes, Red,' she said, 'life demands chocolate roulade and a black and white film. I'm hoping for something with Cary Grant.'

'Anything with Bette Davis does that for me.' He turned to me. 'What about you Tab,' he said. 'Who does it for you?'

'Um...' But I knew exactly what film I could watch over and over again.

'Listen,' said Clodagh, 'I'm going to head off. See you all soon.' She put on her sunglasses and squeezed me goodbye. 'You're worth a million Bridgets,' she said into my ear.

'Thanks for coming.'

When she was gone, Red was still waiting for an answer. 'In old films? Um, probably anything with Jack Lemmon. *The Apartment?*'

We'd watched together years ago, loving every moment of it. Every time I'd seen it since, I thought of Red. He nodded, slowly. 'Great film.'

'Great film,' I echoed.

'I'll finish sweeping,' he said, taking the broom. 'Give me something to do.' For a moment, he stood there and we looked deeply into each other's eyes. It was all there, in a flash. I knew what he wanted. He wanted to know why. I would have wanted to know the same. All those years on, if it were me, it would have dug away until I got answer. We were going to have to talk. I was going to have to explain exactly why. 'We should... I want...' I began but my phone rang.

'Do you mind if I take this? It's my Rosie.'

I could barely make out what she was saying. She couldn't speak and she was sobbing. She sounded terrified. I could feel the panic rise within me as well.

'I'm coming home, Rosie! I'm coming home, sweetheart.' Oh God, I needed to get home. My daughter needed me.

'What's wrong?' Red said. 'Is she all right?'

'Rosie... she's having another panic attack... I have to go...' I suddenly remembered my car was in the garage that day having its annual check-up. 'My car! I don't have my car! I walked down...' Tears were in my eyes as I started to panic, calculating how long it would take me to get home. Half an hour at a quick clip, if I was lucky.

'I'll drive you. Come on.'

* * *

I raced into the house to find Rosie was tucked into a ball, on the bottom step of the stairs in the hall, arms wrapped across her body, head on her knees. I sat on the step beside her and put my arm around her back. 'It's all right, my darling,' I said, gently, softly, my head close to hers. 'It's all right, everything's all right.'

Her head shook, no. No, everything is not all right.

'Breathe, that's it. Come on. Keep going.' I could feel her back rise and fall, juddery and shuddery, jagged, tortured breathing. 'It's all right.' Her heart was jumping around, I could feel it through her T-shirt, beads of sweat around her hairline, her breathing still short and panicky. And then she lifted her tear-streaked face, her eyes watery and bloodshot.

'Mum...' she began to cry. 'It was so scary... I thought... I thought...'

'It's all right, it's all right,' I soothed and shushed her, finding a rhythm to my voice, low and hypnotic while I could feel her breathing become calmer and more regular. 'That's it, that's right...'

Eventually, she pulled away and lifted her face. 'It hurts,' she said.

'What does?' I said, scanning my beautiful girl's face and smoothing her hair, tucking strands behind her ear, her skin was hot.

'Everything. My chest. My whole body. And inside.'

'You're going to be all right, okay? I'm here now.' My mind was working overtime, making plans for the next five minutes, thinking further ahead and trying to decide if sitting her exams was a good idea, could/ should she resit next year? Maybe I should give up my job and just be here. I'd been so selfish going out to work while she was struggling. Why hadn't I done anything before?

'It's like a real thing,' she said. 'Everything inside is real.'

'What do you mean?'

'Everything I think becomes real.' She looked at me, willing me to understand.

'Sweetheart...'

BEFORE

Red and I swimming in the Forty foot, laughing. The sun overhead, one of those rare perfect summer days. Him swimming over to me and kissing me. 'I love you, Tabitha Thomas,' he said, 'and I will love you forever.'

*   *   *

'Rosie, listen to me. Maybe you should think about not doing your exams. Take a year off, you know, a breather.'

'No way...' there were tears in her eyes again. 'I have to. You're making a big deal out of it. Please? Anyway...' But immediately tears began running down Rosie's face. 'I don't know what to do... I can't not *do* my exams. Nobody drops out.'

'Ro...' I said, gently, 'what triggers it?'

'I don't know,' she said, 'it can happen anywhere.' She stopped for a moment and was still, as though she was summoning up something deep inside, as though she was drawing on a reserve of strength of inner power, I didn't know. 'I've just got to eat better and sleep better.'

She was working so hard. Always in her bedroom. She had stopped going out, meeting her friends. Anxiety was affecting teenage girls, I knew that. But for some reason, I thought that Rosie was immune. She was clever and confident. She had always sailed through life, always popular, always successful. She was on the hockey team, the school debating team, the drama society. Parents' evenings had always been a joy; a fifteen-minute chat about how lovely my daughter was. She had been Mary, for God's sake, in the school nativity play not once but *twice*. I had searched online for information; it all said the same. She needed help and support, she needed to take the pressure off, and she needed to stop trying to be perfect.

* * *

The next day, there was a knock on the front door. Red was standing there.

'I hope I'm not intruding on a Sunday morning,' he said. 'But I've bought a book for Rosie. I was just going to leave it on the doorstep and then I thought I'd just try once...' He looked at me. 'I hope you don't mind...'

'Not at all,' I said. 'It's very good of you.

'Hello.' Rosie had joined us.

'Hello,' he said, gently. 'You must be Rosie.'

'This is Red,' I said, realising that Rosie had no idea who he was. For all she knew, he was some random man who was now in our hall. 'He's an old friend. I used to know him years ago. He's now a teacher in the school. And he gave me a lift yesterday.' She nodded again, only half taking it in.

'Listen,' he went on. 'For what it's worth, life does get better, as you grow up. It's really hard being a teenager. Too many pressures being heaped on you. But the thing is, exams don't matter. You think they do and everyone around you is telling you they are the most important things on the planet. But they're not. They don't mean anything, they don't say anything about you and they are no guarantee of future success. The most important thing you can be is true to yourself and find something that excites you, something that makes you happy, that you cannot wait to do each day. That is true success. That's all you have to do, find that thing and, when you do, grab on to it.'

'Thanks.' Rosie tried to smile at him.

He smiled back. 'I'll go now,' he said. 'Before I start expounding my other theories on life. I've got a great one on food and lots on politics and football. Lots on football.'

She smiled again. 'What's the book?'

He handed over a well-thumbed copy.

'*The Road Less Travelled*. It's just one of those books that reminds you that everything you do is okay...'

Rosie was reading the blurb on the back. 'Thank you,' she said. 'I'll look after it.' She looked at me, wonderingly, why wasn't I inviting him in?

'Would you like a cup of tea?' I said. 'We're just having one.'

'Well, if it's not too much trouble...'

'Actually, Mum,' Rosie said. 'I'm going to go upstairs, to start working again.'

He followed me into the kitchen. 'How is she?' he said. 'Was she okay afterwards.'

'I think so,' I said. 'She keeps telling me she's all right but then this happens. I don't know what to think. I wish she had better support. I think talking to someone might be a good thing to do. Or maybe not.'

He nodded, understanding. 'I don't have a child,' he said, 'but I do remember what it was like to be at an age where you don't feel you have any control over your environment. You are being forced into situations that are incredibly challenging but you didn't choose them...'

'Exams?'

He nodded. 'And everything really. When you are young, like Rosie is, or in your 20s, you aren't really living life for yourself, not knowing what you truly want... you are just doing what everyone expects of you.'

'I know... getting older is so much better.'

'You know what you want,' he said. 'And even just knowing it, even if you can't have it, is very liberating.'

'How was the film?' I said, changing the subject. Thinking of Red and Mary, I felt a bit put out by their friendship, childish of me, I knew, but I wanted to have that same easy relationship with Red. I wanted to be singing cheesy songs with him and going to the cinema. But I also wanted to be holding his hand and coming home with him. And that just wasn't possible.

'Dad says hello,' he said.

'How is he?'

'Working on a new poem. Says he feels inspired by the protest.'

'Oh God, really?'

A key in the door. 'Yoo-hoo! I'm home!'

'That's Michael,' I said to Red. 'I thought he was in Brussels.'

'Mammy! Mammy?'

Red was looking puzzled. 'You?'

I nodded, helplessly, as Michael walked straight into the kitchen. 'Ah, there you are Mammy...' And then he spotted Red who stood up and held out his hand.

'Hello,' he said. 'Red Power, a friend of Tab's.'

'Michael Fogarty, MEP. And what brings you here on a Sunday morning?'

'Just had to drop something off,' he said.

'Red works at the school,' I explained. 'What brings you home?'

'I wanted to see Rosie,' he said. 'I've managed to organise an internship for the summer in Brussels. Now, these are not easy to acquire even for one's offspring. You can imagine how many of the MEPs and the thousands of people who work in the parliament want to organise them for their children, so I feel very lucky to have one for Rosie. This would be the making of her.' He turned to Red. 'She's off to Trinity to do Law in September so a stint in Europe would be extremely beneficial. You see, she'll eventually go into politics, just like her dear old dad.' He smiled, happily, at us both.

'Michael,' I said, 'we can talk about this later, 'but Rosie is taking the summer off. She's got a few things planned with her friends and I think she deserves a break.'

'Nonsense!' he said. 'She'll be fine. Stop fussing Mammy. What have I told you? Now, this is too good an opportunity to miss. Now, Richard...' Michael's famous never forgetting a name trick had failed him with Red, I noticed. Or probably deliberate dismissive tactic. 'Do you like milk?'

Red nodded. 'Yes...'

'Drink it every day?'

'In tea... coffee ...'

'But when was the last time you had a big glass of it?'

'When I was about eight years old?'

'Aha! You see?' He looked up in triumph.

Red was puzzled. 'You see what?'

'It's just a theory I'm working on... why masculinity, in fact, is in crisis.'

'It is? It seems quite healthy to me,' said Red.

'No, it's in crisis,' said Michael definitely. 'All the big thinkers are saying it. And I have developed a little theory which suggests that the crisis began when we stopped drinking milk.'

'Right...' Red looked utterly bewildered. 'I don't think milk has anything to do with anything...'

'How can you say such a thing?' said Michael. 'Vitamins, minerals, protein... our country is built on the back of dairy cows... if we drank milk, Ireland would be an economic powerhouse... and that's my plan. More milk, more money, more milk, more masculinity.'

'Catchy.'

Michael ignored me. 'So what do you think, Richard?'

'I will have to think about it,' said Red. 'I'm not sure yet.' He turned to me. 'I'd better go. Thanks for the tea, Tab. I'll see you in school in the morning.'

'And I'll go up and tell Rosie the good news about the internship,' said Michael. 'She is one lucky girl.'

* * *

'Rosie says she doesn't want it,' said Michael when he came back downstairs. 'She started crying.' He looked utterly perplexed as though he had bestowed her wildest dream only for her to reject it.

'She's under a huge amount of pressure,' I said. 'She just needs a break over the summer. Hang out with her friends. Eat pizza. Go somewhere nice. Be a teenager.'

'But she is a teenager.'

'A proper teenager,' I said. 'Not one who is having to pretend to be an adult, wearing a suit and scurrying around after some MEP.'

'It's the opportunity of a lifetime,' he said. 'I worked every school holiday for Dad, learning the ropes. I used to do carbon copying, heading up to the train station for deliveries... it's much easier these days. She'd only have to take notes and see what it's like. One day, she'd be hooked. That's all it would take.'

'Maybe just leave it awhile,' I said. 'I should go and see how she is.'

Wait a moment,' he said. 'There's something I need to talk to you about.'

'Oh yes? Did I leave the immersion on again?'

He looked up, alarmed. 'You haven't, have you? All that hot water, being wasted.'

'Michael, we don't even have an immersion. It's all on a timer.'

'Don't we? When did that happen?'

'About three years ago, an electrician did it.'

He looked visibly relieved. 'Well, that's okay then. Now...' He looked at me, seriously. 'You're not going to like this... but after great consideration, and soul-searching, I have decided that...'

Was Michael about to end our marriage, I wondered. What on earth would cause him to look so grave? I felt a feeling of admiration. He'd had the guts to do it. He was better than I was.

'It's Brussels. I am going to spend even more time there. I know I get to come home every few days or so but I have to make a bigger commitment to my role there. I know you miss me around the house, I know that it must be hard to do things such as source electricians and the like... I know it must be hard for the man of the house to be absent.'

I wasn't sure what to say. 'Okay...'

'Will you be all right?'

'I think so.'

He nodded. 'That's the attitude. Sacrifices have to make for our country, for Europe. This is your little bit.'

'Thank you.'

He smiled. 'Some people stay at home and watch daytime television. Others waste their lives on picket lines and protests. Others play their part.'

I pretended to be puzzled. 'And which one are you?'

'The latter! Mammy! Were you even listening?'

17

'Will you sign this letter to the parents?' said Mary, as she came into my office. I'd been staring out at the protestors and wouldn't have been surprised if a few tents were erected and this went on for years. All the things we could do with the money kept flashing through my mind. The new surface for the playground, all the bits and pieces that the school needed. But my heart was saying no. But sometimes the head had to rule the heart. And I was, after all, the Head.

'Lovely day, isn't it?' said Mary, letter in hand. 'But that Bridget last night said it might rain. But she also said it might not.'

'That's useful,' I said, turning round from the window.

'She said it was an Irish summer and we all knew what to expect. The unexpected. Whatever that means but she has a point. More a philosophy on life rather than a weather forecast, though...' She passed me the letter. 'So, will you sign it?'

I nodded and took it from her. 'Mary, what do you remember about school? Did you feel stressed at all?'

'I hated it,' she said. 'For all their talk of love, the nuns didn't show one ounce of compassion to any of us girls. It was a horrible place to be, and it made us girls suspicious of each other. They created an atmosphere where you didn't know who you could trust. You didn't know who was on your side. I used to take the bus into Cavan town every day. I was petrified that someone who knew Mammy would see me. But I couldn't stop myself, I had to do something to prove to myself that the world was bigger than the school, than home, than Ballyjamesduff. Cavan town was as far as I got.'

'Did you get caught?'

'Of course I did! You couldn't *breathe* without someone spotting you and telling on you. Mammy went, as expected, quite mad. Bulging eyes, the usual.' She shrugged. 'She thought I should join the Sisters of Charity. She was *that* worried for me. She thought if I was capable of deceiving her, my own mother, then she was terrified about how I'd get on when left to my own devices. She's calmed down now.' She laughed. 'Only took her 30 years.'

'And you headed off to London...'

'Anywhere was better than the twitching curtains of home,' she said. I knew I was gay back then. But wasn't out, you know. London gave me the confidence. But everyone back home thought I'd gone off with a man. But he was gay too and so we both looked after each other,' she said happily. 'Australian, he was. Lovely fella. Martin from Alice Springs. He'd been working in Cavan Town. Took pity on me and was horrified when I told him about having to become a nun. Said he was heading off to London for a bit and told me I could come with him. Helped me find somewhere to stay and I found a job in a pub in Kentish Town. Time of my life it was. There were so many Irish girls, just like me, running away from home. We became quite the gang. Eight of us in all and all still in contact. Two of us turned out to be lesbians. What are the chances?'

'And what happened to Martin?'

'Back in Alice Springs. We still email at Christmas. I will go and see him one of these days...' Her sentence drifted off. 'Life is a series of unending possibilities, Tabitha, you just have to see it as that.'

Was it though? I thought of Rosie, in the four walls of her bedroom. There wasn't much she could do about it. This was the system and it decreed that you must break your arse studying for two years or so and then... *then* only then was life was a series of unending possibilities.

I wondered what she was doing now. Working, I knew. In her room. I vowed, as soon as the exams were over I'd get her out of there. We'd go to

Paris. Mary, I realised, was someone who was still adventurous, still a dreamer. I used to be like that, years ago. But along the way, I'd stopped dreaming. I felt something prickle inside me. I wanted some of that wanderlust for me too.

'Tabitha?'

'Yes?'

'What's it like being a mother? Have you ever regretted it?'

'Regretted it?' I said. 'Never. Not for one moment. I don't think any mother regrets it. Why?'

She shrugged. 'Just wondering. It must be a worry having a little girl...'

Mary was obviously thinking of her own mother and the grey hairs she'd acquired when Mary bunked off school and all her other adventures. No wonder she wanted her locked up in a nunnery. It would make life easier if all our daughters could be protected in such a way.

'Yes,' I said. 'It's hugely worrying and you never stop. It gets worse, if anything...'

Mary had gone pale. 'Are you all right?' I said.

'Quite all right, just haven't much to eat yet... go on...'

'Well, I was going to say, there is nothing which can bring you more pleasure than a daughter – or a son, I imagine. The deep, real joy of just watching them grow up... well, there's nothing like it.'

There was a knock on the office door.

'Busy?' It was Red. 'I just wanted to talk to you about... oh, hello Mary,' he said, smiling. '*A Bout de Souffle* this Saturday, you still on?'

'Is that about soufflés?' I said, giving Mary a wink, 'because if so, your Dad will want to come along.'

'Is he still going on about soufflés?' said Red. 'Honestly. He's always fancied one but has never had one.'

'Never?'

'He doesn't go to restaurants that are posh enough for a start,' said Red. 'And I can't make one. I mean, I could try but I'm not into precision cooking.'

'I could make one for him,' I said. 'I mean, I wouldn't mind having a go...'

'Really?'

'How difficult can they be?'

'Very,' said Mary. 'It's getting the eggs right, they need to be exactly three days old and at room temperature. It helps if you are making them in a French farmhouse kitchen because of the thickness of the stone walls creates the perfect ambient temperature. And then it's all in the wrist action...'

Red whistled, impressed. 'How do you know this?'

'I did a cordon bleu course in Paris,' she confessed modestly. 'Years ago. I do know how to make a few classic French dishes.'

'Johnny Logan and soufflés. You are quite the catch Mary Hooley,' he said, teasing her.

'I just happen to be a Europhile,' she said. 'I'm quite envious of my young cousin Lucy, living in Brussels, being at the centre of Europe,' she said.

'I think you might be getting Eurovision mixed with the European parliament,' said Red, ignoring the reference to Michael. I wonder what he thought of him when they met. 'Easily done.'

Mary laughed. 'Did you know that Red eats sweets in the cinema?'

'What's wrong with that?' Red was laughing. 'Anyone would think that there was something wrong with a small sweet now and then. Mary, however, frowns at anyone who dares to rustle a wrapper or crunch their popcorn. I bought some pick-n-mix and Mary almost fainted with shock.'

'I never had you down as a pick-n-mix kind of person,' she insisted, laughing. 'I didn't know that grown men ate *sweets*.'

'Sorry to disappoint you, Mary,' he said. 'Real men do eat sweets.' He turned back to me. 'Anyway, so I had to eat each one so slowly and carefully so as not to make any noise. I was terrified that I would be subjected to the Mary death-stare. In the end, I was sucking on them as if I had no teeth.'

They were both laughing now, behaving like two old friends. He was always good for a laugh, was Red.

'*A Bout de Souffle*, next Saturday.' Mary gathered up files and went to leave. '*Don't* forget. Now, I must be off, and stop all this gassing.' She turned to me. 'Tabitha, I wonder would it be possible if I made a long-distance call? Just with the time difference and everything, I have to make it now. I can leave the money. I wouldn't like all our fundraising to go on phone bills.'

'Would you like to use my office? For privacy?'

She hesitated. 'No, no, it's all right. It's not a big deal. It won't take long.'

'Is everything okay?'

'Oh yes.' She smiled her bright efficient smile. 'Everything's fine. Just something I need to do... that's all. I'll be quick as quick.'

Before she left my office, I noticed that Red gave her a look, an encouraging 'go on' kind of nod. She gave a short tilt of her head and she was gone. Red knew what was going on, I realised.

'So,' I said, 'what did you want to talk about?'

'*Annie*. I was hoping we could perform some of the songs at the last school assembly.'

'That sounds good. Who's playing Annie?'

'We're working on it, everyone wants the lead role. I think I might share it out a bit. Have lots of Annies. Just need to buy a job lot of red curly wigs on eBay.'

I smiled, feeling better already. 'Annie is theatrical catnip to girls. Annie is their Lady Macbeth, their Medea.'

He laughed. 'Totally. I remember at school, we all wanted to be the Artful Dodger. All of us, practising our cockney accents in the playground. It was given to someone who didn't want it. He wanted to be Fagin and was furious. The rest of us had to be nonspeaking urchins. Hours of accent-practising wasted.' He grinned at me. I found myself grinning back.

'How's your cockney accent now?' I said.

'As bad as it was then. No wonder I didn't get the part. Dick Van Dyke's was better.'

I laughed. I wondered if he and Mary would mind if I asked to go to the cinema with them. Maybe they would. Maybe they wanted it to be just the two of them. But... I couldn't just be friends with Red. It wasn't that simple.

'By the way,' he said. 'I was wondering about Rosie. How is she?'

'I don't know,' I admitted. 'She keeps saying she's okay and for me not to worry. I don't know what to think.'

'She's obviously under a huge amount of stress. Have you talked to your... your husband about it?'

'Well, he's very busy. Very busy. He's very rarely around and...' I looked at Red. I wanted to tell him everything about Michael. But it was all so pointless. Red wasn't just some friend I could confide in. 'Michael is... well, he's determined that Rosie will do Law in Trinity, like he did... but I am starting to wonder if it's what she wants. Or is she just doing it for him. And for my mother-in-law.'

'Well...' There was nothing he could say. He couldn't pass judgment on any of us. He'd only briefly met Michael, but Celia not at all. 'I hope,' he said, 'she's feeling better, soon.' He went to go. Oh, but I wanted him to stay. There was so much I wanted to chat about, innocuous things like cockney accents but seismic life-altering events as well. Everything.

'Listen,' he said, pausing, gratifyingly, at the door. 'I know it's none of my business, I know that. I'm just a supply teacher who is pushing my nose into places where I shouldn't and I have no right. None whatsoever. So please tell me to butt out or whatever. But...' He stopped, and looked at me, right into my eyes. 'I was just wondering if *you* were all right. I'm worried about you.'

'Worried. About me?' I said, swallowing. 'I'm all right. What makes you think I'm not?'

'Listen, forgive me if I'm overstepping the mark. You look so different, Tab. I mean, you *look* the same, as though not a day has passed, but I can see it in your eyes, how much you've got on your plate. There's a lot going on. And you keep on going...'

For a moment, I thought I was going to cry. When was the last time anyone cared how I was doing? 'I'm fine,' I said, sounding just like Rosie. 'I'm absolutely fine.'

He took a pen out of the inside pocket of his jacket. And ripped a corner from a little black Moleskine diary. 'Here's my number,' he said, writing it down. 'Call me if you need a friend.' He handed it to me. 'I'm still that, you know.'

'Thanks.' I didn't trust myself to say anymore.

'She's the image of you,' he said. 'Rosie.'

'Really...' I suddenly felt embarrassed. 'I can see Rosaleen in her but I thought she was *like* her dad, but maybe... maybe she isn't as much as I thought.'

'There's a definite look of you in her, it's like going back in time,' he said. impassively, betraying no emotion.

And then he smiled, the kind of smile that makes you feel as though someone is on your side. Encouraging you, cheering you on. And there he was being nice to me, when I hadn't been nice to him.

18

18

Rosie had been upstairs, as usual, but I brought her up a cup of relaxing tea.

'Sweetheart?' I called gently through her door. 'How's it going in there?'

Silence. I pushed open the door.

'Rosie, I have some nice camomile...'

She was asleep on the bed, her breathing light and steady. For a moment, I just gazed at her. The poor girl. Fully dressed, her long hair falling over the pillow.

I remembered when she was a little girl and we'd walk to school together, knowing so clearly that this was a golden moment in my life. You, as their mother, define their world, you shape it and make sense of it for them, sharing the life so intimately with your small child. I stayed in my marriage for her, I became a teacher because I thought it was more family friendly, I wanted to make the world perfect, or as near perfect as was possible, for her but it seemed it was never quite enough.

I hovered for a moment with the cup of camomile tea. Should I leave it or bring it downstairs? Leave it. I went to her desk to place it down.

One notebook was open, the pen lying across it, as though she'd been writing and, overcome with tiredness, had fallen asleep. It was just a glance, but something made me take a second look. It was the uniform look of the writing, the fact that it looked so unlike a piece of revision work or an essay of any kind. It was Rosie's handwriting, though, her loopy biro, the way she did her a's, the slightly embellished f. But it was the same sentence, over and over again, the same phrase, over and over.

I hate my life. I hate my life. I hate my life.

The same words covered the page. I flicked through the whole book. Everywhere, the same sentence, filling the pages. This must have taken weeks and weeks. Months.

I hate my life. I hate my life. I hate my life.

I looked through other papers on her desk, the ream of foolscap, all covered with that phrase. The same, page after page after page. Months of work, the careful writing of this horrible sentence. She hadn't been revising, she had been filling notebooks with this one thought.

I hate my life, I hate my life.

On the shelf above her desk were other A4 pads, I flicked through them, all of them, the same.

I hate my life. I hate my life. I hate my life.

My darling girl. My beautiful girl. The person I loved more than anything, my absolute pride and joy, the girl who had everything, was good at everything, the person who had the world at her feet, laid out like the finest carpet, hated her life, and had become stuck on this one thought and couldn't move forwards. She must have been so terrified. Why hadn't I realised? Why hadn't I checked, helped her, asked more about how she was getting on... there were so many signs. So many obvious signs and I just assumed – hoped – that it would be okay.

I stood there, for a few moments, not quite knowing what to do. I thought back to Celia's party, and then when she called me at the cake sale. And the fact that she hadn't gone to see any of her friends for months, or been out of the house.

But all the time, I had thought she was getting closer and closer to the end, when in fact she was getting further away. Because the one thing I wanted for her was for her to love her life. That's all I had ever wanted and if she didn't, then I had failed.

'Mum. What are you doing?' Rosie was sitting up, furious.

'Rosie... why didn't you say?'

She stood up and angrily grabbed her notebook from my hands. 'Why are you going through my things? I can't believe you'd do such a thing!'

'Rosie, wait...'

'Everything's fine, Mum. Don't look at me like that.'

'You can't keep saying everything's fine when obviously it isn't. You should have told me. I could have helped. I could have helped you.'

'And done what exactly?' Rosie started to cry, great rackety sobs, the kind I hadn't seen her take since she was tiny. They were filled with hopelessness and devastation, as if her life had come to an end.

'Rosie... Rosie...' She stood trembling and shaking in my arms, her head pressed onto my shoulder.

'Mum...' was all she managed. 'What am I going to do?'

I pulled her onto the bed and we sat side by side, both her trembling hands in mine, and we waited until her breathing slowed down.

'Right, Rosie, whatever you are thinking now, that none of this can be fixed, it can. It's a case of how you recover. Setbacks are just that. Until your comeback. You get up again, you move on and you *learn*. Do you understand?'

She nodded, her lip wobbling.

'Because it doesn't matter. Exams don't actually matter. Going to college doesn't matter. None of those things will make you happy. Not really. Well, they will but true happiness is something that comes from in here.' And I pressed my hand to her heart. 'Get that right, and the rest is easy.'

She nodded again.

'Do you want to tell me what happened?'

'I was doing all right... I thought. All last year, I kept up with everything. All the work, the study events. I did well in my mock exams... remember?'

'You did brilliantly.'

'I thought I was going to be okay even though there was this feeling starting to spread inside me. It was like it had taken root and every day I could feel it getting bigger. Not hugely but there was a feeling every morning, when I opened my eyes.'

'What was it?'

'Like a ball or a knot or stuff, right in the middle of me. And I couldn't concentrate. Or eat. It was like it was this alien inside me...' She gave a wonky smile. 'That sounds weird.'

I shook my head. 'No it doesn't. Nothing you say ever sounds weird. Go on.'

'Well, I first felt this thing, this alien, last summer. All I could think about was September when this year would start. The *last* year. The most important year. No one has been able to talk to me about anything but the exams for ages now. It was all, *when are you doing the Leaving, what subjects are you doing? What college?* I felt like screaming and all the time I had to be nice and polite and tell them over and over again. Everyone asks you, Mum. Not just family members but people in the shop, the guys down in the sailing club. Even the postman asked me!'

'And then...'

'Well, I didn't do any work all summer. I kept convincing myself that I would start in September and that I would be brilliant, keep to study timetables and go for walks and just be... you know... methodical. Cool. But... I don't know. I just didn't. And then Jake finished with me...'

'It's not easy, is it? A relationship ending like that.'

She shook her head. 'No. No, it's not. And, it didn't help my alien. It just kind of doubled in size overnight. Sometimes I would feel as though it was going to take over my whole body. I felt so scared. I mean, we haven't had to be in school since January. All the study events were optional, if you were able to do it at home, then they didn't bother you. And I just let it all get on top of me.'

'Don't they have counselling services? Someone you can talk to?'

'Yeah, they are always saying, if you need help, you can go and talk to Miss Byrne.'

'Oh, sweetheart, why didn't you?'

'I felt ashamed,' she said. 'Embarrassed. Like I was a failure. Which I am.'

'You're not. You're absolutely not. Doing well in exams does not signify success in life, just in exams. It's how you deal with things when they go wrong. What you learn, how you bounce back, what you take with you to the next experience. Do you see? But why didn't you talk to me? I could have helped...'

'I kept thinking, if I could just get working, I'd be all right. I kept thinking, I would start tomorrow. It wasn't too late. And then it was Christmas...'

'Christmas!'

'Yeah...' She hung her head. 'It goes back as far as then. But I thought, I'd just take that time off and then start in January. It wasn't too late. But I just couldn't do it.'

'And the hating your life... when did you start doing that?'

'Once I wrote it, and then wrote it again, I swear it helped... just naming what I felt was good for me.'

I put my arm around her and squeezed her. 'Couldn't you have talked to your friends if you couldn't talk to me?' I said gently.

'It was easier not to see them. I couldn't do with all their exam talk and college talk. So I said that you had said I couldn't go out or contact them...'

'Really?' I said.

'It was just easier that way.'

'Okay, let's not worry about any of that now. You've got your first exam in a week.'

'Oh mum,' she wailed. 'I can't do them.'

'Really? You could try and just see how you get on?'

She shook her head. 'Don't make me. Please don't make me.'

'First thing's first, I'll call the school and chat to them. Miss Byrne for one, okay?'

'I can't do them,' she said. 'I'm going to fail everything.' And she began to cry again. 'And I'm never going to go to Trinity. Or do a stupid internship. Dad's going to be so mad.'

'No, he's not... he'll be fine about it.' I hoped he would, anyway.

'But, Mum, I didn't actually want to go anyway. I don't want to do Law. It's not me. It never was. But Dad's never shut up about it. Ever.'

'He just wanted something nice for you and this is what he thought was something nice.' Bloody Michael, I thought, though. Not only has he compounded her stress and panic by talking incessantly about Trinity and the following in the Fogarty footsteps, but he was never around. He hadn't actually taken a proper interest in how she was going to get there. 'Well, thank God for that,' I said. 'It took this, all of this, for you to admit you don't want to go to Trinity to do Law. Bit of an elaborate way of going about it...'

'Yeah...'

'I got stuck, just like you have, once. And you think that you are never going to be unstuck or even how on earth you are going to move on... is that how you feel?' She nodded. 'I think finding that way of writing something down, like you did, was really clever of you, because I didn't do that, when it was me. I just stayed indoors for weeks and weeks.'

'What happened?' Her eyes were wide, listening.

'Oh, it was a long time ago. A really long time. Before you were born. But it changed me, that experience. Reshaped me. My life wasn't the same again. Couldn't be.'

BEFORE

Nora was at home with me, taking care of me as I lay in bed, facing the wall. She'd never been particularly maternal before and neither of us knew if she even had it in her. Seemingly she did.

'Red phoned,' she said. 'I told him you were out, like you said.'

I didn't respond, just stared at the intricate flower patterns on the wallpaper, the curls and curlicues, the swoops and sweeps of colour. Rosuleen had chosen it before it became my room. It was in her colours, the greens and the turquoises.

'He sounded really upset,' she said. 'In tears.'

The feel of the ruffle on the pink bedspread against my face, the sound of the starlings gathering in the tree in the churchyard behind the house. The nothingness, the emptiness, the deadness in my belly.

* * *

Where do you start, how do you even tell you daughter this thing that happened? How do you put it into words that she might understand, that might explain who you are to her but will certainly make her feel differently from you?

'Rosaleen was ill for at least a year before she died,' I began. 'She was diagnosed with cancer and initially she didn't tell us. We noticed she was getting thinner and paler. And she stopped going swimming. She'd head down to the Forty Foot, get changed and then just stand there, on the top step, and let the sea wash over her feet. "That's enough," she said. "I don't think I'll go any further," as if she was talking about her own life. But then when Nora and I were told, we assumed she'd get better, as you do. We were certain she would be fine because Rosaleen always was. Somehow. Anyway, Red and I had both finished our teacher training...'

She sat up a bit. 'Red, as in that man Red? Who brought the book round?'

'Yes. As in that man Red.' I half smiled at her.

'You were going *out* with him? I thought it was a bit of an odd thing to do, bring a book to a stranger's child.'

I nodded. 'There you go...'

'And you never told me? I didn't know any of this!' She was half-shocked, half-thrilled with this previously classified information.

'Ro, I didn't tell you *then* but I'm telling you *now*... So Rosaleen was dying, but I was meant to be going to San Francisco with Red so I stayed just to see her back on her feet again and I would join him later. But her dying, well, it kind of put a spanner in the works...'

'You were going to *live* together?' Rosie was delighted with this idea of her mother. 'You and Dad didn't, did you?'

'Red was different, okay? It was an entirely different relationship.'

'Obviously,' she said.

'Rosaleen was chatting to all her friends at the Forty Foot. She hadn't been in the water all year. And everyone was so happy to see her back and I had to wait for her for ages before she finished talking to them. But I didn't mind really because the sun was out.'

* * *

I stopped speaking for a moment, thinking of Rosaleen and me. We walked home, my arm in hers, because she wasn't able to cycle, her asking me all about the phone call I'd received from Red. He'd found a place for us. Haight Ashbury. Not luxurious, he'd said. But it was perfect. Perfect for us. I hadn't told him my secret. I thought I'd tell him when I was there. It might mean coming home to Ireland sooner than we'd thought. Or we could stay there. I imagined us, our lives together, getting jobs and buying a house. Bringing up a little American child. Who would never know the delights of Cadburys or Tayto crisps but would race home-made go-carts and have lemonade stalls. I'd walked home in the sun, thinking that I could never be this happy again. I'd see Red next week and I'd tell him and... and...

'So, Rosaleen and I went home, together, talking all the way, about San Francisco and my plans. It's funny because I always thought she and Nora were chalk and cheese but Nora is so like her in so many ways. Maybe I'd just never noticed and she always was. Or maybe it's just getting older. Anyway, when we got inside, we had a cup of tea and I told her...'

'Told her what?'

'That I was pregnant.'

'What?'

'Pregnant. I mean, it was an accident, it wasn't meant to happen but I wanted it. I mean, I loved Red and I knew he loved me. I wanted the baby.'

'Oh my God...'

'But she died that day. Granny Nora and I organised the funeral, got everything organised... but I hadn't told Red about the... you know... the baby.'

'Did Granny Nora know?'

I nodded.

'But why didn't you tell Red? It was his baby too.'

'I know. But it was going to be a surprise and I thought I'd wait and then... well, sometimes you don't think straight... Anyway, I was still meant to be leaving right after the funeral. I was determined to go. And then I would tell him. It was only a week. And even all that week, being so sad about Rosaleen, the baby kept me going. My lovely baby... it was like I knew him or her – I never knew which – it was as though we already knew each other.' Rosie's face was full of sympathy.

'I thought about what he or she would be like,' I went on. 'Would they look like me or Red, or be entirely their own self? I couldn't wait until I was able to bring my baby to the Forty Foot and swim there, just like Rosaleen and I used to. So, the morning of the funeral, I woke up and for some reason I wanted to go swimming. It was the one place which I most associated with Rosaleen. But...' I stopped, not wanting to cry or do anything that might upset Rosie.

'Go on...'

'Well...' I could still feel the cold instantly leeching into my skin, soaking my bones, so cold, it made me gasp as I paddled around, trying to get warm. 'Well, I lost the baby. And I thought it was because I went swimming. I thought the water had done something, like it was powerful.'

'Really?' Rosie's eyes were wide-open, as she tried to make sense of everything. 'Oh Mum...'

It was devastating. Red and I were over. Life shifted entirely in a different direction. Permanently altered, forever scarred, I thought I was an entirely new Tabitha but it was only recently, since Red had come home, that I had realised that she was still there. She'd just been hiding.

BEFORE

Me, floating on my back, feet sticking up out of the salty blue of the sea. I put my hands on my belly. I don't feel any different. Or wait... was that a flutter? The shift of a million cells working day and night to create this new life, this baby inside me. 'I can't wait to meet you,' I say to myself, to my baby. But when I turn over and plunge again under the water, I gasp with the shock, my body immediately numb and a strange feeling in my stomach, cramp gripping my insides, cold settling into my bones. Eventually I pull myself out and shiver while I get dressed, my body getting colder and colder on the cycle home.

Later Nora and I stood in the church together, my body frozen, teeth chattering under Red's old winter jumper I'd pulled from my wardrobe. I thought of Red in the warmth of San Francisco. I'd be there too, just as soon as Nora and I organised everything here. It would do me good to get away. I didn't want to be in this house without Rosaleen.

But it was later that evening when I began to feel really unwell, when the pains in my stomach began to jar, causing my legs to wobble. Eventually, I fell onto my bed, the pain making me double up. I knew what was happening, but even when I saw the blood, I didn't believe it. I didn't want to believe it. And I lay there, quiet in that moment, when no one could tell me for sure that everything wasn't okay. I had lost my grandmother and my child in one day. Lying on my bed, the house dark, writhing in agony, too much in pain and too confused to turn on the lights. Knowing I should go to hospital but that would make it real, official and all I wanted was a few moments longer with my baby. I was still a mother. In that space between life and death, between fantasy and reality, where a tiny part of me could still pretend that everything was all right.

* * *

Rosie was holding my hand. 'Who looked after you?' she said, quietly.

'Nora. She... well, she was amazing. Stayed with me for months afterwards, refused to go down to West Cork,' I said. 'Which itself was a miracle, knowing that a tepee in Mizen Head was waiting for her. And a vat of something unspeakable involving lentils...' I was desperately trying to make light of what happened. I didn't want to burden Rosie. I didn't want her to worry about *me* as well. 'Yes. I remember she brewed me some kind of tea, involving liquorice root. She says it had healing properties. She was wrong. It just made me think I could never have a sherbet dip-dab ever again.'

Rosie very nearly laughed.

'The thing is,' I went on. 'I didn't think I'd recover, really. I had never thought that losing a baby, someone you had never met, something that was an accident, not planned, could mean... could mean so much.' I managed to keep my voice steady, well aware that I didn't want to freak Rosie out too much.

'And that's why you never swim there?'

I nodded. 'I can't. I just can't.'

'The point of all this, Rosie, why I'm burbling on, is that I do understand. I know what it's like when you don't know what's coming next and you feel overwhelmed...'

'That's how I feel. I'm scared.'

We were still holding hands.

'We all feel like that. Life *is* scary. The trick is just accepting that. Feel the fear, but know that things do get better. After all, I had you.'

19

Early the next morning, I rang Michael's phone. I hadn't slept well and had laid in bed wondering and worrying, thinking of my past and Rosie's present and our future, wondering what it looked like. Michael needed to know what was going on in Rosie's life and the fact that she very well might not be sitting her Leaving Cert this year and the sooner I told him and prepared him for disappointment the better. He was in Brussels as far as I knew.

'Tabitha?' He sounded half-asleep. It was eight a.m., surely, there was some kind of high-powered breakfast meeting he should be at?

'Hi Michael,' I said. 'How's it going?'

'Pretty good,' he said. 'Just checking something. This thing is saying I slept for nine and half hours. No, sorry, nine and three-quarters. I could sleep longer. Getting ready for my big presentation tomorrow. And then there's the vote at the end of the week. I'm not so much up to my eyes but am submerged.' He paused. 'So why are you ringing? Is there something wrong? A fuse gone? Your mother arrested?' He laughed at his own joke.

'Michael, this is actually pretty serious.'

'What? She has been arrested. Listen, I can't pull any strings. It would be against SIPL. If she is in some cell somewhere justice will have to be seen to be done.'

'It's Rosie,' I said, 'it's about her exams.'

'Tabitha,' he said. 'Anyone would think she was the only person who'd ever done an exam. It's you, it is. Fussing. Just let her get on with it. She does so much better when you are not hovering around looking worried.'

'Michael!'

'Well, sometimes it has to be said. I'm not being personal, it's just mothers. They're rather suffocating at times. I mean, look at mine.'

'It's Rosie,' I said, keeping my voice calm. 'Just to let you know that she's not going to be doing her exams. Not this year anyway. I've been thinking and thinking and maybe she can start again next year, this time with different expectations and goals.'

There was a noise that sounded like Michael falling off the bed. 'What?' He was muffled, and then clearer as he wrested back control of his phone. 'Of course she's going to do her exams! How can she not do them? It's what you do. It's what we all did.' You could practically hear the whirring of his brain, as he tried to assimilate this new information. 'You are born, you go to school, you learn how to read and write and then you do your exams. It's how it's been done for millennia. Unless you are mentally incapacitated or the academically disinclined and, as far as I am aware, our daughter is neither.'

No one witnessed my eye-roll. Michael was on another planet entirely.

'She hasn't been working,' I said. 'She's been far too anxious.'

'Anxious? It's called the Leaving Cert. It's *supposed* to make you anxious. It's no walk in the park, you know. It's not like *Who Wants Be A Millionaire*. Nice easy questions and phone a friend!'

'She's been having panic attacks,' I pressed on. 'Remember at your mother's party?'

'That was nothing. The room was too hot and she was being forced to talk to Imelda Goggins. That would induce panic in any right-minded person. I've spent my life perfecting disinterested interest and a healthy internal world when talking to people like her. Rosie just needs a bit more practice.'

'Michael, listen to me.' I could feel myself getting annoyed. 'Rosie hasn't actually done any work.'

'But every time I ask, you say she's up in her bedroom. Working.'

'I was wrong.'

'*Wrong*? I leave my daughter in your care and this happens!' He blustered. 'I am off trying to make Europe a better place for our citizens. And upholding standards in public life. And supporting the dairy farmers of Ireland and you take your eye off the ball...'

'Michael. Just stop this. Okay? It's no one's fault. We've just got to look after Rosie...' But then I heard his voice break. A wobble? Michael never wobbled. He was Teflon.

'I'm sorry,' he said, dropping his voice so low I had to strain my ears. 'I'm under a great deal of pressure, that's all,' he whispered into the phone. 'This couldn't have come at a worse time for me.'

'What do you mean? It's not about you. I think, Michael, that it might be a good idea if you...'

'It's just... I'll talk to you later. Okay?'

'Are you going to call Rosie, tell her that it's okay, that you understand and that you love her despite her not going to college? Well, not this year anyway.'

'She knows that anyway. She knows that I support her whatever she does. Even if she doesn't...' He stopped, as if the enormity of what he was contemplating was hitting him for the first time, his voice cracking at the horror and enormity, 'even if she doesn't go to Trinity.'

'It's disappointing, I know,' I said.

'I won't be able to go back to sleep now,' he said. 'I may as well get up...'

'And phone your daughter!'

* * *

After I'd put down the phone, I heard Rosie come downstairs. 'Morning, sweetheart,' I said. 'I'm making pancakes.'

'Oh God.' She began to cry. 'You're trying to be some mum in an American sitcom.'

'Oh Rosie...' I went over and gave her a hug.

'But no one made you pancakes when you had your... your miscarriage. I've been thinking about you. That was horrible. You were so young. I can't believe you were so young.'

'It happened. It was really sad. It changed my life, yes. But I've no regrets. People have miscarriages and I do think of the baby and wonder about it, but it wasn't meant to be. *You* were meant to be. And everyone needs someone to make them pancakes.' I placed one in front of her, not wanting her to realise that I had thought about the baby I lost every single day since. 'There we go. So tell me, how was your night? Did you sleep?'

If she had, then she was the only one of us who had slept that night. I had lain awake thinking about her, about what had happened and why, how much of it was my fault (pretty much all of it) and where we would go from here.

'Not really,' she admitted. 'But I feel a *bit* better. Like the alien is shrinking. Just a bit.'

I smiled. 'Glad to hear it. You know why?'

'Why?'

'Because you've started talking about it. You're not alone with what you might think of as your shame. Once you start telling people, the shame – or the alien – is exposed. It has no power.' I took a deep breath. 'This is where it ends right now, okay? This is where this stops. We have to work out what kind of help and support you need...'

'But I don't want to leave the house. Not ever. It scares me to think about going to the shop. What was I thinking that I would be able to go to college? Or inter-railing. Or anywhere. I am seventeen years old and I just want to stay with my mum. Isn't that crazy. I'd die if anyone found out. Every time you left the house lately I'd be scared that you wouldn't come back, but if I just stayed in my room, doing nothing, it was as though I could control that tiny part of my life.'

'I always came back though, didn't I?'

She nodded.

'And I always will. Sweetheart, you don't need to leave the house. Not until you're ready.'

'Okay.'

'But we do need to get some help, okay? I'm going to call the school in the morning and tell them what's been going on and talk about a few options. I think you need to talk to someone...'

'It was as though I was the only person in the world,' she said, tears forming in her eyes. 'Every time I went out, I could just see faces, you know, people everywhere all doing things, being functional and normal and happy. And there was I, all weird and strange and not normal. I thought something might happen, like another panic attack, or worse, that I might die, you know, from not breathing. Staying inside was safest...'

'I wished you'd told me.'

'I couldn't... I was just trying to manage it. Anyway, I didn't want to let you down...' She almost smiled. 'I made everything worse, didn't I?'

'No.' I took her hand again and I kissed it. 'No you didn't.'

'I just want to be normal, Mum? Everyone else I know is normal, they are all working so hard. What is wrong with me? Why can't I do this? Every time I tried, every time I sat down at my desk, I could just feel this horrible feeling inside me, rising up, like some kind of wave that I could actually taste. It was disgusting. And it was like that was who I was, who I am, this horrible disgusting person who can't be...' she began to sob once more... 'who can't be normal.'

'You are normal...' I was crying too now. 'You are normal. This is normal. What's happened is normal. Panicking, feeling scared, things going wrong are normal. What's *not* normal is the way other people present themselves to the world as if there's nothing wrong. Everyone is scared, everyone makes mistakes and no one is perfect. But life is not crap forever. It's not ongoingly crap or awful. But without crappiness, you don't get the happiness.'

'Oh my God, did you just make that up?'

'Yes! It just came out. Genius? No?'

'No.' But she smiled at me.

* * *

I had no choice but to leave her when I went to school and that morning, the first face I saw was Christy, sitting in one of those large picnic chairs, a mug of tea in the cup holder, notebook on his lap. When he saw me, he signalled to Leaf to give him a hand up and she hoisted him to his feet. 'Tabitha!' He hobbled over to me wearing a t-shirt which had a vaguely recognisable face on the front and the words *Leonard Cohen is how the light gets in.*

'Beautiful day,' he said, when I'd rolled down my window. 'The kind of day that makes you feel like you don't ever want the day to end.'

I nodded, I supposed it was. 'Nice t-shirt, Christy,' I said, getting out of the car to talk to him properly.

'Red bought it for me,' he said, 'from California. He knows I am a disciple of the great man.'

'And what would Leonard Cohen have made of Nora's Last Stand?'

'My poem or the point of principle?'

'Both.'

'He would have been impressed by the latter and I would say encouraging about the former. He might give me a few tips, though, on how to write a great poem. It's a very creatively inspiring space, Tabitha, I have to say.'

'Really?' Was heating Heinz tomato soup really so inspiring? Forming a human blockade, pitching mother against daughter, really so exciting. I was feeling decidedly weary regarding the whole thing. 'That's nice for you. It's great, Christy, it really is that so many people are having the time of their lives while making mine really difficult.' I thought of Rosie at home. She'd cried that morning when I said I had to leave, making me promise that I would be home at lunchtime to check on her.

Christy nodded. 'You're right, Tabitha,' he said, gently. 'It seems very unfair, doesn't it?'

I nodded. 'Yes it does. And how am I meant to make a rational decision *in either direction* under these circumstances?'

'I don't know. But you will.'

'What?'

'Make the right decision – whatever it is. If it's to sell the land, then I know it is the right decision.'

'Why?' I said suspiciously. 'What do you mean?'

'I've always admired you, young Tabitha,' he said. 'You are one of those people who aren't afraid of anything.'

'Thank you, Christy.' If only he knew. I had lived my life based on fear.

'As Leonard would say,' he went on, *'poetry is just the evidence of life if your life is burning well, poetry is just the ash.'*

Did he expect me to start writing poetry now? Just being me was struggle enough. 'I think I'll leave the composing and the musing to you, Christy,' I said. 'And I'll...' I'll what? Carry on being the bad guy? The one on the wrong side every time?

But he chuckled. 'You'll do the right thing,' he said. 'Whatever it is, you'll do the right thing. You know it's much easier to be us,' he said, pointing to the protestors. 'We're just speaking out. We don't have anything else to do. You are the one with the weight of decision on your shoulders. You are the one with the weight of responsibility.'

I shrugged noncommittally.

'This situation...' He gestured to the protestors. 'And all you can do is find a place of peace.'

'Peace?' I said, sulkily, but realising how much I loved Christy. He was right. Fighting never got anyone anywhere. This was democracy and however much I would have like to live in a totalitarian state, we didn't and I would have to suck it up. Also, the energy I had for the sale of the land and all the improvements was waning. Our pupils, were, on the whole happy. If I didn't make any more speeches which would make them cry, then we weren't doing too badly. Rosie was alone and upset. All anyone needed was love. Soppy but true.

'Have you written any more about the protest?'

'I have a few,' he admitted. 'Well, more than a few. Seeing these people, never giving up, standing up for what they believe in... it's been quite the inspiration.'

'Really?'

'Really,' he said. 'And that's what I want to talk to you about. You see, my book is going to be published and I wanted to know if I had your permission.'

'For what?'

'To publish it. *Nora's Last Stand* could be out by Christmas. I'm finishing a few poems off and I have one more to write. But it won't happen unless...'

'Unless what?'

'Unless *Nora's Last Stand* has your blessing. I won't publish it if it makes you unhappy or uneasy or uncomfortable.'

'Congratulations,' I said. 'That's great news.'

'And your blessing?'

'Why not?' I couldn't think of any reason why I wouldn't give it. It was slightly irksome but if something good, such as Christy getting a book published could come out of this, then who was I to prevent it?

* * *

'I have something to ask you,' Mary said, standing at the door of my office. 'I need to go away. I know it's short notice but...' She looked at me pleadingly.

'Come in,' I said. 'Come and sit down.' We were two weeks to the end of term. Something must be wrong. 'Are you all right?'

'I am so sorry, Tabitha,' she said, sitting down in the chair in front of my desk, her hands twisting in her lap. 'But I have to go. I don't have a choice.'

'Okay...'

'But,' she said quickly, 'everything's in order. I thought that I might have to go and so I've been getting everything ready just in case. Just in case. The school reports are ready to send out, all the notices for next term, the filing... everything's done. I stayed late, all night, actually, yesterday. It's all done.' She looked at me. 'Please?'

'Of course,' I said. 'If you have to. But what is it? Where are you going? Are you ill?'

She shook her head. 'No, not ill. I'm fine but I can't tell you, Tabitha, but I will, as soon as I'm home again I will. I just can't. It's too important and...' There were tears in her eyes. I'd never seen Mary well up before. 'I can't tell anyone anything. Just in case...'

'Just in case what?'

'Just in case I jinx it.'

Maybe it was financial trouble? She wasn't about to join the Sisters of Charity? Never to be seen again without a wimple.

'It's all I've ever wanted,' she said. 'I can't tell you what it is because you'll tell me not to do it or that it's too risky and I'll only get hurt like the last time...'

'If there's anything I can do to help you... anything at all... Please call me. Money... whatever you need.'

'Tabitha, you make it sound like I'm dying.'

'You're not are you?'

'My time will come but, as far as I'm aware, it won't be anytime soon.'

'You will look after yourself, won't you? And call me, any time. Please?'

She nodded. 'I've never been so nervous in my entire life,' she said, standing up. 'Wish me luck, Tabitha. Wish me luck.'

'Good luck Mary.' It was like she was off to war. Oh Jesus. She wasn't heading off to fight terrorists, was she? I went over to her and we grabbed each other's hands and hugged tightly, her tiny body shaking like a leaf.

20

The situation with Rosie just didn't compute for Michael. He arrived home in a state of near hysteria forcing Rosie, who I'd managed to coax out of her room, like a shy animal, to retreat, and close her door behind her.

'I don't understand,' he said. 'How could she not do her exams? She should at least give it a go... she could *fail*...' He blanched at the thought but carried on gamely, 'but it would be better than not doing them. There was a lad in my year. Failed the whole lot. Estate agent now. Makes a packet. Lives in the South of France, drives some tiny, red car and roars about Ville-franche.'

'And that's what you want for Rosie?'

'No! It's just that even if you don't think you are going to do well, you should just do them. Never give up. Don't cop out. Failure is not an option. Us Fogartys...'

'Fogartys can't give up. Fogartys are made of sterner stuff. Fogartys aren't allowed to be seen to fail, is that right?'

'Well, it's just that Lucy...'

'Lucy? What's her advice? Lucy is just like you, Michael. She never shows weakness, vulnerability, never puts a foot wrong. She's not going to know what to do...'

'Lucy suggested it was vegetarianism. Don't look at me like that. Hear me out because I think she might have a point. Milk. Does Rosie drink milk? Big glasses of it?'

'I don't know,' I said wearily. 'She has it in tea and on her granola, but...'

'Lucy says all the young ones like to drink almond milk or whatnot.' He put his hands up as if to present an open and shut case. 'Is that what she's doing?'

'Michael,' I said, 'I don't think milk is the answer.' He looks shocked as though I'd said that the sky wasn't blue or Brussels wasn't the centre of the universe. 'I think it's something that will take a bit of time...'

'Time... but we don't have time. Life is short. She...'

'She needs time. Things are going well with her counsellor...'

Michael's brow furrowed. 'Counsellor... clap trap. Milk would be better Vitamins and minerals and a good dose of protein. I think Lucy might have a point...'

* * *

All week, before I left for school, I'd check on Rosie. She was permanently tear-streaked and washed out. At lunchtime, I'd come home to make her something to eat, and later find the sandwich only half eaten or the soup untouched. But she was getting a little bit stronger. The school had been immediately responsive, full of empathy and practical support and organising a counsellor which Rosie had seen on Friday. She hadn't said too much about it but she had appeared slightly brighter yesterday evening and had watched the news with me.

This day, when I stood at her bedroom door, my heart broke at the sight of her, still in her pyjamas, lying on her bed. She didn't seem to be doing anything not reading, not watching television, just sleeping or staring into space.

'Why don't you talk to Alice?' I said. 'Give her or Mary a call.'

'I can't. They're working.'

'But a quick phone call or a pop round would be okay, surely?'

She nodded. 'The counsellor said I should tell people.'

'And why don't you?'

'Shame,' she said. 'Apparently. It's what stops all of us from doing emotionally healthy things. And I'm quoting. That's what she said. I'm to tell people and that will rid me of shame.'

'So?' I asked. 'So, are you going to tell people? You could call Alice. Call Mary. Put it up on Facebook.'

'That's what I should do. But I'm working towards it.' She looked at me. My battered and bruised baby.

'I've got to go out. Board meeting. I'll be two hours. No longer.'

'Promise?'

'Promise.' I smiled at her. 'Love you Ro.'

'Love you too.'

* * *

'Sister Kennedy, these are for you.' Brian placed a box of Black Magic in front of her. 'A little bird told me you were partial to something sweet...'

We were at the board meeting to come to a final decision about the selling of the Copse.

Brian had a formal offer that he was waving around. 'We'll sign all the documents next week,' he said, slipping it back into the inside of his jacket. 'My lawyers and Freddie Boyle's lawyers are drawing everything up. All ship-shape.' He smiled his crocodile smile, his tiny teeth poking over his thin lips.

I'd finally received my formal valuation of the land this morning. It was worth three times what this Freddie Boyle was offering. But the money seemed so unimportant, suddenly. We would survive another winter with a leaky roof. We'd make do with the chairs we had. The playground would remain a little bit gravelly. The children could share the creaky computers we already had. Selling the land was wrong.

And there was something about Brian that I didn't like or trust and I knew he would have known the land's real valuation. I may not have concrete proof that he was conning us but my suspicions were enough. I was going to trust my gut. It was time to halt the plans.

'Chocolates... how lovely.' Sister Kennedy took the box. 'I am most partial to something sweet, Mr Crowley,' she said, going slightly pink. 'How... how *kind* of you.'

'And for you, Noleen.' He presented Noleen's gift with the flourish of Launcelot to Guinevere. 'A Chocolate Orange by the chocolatiers known as Terry's...'

'Thank you, Mr Crowley.' She took it from him, eyes shining, examining it as though it was the Noor diamond. 'They are my favourite. The last time I had one of these was Christmas 1985. Do you remember, Sister Kennedy? Santa paid a visit to the school and he gave all the children one of these and there was one left over. And he gave it to me.' She stopped. 'Obviously, it wasn't the real Santa, just the caretaker dressed up. I've never forgotten it.' She looked misty-eyed and lost in memory. 'He was made to leave, though, soon after. He'd been stealing from the lost property. Selling the items on a market stall at the weekend... such a shame... he was a good man. A very good man...' She drifted away, lost in 1985.

Brian ignored her and turned his attention to Brendan. 'And for you, sir, I've bought you some whiskey liqueurs. A man like you must like a tot from time to time. You have, I would imagine, a palate for fine Irish whiskey.'

'Well... I would like to think... oh, well, that's, that's very kind of you, Mr Crowley.' Brendan looked so pleased that it was as though he'd never been given a present before.

'I'm afraid, I don't have anything for you Tabitha,' he said to me. 'Your office is well stocked with sweet things as it is. I don't think you need any more.' He smiled, baring his miniscule teeth. 'All those biscuits I see waiting to be scoffed.'

'Brian, I don't think gifts are appropriate at this meeting. They are unnecessary and could be construed as bribery,' I said.

'Should I ask for them back?' he smirked. 'Is that what you think? Take them back from these good souls here when all I want to do is bring some sweetness and light into people's lives.'

Sister Kennedy, Noleen and Brendan were clutching their gifts. They looked at me as though they were children and I was trying to take away their Christmas presents.

'It's a very nice gesture,' said Noleen, going pink and looking to Sister Kennedy for approval. 'Very kind, Mr Crowley. Very kind of you indeed.'

'Very kind,' said Sister Kennedy. 'You remind me of one of the *Magi*.' She took him by the hand. 'The kings who traversed afar to give gifts to the

Holy Child.' She smiled. 'Such a simple act, to give a small gift to someone else. But a beautiful one. Thank you.' She picked up the chocolates. 'And the name of them...' she laughed. 'Black Magi... so appropriate.'

'They're Black Magic,' I tried to correct her. 'The chocolates. Black. Magic.' I had lost this one and all I was achieving was making myself into someone seeming jealous and Grinch-like. 'Let's just not make this a regular part of the meetings,' I ended.

Sister Kennedy bestowed upon Brian her most beneficent of smiles, as though he was the naughtiest boy in school but also her favourite. 'I'm going to share these with my meditation group. I think that a small chocolate each wouldn't go against any rules. I think that Tabitha is warning us against bribes and incentives, but we all know, Mr Crowley, you're not trying to influence us. They are hardly brown envelopes, which I think is the preferred way of doing business in this country. Or so I hear on the radio.'

'Envelopes full of cash can be arranged,' winked Brian and the two of them shared a laugh.

'Can we get on?'

'Yes, I can't stay late either,' said Sister Kennedy. 'Regretfully. I have a most pressing arrangement.'

'Not before one of these,' said Brendan who was opening his liqueurs and passing them around. 'We'll be drunk if we're not careful.' He held the box in front of me. The smell was overpowering, the Proustian experience of a 1970s Christmas.

'No thank you, Brendan. I really want to get down to things.'

'Some lady's in a hurry,' said Brian, who had two liqueurs in his mouth, one in either cheek, the words barely discernible over the chocolate and whiskey mushy spittle. 'Well, maybe I'll take over... hmmm? This meeting is to bring the board up to speed, vis a vis, ergo, veto the *situacion* the sale of the rubbish ground, erstwhile known as the Copse. Not cops. That's something else entirely...'

This was met by polite smiles from Brendan and Noleen as Sister Kennedy looked merely confused. Brian continued, unabashed by the lukewarm reception to his attempt at humour. 'As you know we have our buyer – or Good Samaritan, Sister Kennedy...'

'You are clever Mr Crowley,' she said carefully laying her liqueur in front of her to enjoy later. '

'These chocolates are a celebration, really. And he's a perfect buyer. Freddie Boyle is his name. I think, if you don't mind me saying, Sister Kennedy, I think that you would particularly like him. Boyle has a priestliness to him. A spiritual quality that would not look out of place giving Mass on a... on a...' For a moment, he looked confused, as though he couldn't quite remember the usual day for Mass.

'Sunday?' I suggested.

'Yes! Sunday!'

'I had a dog called Freddie,' said Noleen. 'When I was young. Lovely little thing he was. Used to wait for me to come home from school. We had to put him down in the end.'

'A woman like you,' Brian went on, looking at Sister Kennedy, 'who has known such goodness in your life, has shown such charitable spirit, would recognise a kindred spirit and Freddie Boyle is such a man. You two would have so much to talk about.'

'Our Good Samaritan,' she said, wide-eyed at the thought of such goodness come to life.

'Indeed,' he nodded. 'Like the story in the Bible when Jesus does that thing. And the thing happens. And the Good Samaritan saves the day.'

'He does,' said Sister Kennedy. 'He saves the day. That's a lovely way of putting it. It's my favourite parable.'

He smiled. 'Let's make this happen, Sister Kennedy. Let's make this happen.'

'Well,' she said. 'I vote yes to this Freddie Byrne.'

'Boyle,' he corrected.

'Aye too,' said Noleen.

'And me,' said Brendan, who was on another liqueur.

Brian looked delighted. 'Well,' he said, 'that seems as though we're...'

'Wait a minute,' I said. 'We have to discuss this. We need to talk about it properly...'

Sister Kennedy looked at the clock. 'Oh my goodness, it's time to go. I told you I couldn't stay long tonight... it's my book group. The Thorn Birds. My goodness. So much to say. I just don't know where we'll start.'

Brian stood up and pulled out her chair and helped Sister Kennedy to her feet.

'I'm so glad you approve of the plan,' he was murmuring. 'It's practically holy. For us to give the land to Freddie Boyle, I think it's a holy thing to do. God would be pleased with the plan, if I may be so bold.'

'You may,' she said, 'for He moves in mysterious ways.'

'Indeed he does,' said Brian. He glanced at me and there was triumph in his eyes. 'Looks like there's just the i's to cross and the t's to dot. Sharpen your fountain pen, Tabitha.'

For a moment, I felt rather alone. Mary was perhaps a world away, Clodagh was fighting her own battles and my mother was pitched against me. I needed a friend. Well, I needed Red. And once I was in the car, I found the scrap of paper he'd written his number on, and dialled it.

21

The choices we make, the million decisions we take every day, are often unfelt, unnoticed. But sometimes, the after-shocks are felt for years and years. If I hadn't gone swimming, maybe I wouldn't have lost the baby. If I had told Red about the baby in the first place, I would have had to tell him about the miscarriage. If I'd just been honest, then maybe our lives would have been so different.

'Red... it's...'

'Tab?' He interrupted. 'Are you all right?'

'Yes... fine.' Where to start? What to say? Just, *I wanted to hear your voice. I really want to see you.* 'Have you heard about Mary? She's had to go away. I don't know if she told you.'

'Yeah...' He hesitated and I knew immediately that he knew her reason. 'Yeah, she cancelled our film club so... so, I was aware.' He wasn't going to betray any confidences that was for sure. There was silence for a moment.

'And you, Tab?' he said. 'How are you? And Rosie?'

'She's not... she's not so good.' I could feel my whole body unfold as I began to confide. 'Red, she hasn't been doing any work. None at all. She's just been sitting there in her room, writing over and over again that she hates her life.' He was silent as I spoke and all the worry I had been feeling for the last months bubbled up and I started to cry. 'It must have been so awful for her. I feel that it's my fault. I didn't ask any questions. I just assumed she was okay and she was upstairs in her room and I didn't bother to check on her. I should have done. And now Michael thinks milk is the answer. And so...'

'I'll come round,' he said, firmly. 'We could go for a walk.'

That was exactly what I needed. I breathed out in relief. 'Thank you Red. I'll just check on Rosie and see if she's okay with me popping out.'

If I could turn back time, I would never have gone swimming. And I would have told Red from the moment I found out I was pregnant. But then I became someone else, the girl who lost a grandmother and an unborn child within a week. And if I could turn back time, I would have noticed what was going on with Rosie. I would have seen it, she wouldn't have been so alone.

Red wasn't my answer, my knight in shining armour. And I could never tell him about what had happened. I should have told him years ago, *when* it happened, but it was too late now.

But we could still try and be friends. Not *friends* friends but acquaintances who shared a special history. That counted for something, didn't it? And I wanted to see him. In fact, I wanted to see him more than anything, however awkward and strange and weird it all was.

Rosie was sitting downstairs, watching television when I got home.

'Hello,' I said. 'You're looking... better.'

'Am I?'

'Yes. How are you feeling?'

'A bit better.' She gave a smile.

'Well, then, that must be why.'

'Would you be all right, if I went for a walk. With Red?'

She nodded. 'Yeah, I think I'll survive.'

'Sure?'

'Sure.'

Doorbell. I ran to open it.

* * *

'We could go down to the harbour? It wouldn't take long,' he said.

'Yeah, that would be nice.'

We began to walk, side by side, the closest, physically, we'd been in years. I was so aware of his body, one that I used to know every inch of. His arm brushed mine for a moment and the warmth, the intimacy of that movement was all too fleeting.

'So, Rosie...' he began.

I remembered how this felt, talking and walking. One of us listening, while the other unburdened or entertained or explained or whatever we used to do. He was a good listener, was Red. All those years away had not dimmed his ability to listen as though there was only one thing in the world he was interested in, and that was what you were saying. And with everyone else, you were just imparting information, bringing them up to speed on certain life events. With Red, it always had been, an unburdening, an opening up. And he was there, listening with his whole body.

We sat down on a bench, just inches from each other, overlooking the sea where the trawlers and the small fishing boats were tied up for the night. Him, as he always sat, right ankle resting on left knee.

'I should have known how bad it had got, Red,' I said. 'I mean, all the signs were there.'

'It's not your fault,' he said kindly. 'People need to ask for help. All too often, we just try and cope on our own, thinking that that is the best way. But it's really the worst.' He smiled at me. 'It's the least effective way of getting better.'

If you only knew, I thought. 'Yes, yes... but sometimes we can't. Sometimes we don't know what to do. And it's easy for me – for us – to sit here and say you should talk, when we're rational and not in the middle of some crisis. When you are... well, it's hard to do all the right things.'

He nodded. 'I know. But you shouldn't blame yourself.'

'She's always been a perfectionist, always wanted everything to be nice and good, always had the best marks in school, just so easy. But when Jake finished with her... that was a bit of a point of no return... a kind of loss of innocence that life can be really awful.'

'I suppose it builds resilience,' he said thoughtfully.

'The school have told me that she doesn't have to sit the exams this year but that we should have a total rethink about next year. Reapply to different colleges, make sure she's on a course that she really wants to do.'

'You're a really good mother, Tab,' he said. 'I always wondered what...' He trailed off.

'What?'

'Nothing...'

I let it go. I was loving talking to him, as though nothing bad had ever happened, that we were still Red and Tab, that there was no painful elision in our lives. And that in a moment, I could lean over and he'd put his arm about me and we'd sit there and watch the boats and the sea, together forever, as we'd always meant to be and there was no way I was going to spoil this moment by talking about the past.

'She's sort of lost her footing... you know?' I carried on.

'I'm still losing mine, all the time,' he said. 'Literally and metaphorically. We were rehearsing the songs from *Annie* and I ran down the steps from the stage and misjudged them.'

'Not in front of the girls?' Red always made everything better. I should have remembered that.

'Oh yes... how they laughed,' he said, grimacing. 'And I had to pretend that I wasn't embarrassed and that I hadn't bruised my arse.'

I laughed. 'And metaphorically?'

'Oh you know, in the way that we all do, us humans, doing the wrong thing, saying the wrong thing, wondering if the life you are living is the life you are meant to live, that kind of thing.' There was a look in his eye that I couldn't quite read.

'Why? What makes you think you're not?'

'I don't know,' he said, looking at me. 'Just a typical ongoing existential crisis. I just wonder sometimes. But you have Rosie. You have *her*.'

We looked at each other, unable to break eye contact, a huge swell of feeling washed over us, so much unspoken, so much unresolved emotion. The detonating of our relationship had been brutal for both of us.

'Red...'

He looked away. 'It's been tough, you know,' he said. 'I mean, I'm a grown-up now. And I've learned to live with it.'

'With what?' I said gently.

'The disappointment,' he said. 'It never went away, *the disappointment.*' It was clear he meant only one thing.

'Red... I'm so sorry.'

He shrugged it off. 'Part of me was frozen, numb,' he went on, looking out to sea, as though I wasn't there. 'When you didn't come to San Francisco, when you didn't answer any of my calls. When there was no explanation. You should have just told me. If you had met someone else, or if you'd just gone off me. Or whatever.' He said sadly, as though resigned. 'That would have hurt, sure, but it would have been better than nothing.'

'I know... I'm sorry.'

'What's done is done. I don't blame you. I'm not angry. I've never been angry. I was just so bloody sad about it. It was like it took root, this sadness. I mean I went out, I was sociable, good to be with, made jokes, the usual Red, like I am now but I was never able to shake the sadness' He shrugged again. 'It doesn't matter now. But I've always wanted to tell you how I felt. I mean, I know you were grieving for your grandmother... that must have been hard. But not to tell me. To just disappear like that.'

I sat there, not knowing what to say, certain though that any explanation may be redundant and I didn't want to try and excuse or to explain away what I'd done. I needed to feel his pain, his sadness.

'Tab,' he said, quietly. 'There is one thing, though. Why did you marry Michael? I'm sorry. That sounds rude, I know it does and it's none of my business. But I knew you once and, going by that, I just don't get it. I mean, you're the daughter of Nora. And you marry a *Progressive Conservative.*' He stopped. 'I know I shouldn't ask, but it never made sense. None of it did and then you marry someone like Michael Fogarty. When Dad wrote and told me... it made me think that I didn't know you. And that was really difficult. But maybe I didn't. And maybe you're happy now and you made all the right decisions and then that's good. But reassure me, tell me that you're happy.'

He was looking at me intently, puzzled, curious. When I didn't answer immediately, he broke away and stared out to sea.

'Tab, it's none of my business. But I've never come up with an answer. Not...' he gave an awkward smile, 'that I'm so amazing. But I thought *we* were amazing. And so...'

'I know. I thought we were too.' I let his words and his feelings soak into me, hearing every word, every nuance. His loneliness and pain. His disappointment. I'd felt it too but mine was a different story. I needed to hear his.

'And as soon as I saw you again, I involved myself in your life. Like I used to. It was just instinct, wanting to be there, taking care of you. The protest, me tackling you about it when I'd been in the school for less than twenty-four hours and you being so gracious by my intrusion. And then calling round to give that book to Rosie because I felt so worried about you. Both of you. It's crazy.'

'Red...'

'Being back here is a mistake. I know that now,' he went on. 'I thought we could be friends because there was so much I still liked, the way you try and make people laugh. The way you play with your hair. Your beautiful face...' He looked at me again. 'I thought I could do it. I would take anything, any crumbs you would give me. You were all I thought about for all those years and from that first moment I felt that same pull towards you, stronger than ever, and I didn't know what to do, to ignore it, to ignore you or try to find a way of being close to you. As a friend. I *wanted* to. I wanted to so much... And here I am now, still lonely, still on my own and I get nothing. Again.'

'Red, please...' I was trying to process everything. He still cared about me? He felt the same way? But I couldn't say how I felt because what would he say when I told him about my miscarriage. How angry would he be then?

'Forget it Tab,' he said. 'My fault. All of this. My messiah complex, think I can sort everyone else out and not look after me. You'd have thought I might have learned something in the intervening years. But it seems not.'

'Red...'

'I missed *you*, Tab. More than anything. More than tea. More than Irish chocolate.' He didn't smile. He meant it. 'More than watching the Irish soccer team play an international. More than *Dad*. I missed *you*. But I can't do it. I'm not coming back next term, I don't even know if I'll stay in Ireland.'

'Me?' The full force of my action hit me. His words didn't just permeate, they fused themselves to my cortex. He had loved *me*?

'And I still do,' he said. 'All the time. You know at Clodagh's party? I was standing there, chatting to you, acting as if we could do this, be friends. I was enjoying myself. I like being with you Tab. Always have done. But then it hit me. Again. That love, full force, full on love. I mean, I can't do this... I can't. I don't want to be friends with you. I want *everything*.'

'Red, I'm sorry...' I *feel the same*, I wanted to say. *I feel exactly the same. I love you too.* But how could I say it when I was married. I couldn't say it. My throat dried up and I sat there, slightly stunned.

He turned to me. '*How can I begin anything new with all of yesterday within me?* Leonard Cohen wrote that and it was all I could think about for years... I couldn't move on because I was still consumed by you.' Angry and furious now, he went on speaking, 'I didn't want to become bitter,' he said. 'It took all my strength, is taking all my strength, not to be angry and bitter. But I think I am losing that particular battle.' He stood up, hands pushed into his jeans pockets. 'I tried. I thought that I was over it enough. But... it's hard, you know?'

And he stood up and walked off, leaving me sitting on the bench as seagulls circled overhead. I didn't call him or run after him. I didn't know what to do, I didn't know where to begin, so I just watched him walk away.

BEFORE

'I'll see you in three months,' Red had said. We couldn't stop kissing each other at the departures gate. 'Will you be all right?'

'Yes, fine,' I said. 'I told you. I've got so many things to do and then I'll come and join you.'

'I don't know how I'm going to survive without you.'

'Me too.' Our foreheads were pressed together, our lips nearly touching. 'I love you Tab,' he said.

'And I love you,' I said. And I did love him. And I never stopped.

22

I deserved that. Being abandoned on a bench. It was the least he could do, the least I deserved and, after taking a moment to gather my emotions, I walked home. But as soon as I'd said hello to Rosie, there was a knock on the door belonging, I was sure, to Red. I was ready now to talk, really and truly about everything, to open up to him... to try to explain. I felt a sublime gratitude to whoever or whatever was owed it that he hadn't given up on me. But it was Clodagh, crying, her mascara and make-up was running down her face.

'I've been dumped. Sacked. Booted out. Removed from office. My contract was not renewed. It's been renewed every three years for the past fifteen and now...!'

'What do you mean? Who's done this?'

'Max. The tiny, miniature bastard. Personally. And. Professionally. Personally, I can deal with. Professionally, I am livid. Bridget is taking over the reading of the news.'

'What? But she's not a journalist...'

'No. But she's popular. People want to see her. More than they want the news. My services are not required.'

'What happened?'

'So, I'm standing in his office, ready for our standard contract renewal chat but Max tells me I am no longer needed or wanted on the six o'clock news and that Bridget is going to be reading it because, and I quote, *a monkey could read the bloody autocue and someone else can write the copy*, and then he says that this won't affect our personal relationship and, at that point, I laughed and said it bloody well did.'

'Clodagh, slow down and start at the beginning.'

She breathed in. 'First of all,' she said. 'Do you have any cake?'

'What kind? I have coffee and walnut, mini rolls and baklava. Which would you like?'

'All of them.'

This was serious, I thought, as I watched Clodagh systematically demolish the sugar smorgasbord.

'After the meeting with Max, I went straight to the vending machine which I had passed several times a day for the last decade but had never sullied with my hard-earned cash. I flung in the coins, pressed the code for a Mars Bar and waited for the drop. I ate it standing there. And I haven't stopped eating sugar since. God, this coffee and walnut is good. I'd forgotten how nice food can actually be. Why did I ever think it was a good idea to go out with Max? I think I was desperate.' Sugar had made her slightly hyper, I noticed. But maybe that was the whole point.

'After I'd eaten the Mars Bar, I was practically buzzing with the sugar. I felt almost luminous like ET or something, like I could take off. I barged right into his office and I could swear he was playing a game on his phone. Sudoku or something. Anyway, Max says...' She couldn't quite get the words out. 'He says that I'm not the right fit for the news anymore. They want a new look. *Freshen it up*, that was the phrase he used. It's a euphemism for using younger talent, that's all. He said that I had to be realistic, now I'm *forty*. He said that no one wants to see a *mature* woman on television except for notable exceptions. And I'm not a notable exception.'

'That's outrageous.'

'He said that there's always going to be someone younger and prettier and more talented so just get on with it. Which I think, in his weird little world, was him actually trying to be comforting, but I told him to fuck off.'

'Would you like a drink? There's still the Baileys in the cupboard. Cake in alcohol form.'

'Yes please,' she said. 'I may as well become diabetic as well as jobless, old and single.' She shrugged. I poured us both a drink, thinking I needed one too after the conversation with Red and worrying about Rosie. 'How could Max do this to you?'

'He's ruthless. Told me not to take it personally. It's business. He's not a very nice person, you know. And mad. Quite, quite mad.' She sipped her drink. 'Christ on a bike. What am I going to do?' she said, mascara-streaked, her hair all over the place, her silk blouse had signs of chocolate and cake over it. 'God knows what I'm qualified for? Reading an autocue. Wearing make-up. Pronouncing unpronounceable names.'

'Those are important skills.'

'Right.' She picked up her Baileys and drained the glass. 'I *used* to be a journalist,' she said. 'I used to know things. I *still* know things. And I know a damn sight more than Bridget fecking O'Flaherty. So what if I can't leap around the stage in ringlets.' She waved her glass at me.

'More?'

She nodded and tears began to trickle down her face. 'Bridget came to find me,' she said. 'I was getting my make-up done and she gave me a big hug. Said she was sorry and hoped there were no hard feelings. I said there wasn't and I wished her the very best; that I was delighted to be given the opportunity to try out something new, that I was thinking of going back-packing with a yak in the Siberian Steppes for a year, was renouncing all my worldly goods and if she wanted my biro she could have it.'

'Did you really?'

'No, I just said I was delighted for her and the best of luck.' She paused. 'I had my fingers crossed behind my back, of course. But Nicky says to lay low, go on holiday... maybe a Saga cruise or something suitable. Says she'll come up with something. But I can't think what.' She began to cry again while I topped up the Baileys. 'I've got a week to go. And then that's it. News-reading career over. And it'll be in the papers tomorrow. I've already been tipped off. Can't wait for that.'

And she swigged back the drink in one go, a Baileys slammer.

23

Clodagh had been right, she made all the front pages in the morning, leaked no doubt by Bridget, because there was a picture of Clodagh, looking slightly worse for wear, taken the night of her party, shoes in one hand, hanging onto Lucinda. Caption: 'Clodagh given the boot'. And next to it, in an evil kind of compare and contrast quiz, they had a picture of Bridget, the whites of her eyes and teeth glinting with youth and vitality and the caption 'TV's new girl'.

The paper was on the seat beside me as I headed into school. Christy, Arthur, Robbo, Nellie and Leaf all gave me a wave as I drove past. Nora flagged me down.

'How's Rosie?' she said.

'She's... okay. I mean, I think she will be okay.'

'Of course she will!' said Nora confidently. 'Us Thomases...'

'Michael says Us Fogartys in the same way' I told her. 'Us Fogartys never surrender!'

'He always did sound like a cut-price Winston Churchill,' she said, dismissing him. 'But us Thomases actually don't.'

'That sounds ominous,' I said. 'You at the battle of Little Bighorn. Me as General Custer.'

'You see, Tabitha,' she said. 'That's where you're wrong. You're one of us.

You thought you could be on the side of the bluecoats and soldiers. But really you're an Indian just like us. Us Thomases...'

Can we drop the Us Thomas thing, please?' I was growing weary of sides and stands and everyone jostling for their place in history.

She grinned at me. 'Now, is Rosie decided on not doing her exams?'

I nodded. 'I think so.'

'Good. Because I have just the thing for her. A trip. To West Cork. It's Finty. Nothing has got him so far. Cancer, pneumonia, malaria, falling off scaffolding, knocked over by a Hell's Angel on the road into Glengarriff, only one kidney. But it's his liver, now.'

From one of the pockets in her Barbour, she pulled out an envelope. 'Here it is...' she scrunched up her eyes, squinting at the words. *'I would like the chance to say **slán go fóill** before I slip off to the green fields of eternity,'* she read. *'We spent some good times here and I wouldn't like to go without saying goodbye to my **Nora**...'*

Would Rosie come? I wasn't sure spending hours in a car with just me and her grandmother was a good idea. It would tip the Dalai Lama over the edge. But I suddenly fancied a trip away, getting away from the protest, Red and it might do Rosie some good. A break from her bedroom.

'Yes,' I said. 'Let's go. Saturday morning. But only if Rosie comes.'

'I'll call her, said Nora. 'Tell her an old man's dying wish depends upon it. We will have a great time. It'll be a road trip, isn't that what they are called. Like Bonnie and Clyde.'

'No, please not like Bonnie and Clyde.'

'Who do I mean then?'

'Thelma and Louise?'

'Thelma and Louise, those are the ones.'

'You do know what happened to them at the end, don't you?'

'They lived happily ever after? And Rosie needs a bit of West Cork, I think. It will weave its healing magic on her, it never fails.'

* * *

I had hoped to hear from Mary, just to let me know if she was all right. She had left the office and the school well prepared for her absence but it wasn't as enjoyable without her calm, pleasant presence. At lunchtime, I walked passed the staff room and hovered for a moment, as I heard laughing coming from inside. Red and the other staff members were having their break. I hadn't heard from Red since he had left me on the bench, but I took a breath and walked in and sat down with them, as Fidelma Fahy scooted up to make room. Red nodded hello, no smile, just polite, perfunctory.

'Good to see you here Tabitha,' said Fidelma. 'Redmond is planning the staff night out for the end of term. He's suggested karaoke but I think he might be joking.'

'What about just a nice meal,' another voice said. 'When did a nice meal and a drink go out of fashion?'

'We need Mary to organise it,' said Angela Leahy. 'She always makes sure it's a nice place. Remember when we went to the talk in the National Gallery and then for a special dinner afterwards. That was nice. None of this karaoke nonsense.' She nudged Red and laughed. 'Actually Tabitha, any news from her? When is the family crisis going to be over?'

I shrugged, catching Red's eye briefly. 'I don't know. She said she was hoping to be back for the end of term so make sure she is on the list for karaoke or whatever.'

'What about a night at the Greyhound stadium?' suggested Red to the group. 'Come on. Don't tell me that doesn't excite you all?'

'Redmond,' said Angela. 'I hope you're joking about that. We want something a little more sedate. 'What about a nice pizza at the place in the village?'

'As long,' said Fidelma, 'there's a fair few bottles of vino to wash them down with.'

They all laughed.

Later, before I left for the day, I wrote a text.

Red, you asked if I was happy. I'm not. All that disappointment you had, I had too. But I married Michael because I knew I'd lost you and I wanted a child. I thought that marrying someone so different to you, would help me forget you. I was wrong. I'm sorry for everything but there are reasons. I missed you too. And still do. Tab.

For ages, my finger hovered over the send button, but then, rashly, I pressed it and there was no going back. I gathered up my things, worrying about Rosie and wondering about Red and hoping that wherever Mary was, she was safe.

* * *

'I've told granny, yes,' said Rosie.

Really? What did she say to convince you?'

'She said she was leaving me out of her will if I didn't go and that I would never get my hands on her teapot shaped like a cottage.'

I laughed. 'You've always loved it.'

'So, I said yes. I had to.'

'Good. Because I couldn't go if you don't. Are you okay with it?'

She nodded. 'Yeah, I'll be fine. You'll be there anyway.'

'That's what mothers are for. Secret bodyguards. Just hovering around ready to be needed.'

She smiled. 'I'm sorry that what happened, happened to you. If you know what I mean. I've been thinking about it.'

I did. 'Me too,' I said. 'But I had you. Maybe if I hadn't lost that baby, I wouldn't have had you exactly the way you are. So I wouldn't change a thing.'

'Did you have a name for the baby?'

'No, it was really early days.'

'Granny is convinced I need a bit of West Cork magic. Says I'll come back transformed, that it never fails to work.'

'That sounds ominous,' I said. 'Transformed into what exactly?'

'Who knows?' she said. 'But anything would be preferable to me right now. It's quite romantic though, isn't it? This man's dying wish. That's what Granny said it was, anyway.'

'You make it sound like Romeo and Juliet or something.'

'Granny said she wants to bring me to Rosaleen's house. There's a tree apparently.'

'She's full of it,' I said. 'Never gives up, does she?'

Rosie shook her head. 'She's an amazing woman.'

'Amazingly *awful*,' I said, making Rosie laugh again which was lovely to see. 'And you're happy to subject yourself to a car journey with me and granny?' She nodded. 'Listen, I have to warn you, there may be a few cross words, the odd tetchy comment, a side-of-the-road throttling.'

'Mum, I've been dealing with that since the day I was born. The only thing that would surprise me is if there was no side-of-the-road throttling. And it might be fun. A road trip... anything might happen.'

'Fun? Are you sure that's the right word?' It was pretty heartening to see Rosie's lighter side re-emerge.

'Okay, then, diverting. Tell me about more Granny and this Finty,' she said. 'I can't believe she used to have a *boyfriend*.'

'Finty! Oh God. She was mad about him.' I said. 'He was her long-term on-off-on again fling, fancy-man, lover, whatever. They were together I would say for at least ten years and when the peace camp disbanded, he moved to a tepee nearby. She used to go and see him there. But eventually it all kind of fizzled out. So she left the tepee and came home.'

'Was it really a tepee?'

'Yes, an *actual* tepee. I saw photos. It was like the *Last of the Mohicans*. Finty wrapped in some kind of rug, bare chested and toothless...'

'Toothless?' Rosie was loving this story and she was eating up her dinner, I was so relieved and pleased to see. Maybe the West Cork magic was already weaving its spell.

'Dental hygiene was low on his list of priorities,' I said. 'He was more interested in pursuing a... how shall I put this? Pursuing an unconventional life. Anyway, he no longer lives in a tepee because it collapsed one night, nearly suffocating him to death, so now he's in a caravan.'

'Why did they split up? I think Finty's charms ran out in the end. And Nora did say she'd had enough of his particular bodily fragrance. She said it wasn't so much eau de unwashed man as eau de decaying sheep. I think the passion had well and truly waned.'

She laughed again.

'He would arrive up to Dublin with only an old sweet wrapper in his pocket. Never any money or anything. But Rosaleen would always give him food. And Finty would hold court and tell stories and then always pretend to offer to do the washing up but at the last moment his back would go or he'd remember that he promised to find something in a book and by the time he found it, everything would have been done. Let's just say he's a man who was popular with a certain kind of woman. Hippies, bohemians, free spirits. I saw him in his element down on the Peace Camp that time. He was like a god. Well, one that smelled a little of decayed sheep.'

Rosie laughed. 'Not Dad's sort, then,' she said.

'No, he's the kind of man your father would have to wash his hands after meeting. Celia would be clutching her pearls and passing out. And now he wants to see your Granny for one last time.'

24

Just as Rosie and I were sitting in the car, ready to off on our West Cork odyssey, a text from Red.

Call me

But I couldn't because Rosie was with me. She had had her first counselling session the previous day and had walked to school and home again, no bother on her. 'The counsellor has given me advice about how to deal with a panic attack,' she had said, carrying her bag to the car parked on the road, as we packed up ready to head off to West Cork. 'It's all about staying calm. Not letting your thoughts spiral. Focus on one thing, one object.'

'That sounds like good advice,' I said. 'And you don't mind leaving Dublin for a night. You're not worried about six hours in a car with me and Granny?'

'As long as you talk nicely to each other,' she said and smiled. 'I'm glad we're going. It feels like the right thing to do. And it sounds ridiculous, but it helps that you're going to be with me. I'm meant to be grown up.'

'It doesn't sound ridiculous,' I said. 'It sounds normal.'

'Wait. What?' she said, in mock surprise. 'You called me *normal*?'

'Oh, out of all of us, you've always been the normal one.'

She grinned at me. 'Normal*ish*,' she said.

'That's all any of us can ask for. Today West Cork, tomorrow the world. All right?'

But just then, out of the corner of my eye, there was a flash of light. I looked behind me and I thought I heard footsteps, someone running away.

'Hey!' But he was gone. Was it another photographer, someone trying to capture Clodagh at her low ebb? Hopefully, looking old and haggard and past it.

'Come on Mum, let's go.'

And I forgot all about it.

* * *

Nora, in her usual jubilant mood, talked the whole way down, turning around in the front seat so Rosie didn't miss a second of the stories from the Mizen Head camp.

'It was such a great time,' she went on. 'We were all so free, it was beautiful, all of us young and idealistic. Now I'm just *old* and idealistic.'

'What was the aim of the peace camp?' Rosie said. 'I've always wondered.'

'They were just dropouts,' I answered for her. 'Desperate to sing songs out of tune and slip around in the mud all day.'

'The aim, Tabitha,' Nora said, 'and you should listen to this, Rosie, dear, the aim was to create a movement, an energy, an idea that life shouldn't be about living unconsciously, but that that there were other ways of living that didn't involve the nine to five or the daily commute or the office job. That we could take time out of our lives and create a sense of unity and strength. I'd like to think that we were like the old Celtic people. The pagans. Living in huts and making fires and singing. I taught myself the melodeon and I composed a few songs. I'll try and remember them now and teach them to you, Rosie...'

'Please don't. I beg of you. Please don't,' I implored.

Nora ignored me. 'It was possibly one of the most transformative things I have ever done. I wish we could have lived there permanently, instead of a month here and there.'

'Why didn't you, Granny?' said Rosie.

'Well, I had little Tabitha,' she said, 'and *she*, Rosie, in case you haven't noticed, is not cut out for tent life. That was very clear from an early age. She liked everything neat and tidy.'

'Don't blame me,' I said. 'Anyway, I don't think your free spirit was curtailed too much by me. You practically spent my entire teenage years down there.'

'I didn't,' she insisted. 'You must be imagining it. As far as I recall, it was a week here and week there.'

When we finally entered the county of Cork, after hours of driving and stops for loo breaks, tea breaks, leg stretching, Nora sat up, like a farmer's collie and rolled down the window and sniffed the air.

'Ah, it's good to be back,' she said.

'In Blarney?' We were driving past the castle at that moment.

'Cork. The ancestral home. Spent my happiest years of my life here in Cork.'

'Your *happiest* years?'

But Nora was too busy, lost in thought, looking out of the window, no doubt remembering magical days of mud and melodeons.

* * *

It was late afternoon when we pulled into Schull, the village where Rosaleen had grown up. We parked beside the church to stretch our legs and I managed to get enough of a signal to text Clodagh.

Survived journey so far. No one has been murdered. Yet. How are you? Stay away from the sugar. Back in the morning.

I didn't call Red because I didn't have time to say everything I wanted to. I'd told Rosie about the baby and it was about time I told Red and I was feeling nervous about it. What would he say? The memory of what he said to me on the bench kept replaying in my mind. He had *missed* me. He had missed *me*.

I did text him, though.

In West Cork. Will call tomorrow xxxx.

And then I deleted the xxxx's. And then put them back in and pressed send.

Rosie was more mature than me, I thought.

'That drive wasn't too bad,' I said to Rosie and Nora who were perched on an old wall. Rosie was texting as well and Nora was sniffing the air.

'Not too bad,' she agreed, 'and worth it just to breathe properly. Dublin is too smoky.' She wrinkled her nose.

'Mum,' I said, '*we* live by the sea, the air is amazing.'

'But it's sweeter down here,' she said. 'Honeysuckle and heather and bluebells. It's like a tonic.'

'Mum, I think you might be a little too romantic about West Cork. I mean, it's nice and everything...' But I looked around and I knew exactly what she meant. A robin hopped onto the ground beside us, looking at us, his head on one side. 'Who's ready to go and see Rosaleen's house?' I said.

'Me,' said Rosie, who jumped to her feet and turned to give Nora a hand. Rosie was looking well again. Smiling and happy. Like a weight had been lifted from her shoulders. She seemed to be just glad to be here with us, me and Nora.

'Who were you texting?' I said.

'Alice,' she said. 'We spoke properly last night...'

'That's good news.'

'We were both crying,' she said. 'She said she missed me and she thought I hated her or that she'd done something wrong.'

'So when are you going to see her and Meg?'

'Well, they're in the middle of the exams.' She pulled a face, as though she had been reminded of her awful reality. 'But I thought about going tomorrow, when we get home...'

'That's a plan. Right, next stop, the old house.'

We drove through the village and found the house and once we were out of the car, we stood at the gate, peering in.

'There's her cherry tree,' said Nora, pointing to a low and overgrown beautiful tree in full leaf. 'It could do with a prune.'

'I don't think we can go in,' said Rosie.

'I think Granny was thinking we would just march in and demand to be shown round the house,' I said. 'Not just have a look at the tree.'

'That is not a bad idea,' said Nora. 'House tour anyone?'

'Let's stick with the tree,' I said.

'Should we knock on the door and ask to see it?' said Rosie.

'I'm sure they would let us,' I said. 'What do you think, Mum?' I looked around. 'Mum?'

Nora had darted into the garden and was already pulling herself up onto a lower branch of the tree, her legs disappearing into the foliage and showing remarkable agility. But then she never failed to surprise me.

'Mum!' I hissed. 'Come down! You can't just climb someone's tree... it's trespassing!' Rosie and I looked at each other for a moment and then ran over to her, ducking under the foliage. There she was, sitting on a long flat branch, a beatific smile on her face.

'What took you so long?' she said. 'Rosie, give me your hand.'

But Rosie was already pulling herself up, climbing the lower branch and then sliding herself onto the long and strong branch. She sat herself on the other side of Nora. 'Mum...' she looked down at me. 'Coming?'

'Oh, all right.' I managed to get myself up, and sat down beside Nora. 'We're going to get shot at,' I said. 'Or whatever they do in the countryside. Set the dogs on us.'

'We're in West Cork now,' said Nora. 'They don't do that kind of thing. We've come home.' She swung her legs. 'Well, here we are, Rosaleen's three little birds. She'd be very happy to see us in her tree. She always said it had healing properties,' she mused. 'Do you feel it, Rosie? When I came down here a couple of months after your great-grandmother died, it helped me. It really did. I crawled into it, like we are now, and I just sat here for ages and ages. And when I eventually emerged, I felt utterly and totally at peace.' Nora, in the middle of us, took my hand as well and I knew she was remembering that time we spent together, after Rosaleen died and after my miscarriage. 'You should have come with me,' she said.

'Maybe I should have,' I said, after a pause. I felt her hand squeeze mine. Rosaleen's three little birds, in her cherry tree.

'People pay money to come and feel like this,' went on Nora. 'But there is nothing in the world as healing than sitting on a branch feeling the

power of a tree. We must do all we can to save trees. Not *cut* them down.'
There was no escaping the Battle of the Copse, even here, all the way in
West Cork.

'Mum! They are not going to be cut down! I promise you!'

'Right.' She patted my hand, still speaking in her dreamy voice. 'Just
ensure their protection, all right?' It was as though she was trying to hypno-
tise me into agreeing. 'Just enshrine the rights of the trees into school
policy, that's all.'

'It does sound reasonable,' said Rosie. 'Mum?'

'Can we talk about something else?' I said.

'Did you know, Rosie,' said Nora, satisfied that she had made her point,
'that your great-grandmother was going to be an actress? That's why she
left this beautiful part of the world, where our roots lie deep below the
surface, from where the Thomas tribe hails.'

'But she stopped acting, didn't she?' I added, 'when she went to work as
a front of house manager.'

'Yes, but she was brilliant... she could act. Everyone said so...'

'So what happened? Why did she stop?' I had always thought it was
because she lost interest, somehow, her passion waned and she had Nora to
look after. 'Rosaleen never told me.'

'She had stage fright,' explained Nora. 'It was her great tragedy. She
never recovered. Her life's dream taken away from her. But there was no
way she could get back on that stage. I was very young when it happened,
only one or two, I forget now, but she told me. It always makes me sad when
I think of it, someone not achieving their dream.' Nora paused dramatically,
and looked at us both in turn, enjoying immensely telling us the story of
her mother, drawing it out.

'Go on, Granny,' urged Rosie.

'Well, she was standing in the wings of the Abbey Theatre, about to
perform when she realised she couldn't put one foot in front of the other.
She couldn't move. She said that her throat was dry and it was as though
every word, every thought, every line, had been removed from her brain.
She couldn't do it. And then, in her panic, as she saw her fellow actors on
stage, it got worse and she didn't know what to do. She never set foot on a
stage again.'

'That's what happened to me,' said Rosie. 'That's kind of how I felt.'

Nora took her hand. 'I know,' she said. 'That's why I'm telling you.' She smiled at her. 'It happens to the best of us. Even Rosaleen. It might explain why she was so... so indulgent of me,' said Nora, now looking at me. 'Why she let me follow my dreams, never put limits on me, wanted me to be happy. Never any expectations.'

I nodded, sad to think of Rosaleen now, her dreams and career cut short. 'She was also just a really lovely person,' I said. 'The best, really, wasn't she?'

'The very best.' Nora smiled at me. 'Anyway,' she said, 'I think we need a speech. For Rosaleen. A poem... Rosie?'

'Okay...' Rosie thought of something. 'There's that Patrick Kavanagh poem. We learned it in school. It always made me think of you two...' she smiled shyly at us, 'but this time it's for Rosaleen. Now I can't remember all of it but there's a part that goes... *And I think of you walking along a headland of green oats in June, so full of repose, so rich with life... O you are not lying in the wet clay, for it is a harvest evening now and we are piling up the ricks against the moonlight and you smile up at us — eternally.*'

We sat there for a moment, memories hanging above our heads like leaves, ready to be picked and cherished.

'To Rosaleen,' said Nora eventually. 'So full of repose, so rich with life.'

'To Rosaleen...' we echoed.

From the house, there was a sound, a voice.

'Jesus Christ!' The spell had been broken. 'I think it's time to go!'

And then, one by one, we dropped out of the tree, hysterical with terror and adrenaline. Laughing and shrieking, we ran to the car, scrambling in, screeching out into the main road and sped off.

As she had run from the tree, Nora had managed to pull a small branch with her.

'I'll get a cutting of that,' she said, wrapping the stem in a tissue which she made damp with water from the bottle she had with her. 'And we'll all have Rosaleen's cherry blossom tree in our gardens.'

* * *

Finally, after asking countless people for directions we eventually found Finty's field. There, on the edge of a cliff, the roar of the Atlantic Ocean on one side, tufted grasses, dandelions and rabbit holes the other, was a small, battered caravan. It was late afternoon as we parked the car.

'Ah, yes,' said Nora, stepping out of the car. 'I remember this.' She squinted a bit as she looked around, her back stiff from the journey. Rosie stretched her arms above her head. She was looking better, more like herself, every second. 'Well, that journey was at least two hours more than I had estimated it would have taken.'

'It's not my fault that he lives in the arse end of nowhere,' I said.

'But what a beautiful arse end,' said Nora. 'What do you think, Rosie?' She gathered Rosie to her, giving her a hug. 'Could you live somewhere like this?'

'Perhaps,' said Rosie. 'But it all depends on who I was sharing this arse end with.'

Nora laughed. 'Exactly.' She let out a low whistle. 'Well, are you ready to meet him?' And then, after a moment, we heard the same low note back.

'That's him,' she grinned, waving to a figure who had emerged from being in the caravan. Finty. Wizened and ancient, chest bare and brown as a berry, waving both arms above his head. 'That's him all right,' she said. 'The foxy little fella.' She began climbing over the gate into the field.

'Mum, be careful!'

But she managed it, swinging her leg over as Rosie and I, shrugging at each other, followed her lead.

'Hello there!' Finty's voice carried on the Atlantic air. 'Just in time for tea!'

He hadn't changed in all these years, except maybe got even skinnier, but his eyes were the same, the whites more yellow, matching his tobacco-stained teeth. He didn't look well, though. There was a jaundiced look to him under his sun-bathed skin.

'How are you, old girl?' He hugged Nora tightly.

'About as well as you, you old bugger.'

I was a lucky recipient of another bear squeeze. 'Well, if it isn't young Tabitha,' he said. 'Looking more like your beautiful mother every day. And who is this lovely young lady?'

'Rosie,' said Nora, proudly. 'My granddaughter.'

'Beauty runs in the family,' he said, bowing so low to Rosie there was a moment when we wondered if he was going to be able to get up again. But he did, with an audible creak in his back. 'Tea's on,' he said, recovering himself. 'Come in and sit yourselves down.'

'Finty, we'll head off in a little while,' I said. 'Let you and Nora catch up.'

'If you're sure,' he said. 'Where're ye staying tonight?'

'B&B in Schull,' I said. 'We can go there and leave our bags and get something to eat.'

'Have a cup here first though, won't you?' He brought us round to the front of the caravan where there was a tarpaulin pinned to the edge of the roof propped up by a long stick, creating a canopy. And beyond us was the Atlantic Ocean in all its glory, the Fastnet Lighthouse on the horizon. Seabirds circled above us, down below there was a small cove for landing boats, the water glittered and sparkled in the bright white of the sun. For a moment, we stood there mesmerised.

'My God,' I said. 'What a view.'

'I'd forgotten,' said Nora, shaking her head. 'I'd actually forgotten.'

'Every day, I'm reminded of a greater power than myself,' said Finty, enjoying our delight as he bustled around filling the kettle from a large water canister. 'Here I am in this tiny caravan and around me is nature in all its power and majesty. It keeps a man humble, it really does. God knew what he was doing, he really did.' He set the kettle to boil, wiping some tin mugs out using an old rag, while Rosie and I sat ourselves down on a ramshackle bench which was a long plank on two blocks of wood.

'You gave up on the tepee, then Finty?' I said.

'It fell apart,' he said, turning to me. 'It was just a collection of patches in the end and it wasn't waterproof. And then it collapsed. While I was sleeping. I could have suffocated to death. Which might have been a better way to go than liver failure.' He sounded his usual cheery self. 'But I've been in this van now for the last ten years or so. Leaks in the winter but, at this time of the year, Buckingham Palace has nothing on it. You sit there, Nora.' He found a filthy tea towel and wiped a camping stool, but Nora was still soaking up the view and taking over exaggerated breaths of air.

'Running out of oxygen, Mum?' I said.

She gave me a look. 'Not oxygen,' she said. 'Ozone. And my eyes feel better here. As though I could see forever. Must be the sea air.'

'Mum, we have sea air at home. We live on the coast.'

'Yes, but that's only the Irish Sea,' she insisted, disloyally. 'This is the Atlantic Ocean. It does something to a person does being by the Atlantic.'

'It does that.' Finty was handing out mugs.

'Just breathing it in brings me back to the Peace Camp. Same air you see. It could be twenty years ago. It was only a couple of miles away, wasn't it?'

'Three fields that way.'

'Good times, weren't they?'

He grinned at her. 'I've got some great memories.' He tapped his head. 'They're all up here.'

'How's the health, Finty?' I said.

'Not good, Tabitha. I used to go all over the world, I did. India. Australia. I sailed the North-West passage. Been everywhere. But a few things have gone now. Important things. Heart not good. Lungs on the poor side. Liver is packing up. Got a good doctor up in Cork, though. He's about fifteen years old. But a brain like he's lived a very long time.'

'We're all getting old, Finty.' Nora had moved her stool closer to him.

'Not you, Nora. You're just the same. Haven't aged a bit.'

'I'm getting creaky and my eyes are going.'

'No, you've got years left. I've got a few years on you. Still swimming?'

'Every day. You?'

'You always were hardier than me,' he grinned. 'I might go for a dip in the summer. When it's calm, but for some reason I've lost a bit of the fool-hardiness I used to have. And now I'm a bit spooked. Deep water is one thing I can't do anymore.' He shrugged. 'It's funny the things that leave you, isn't it, when you're getting on?'

'I still swim but I can't do people,' said Nora, which was news to me. 'I have to go shopping in the morning. I can't face buses and cinemas and supermarkets. Everything has to be small-scale.'

He nodded, as though understanding entirely. 'Goleen is as far as I go these days. Except for when I have to be in the big smoke for my treatment. There's a little minibus that collects all of the ailing West Corkonians and brings us up. There's a few cancers on the bus, two strokes and there's me with my liver failure. We're quite the school trip. But before we go, I have to take a deep breath of this air here. Enough to keep me going all the way up, the day in the hospital and then the journey home.'

Rosie and I left them to it, they were reminiscing about the various exploits they'd experienced together, mainly, as far as we could tell, run-ins with police. They barely looked up from their riveting – to them at least - conversation about protesting in the age of social media and Rosie and I went off to the village of Schull to find our B&B.

* * *

Starving, we first found a café on the hill in the town overlooking the harbour below, which had three little tables outside.

'Still no signal, Mum,' said Rosie. She'd been checking her phone every ten minutes, waving it around.

We popped our heads inside the door of the cafe. 'Are you open?'

'You're in luck,' said a woman behind the counter. 'We're open until 7 p.m. What are you looking for?'

'A sandwich?'

'What about crab?' she said. 'Caught this morning. Sit yourselves down, now, and I'll bring everything out.'

In the evening sun, we sat beside each other. 'How're you doing?' I asked.

'Fine,' said Rosie. She was checking her phone for signal.

'I know I keep asking,' I said. 'About how you're feeling.'

'It's okay,' she said, putting her phone down on the table beside her. 'But I'm not doing badly. Now I know what hanging in there means. It means just being able to be somewhere, the best you can, for as long as you can.'

'You're doing brilliantly,' I said. 'Thank you. These look delicious.' The sandwiches had arrived.

'There you are. Let me know if you need anything.'

'We will.'

'Down from Dublin are ye?'

'That's right,' we nodded.

'How were the roads?'

'Grand... clear enough. It's just nice to be back in West Cork.'

'Spent much time here have ye?'

'A little bit,' I said. 'My grandmother was from here.'

'Was she now? What was her name?'

'Rosaleen. Rosaleen Thomas.'

The woman gasped. 'Well, well, well. I used to know. Rosie Thomas. She was a friend of my older sister. Went to school together. We lived outside of the town and had to take the bus in every day.'

'Really? What was she like?'

'I've never seen someone so pretty in my entire life. She had her hair just so, even back then. Used to wrap it in papers overnight. She went to Dublin, as far as I knew, but none of us heard anything else from her, not after her parents passed on. She always said she wanted to act, be in films, and whenever I went to the cinema in Bantry I'd stay to the end of the credits, just wondering if I'd see her name.'

'She didn't make it to Hollywood.'

'Now, that's a shame. She should have done. Beautiful she was. With the personality to match. Actually...' She was studying Rosie. 'You've got the look of her. Same shaped face, eyes. If you hadn't told me who you were I would have sworn it was Rosaleen Thomas, back to see us. Ah!' She smiled at the memory. 'Too big for West Cork, she was. Now, we've all sorts down here. Actors, producers. We've more festivals and arty goings-on than you can shake a stick at. But then, the only thing we had going on was either fish or farming. And Rosaleen didn't want either. She was that talented, she was. She used to make up dances when we were waiting for the bus. And act out scenes. Shakespeare was her favourite.'

'She used to do that for me, too.'

'How is she? Is she still with us?'

'She died. A long time ago. She was only sixty-two.' Ten years younger than Nora I thought. 'Cancer. If it was today, they probably would have been able to help her.' I refused to let the words get stuck in my throat like they always did.

'Well, weren't you lucky to have her all the same? Now, there's the paper, just in. Evening edition, if you would like to have a look. More scandal. The usual gossip.'

'Do you have WI-FI here?' said Rosie.

'We're meant to,' said the woman. 'They say we have it. But it's never materialised. If indeed such a thing can materialise. Patchy at best.'

'No, it's fine,' said Rosie, resigned to life in the sticks and waving her phone around.

25

The next morning, as we sat down to a breakfast of porridge and tea in our B&B, I glanced at the Sunday papers.

Michael was on the front page. The headline was;

'F**K Me Foggy. Politician in love romp'.

I snatched the paper quickly and scanned the words. '*Michael Fogarty admits to affair with his secretary.*' And there, in the bottom of the front paper, was a picture of me, outside our house, taken yesterday as we'd got in the car to head down to West Cork. I looked about fifty, hair all over the place. On the other side of the paper was a picture of Lucy looking splendid, as she always did, smiley and happy.

'What's wrong, Mum?'

'Nothing.' I quickly panicked and tried to hide the paper.

'Mum, you look like you've seen a ghost.'

While we'd been in West Cork, miles and miles from home, the whole nation had been reading about Lucy and Foggy. Lucy and Foggy. Jesus Christ. I was not surprised but now here it was, in black and white and capital letters. And asterisks.

'Rosie, I've just read something... now this is what happens when you have a parent in public office...' I began but she snatched the paper from me. I thought of the piles of papers in all the shops and newsagents of the land, thousands of papers with that headline reaching as far as the eye could see.

Rosie stared at the page, her brain trying to make sense of the headline and the words. 'Dad?' she said and then, turning to me, eyes wide. 'Lucy?'

'I don't think it's Dad they are talking about,' I said quickly, helplessly, 'it must be someone else.'

'Mum, this is Dad. Michael Fogarty. He's Foggy. That's him. And he's having an affair. With Lucy!'

'It's all a mistake, you know how newspapers make things up. Fake news!' My ridiculous and unconvincing smile was stuck to my face and I wondered would I always have to look like this. But Rosie was now reading the paper, scanning it for details.

Inside, on the double-page spread in the paper was another photo of me, this one taken outside the school, looking wild-eyed and crazed on the day the protest began. The caption was *'Wife Tobitha is again at the centre of another unusual domestic drama.'* All sane people would understand entirely why Michael would have chosen the serene and lovely Lucy the Marvel. Lucy the *Mistress*.

'*Tobitha!*' Rosie almost laughed.

'Shhhh!' I hissed. We were already drawing attention to ourselves with our increasing hysteria. 'Let's go back to our room.'

Gathering up the papers, we both ran up the stairs to our room and laid the papers on the bed.

'*Another* unusual domestic drama. Oh my God.' We looked at each other in shock and awe, my right hand gripping Rosie's elbow while we devoured the paper. Poor Rosie, this was all she needed. So much for a magical, healing trip to West Cork. *How could Michael do this to you?* I thought, looking at Rosie. For God's sake. Hadn't she enough going on without her father being plastered over all the tabloids. I didn't care about me, I realised. Michael and Lucy could do what they wanted and, in some weird way, I was glad for them, but Rosie was still a child. How could he do this to her?

'Mum... I can't... I can...'

'Okay, just breathe,' I commanded. 'Just focus on breathing. All this is a shock. That's it, just breathe. Don't worry. It's all going to be fine.'

Her hands were clenched, her eyes closed.

'Come on,' I urged, 'come on, it's okay...'

Finally, she opened her eyes. 'I'm all right, I'm all right...'

'Breathe into it, isn't that what they said. Don't try and run from it.'

Eventually she lifted her head. 'Mum, this is actually worse than me ruining my entire future by not doing the Leaving Cert. It's a sex scandal. The headline is F asterisk-asterisk K Me Foggy. We are now Fuck Me Foggy's family, we are the Fuck Me Foggy family...'

'The Fuck Me Foggy family... oh please not the Fuck Me Foggy family.' And maybe there was something in the West Cork air, but we began to laugh, the horror and the hysterics causing us to lose control of ourselves, for the second time that day. Doubled over and becoming helpless every time the other one repeated the immortal phrase 'the Fuck Me Foggy Family'.

'Oh Rosie...' I had managed to draw breaths. 'I'm so sorry...'

'They called you *Tobitha*.' She pointed again to the picture of me and it started the two of us off again. 'Tobitha!'

Eventually, exhausted from laughing, we began to sober up, reality setting in, we now had to face our new notoriety as the Fuck Me Foggy Family.

'Miss Byrne would say that it's about how you handle situations,' said Rosie, looking carefully at the photographs, reading bits of the paper out. 'You can panic and become hysterical or...'

'Which we just did...' I said. 'You know we can never show our faces here in Schull again... We have now successfully made ourselves persona non-grata in Rosaleen's home county...'

'We should channel our inner Rosaleens. What would she do?'

'Get on with it, I suppose. That's what she did. In all my years knowing her, she never complained, never moaned. She just seemed happy, inside and out, you know? She would have handled it with aplomb.'

'I like that word.'

'I've never used it before. But it's exactly the right word for her. Aplomb.'

'Well, then let's handle this with aplomb. Whatever it means exactly.'

'She was just a handler of things, always unfazed. A glider through life's crises. We're from a long line of great women, you and I,' I said. 'Let's live up to our legacy.'

'Mum, I've often thought that I am more a Thomas than a Fogarty,' she said. 'Don't tell Dad because he's always said I'm a Fogarty, but I've always felt like a Thomas, like you and Grandma... and Rosaleen.'

'Well, perhaps you're the best of both of us,' I said. 'You're a chip off both blocks.' She linked her arm through mine and leaned into me. 'But maybe you are just yourself, the wonderful Rosie.'

She was quiet for a moment. 'It makes a kind of sense, though,' she said, thoughtfully, 'doesn't it?'

'What does?'

'Dad and Lucy...'

I nodded in agreement. 'I hate to say this, but they are perfect for each other. Much better than him and me... I hope that's not too upsetting for you.'

'Not really... well, it's weird, but I'm starting to realise that in my life what's weird is normal and what's normal is weird.'

'But that's what normal is. It's weird. There's no such thing as normal. We tie ourselves in knots trying to be normal when we should just accept the weird.'

'You're weird,' she said.

'I know. Have been all my life.'

'Mum, why did you marry Dad?' she said. 'Did it have anything to do with losing the baby?'

'I liked him. I still do. He's a nice person, a good person. And I admired him being in politics, even if I didn't always share his point of view, because he was actually trying to effect change, to do something and I liked that... and...'

'And what?'

'He seemed so normal...' I laughed at how like Rosie I sounded. I too used to want an idea of normal.

'But now he's weird, like the rest of us.'

'Something like that,' I said. 'But it was a year after I'd had the miscarriage and I thought, that he was going to be good for me. And he was. Because then I had my second chance. I had you.'

She nodded.

'I wish Rosaleen had been around when Jake... when Jake finished with me,' she said, tears in her eyes now. 'She might have helped me deal with it, you know? With her aplomb. In a way, and I don't want to blame him, but that was what started it all off. I was kind of starting to panic at the end of last year in school, knowing that I was falling behind and all I could see was the whole of the following year looming ahead... but then when he told me he didn't want to see me anymore, I kind of took it as a reason, an excuse, really, not to handle things, not to carry on, to sink into myself. Not to be...' She searched for the word. My lovely girl. I had her hand in mine, gripping it, following her words. 'Not to be aplomby.' Tears fell down her face.

'I'm sure that even Rosaleen wasn't like that all the time. None of us are perfect, but let's not beat ourselves up, okay? Just promise me you won't give yourself a hard time, all right? Just be nice to yourself, say nice things to yourself. Please?'

She nodded. 'That's what Miss Byrne says.'

'So you'll do it? Promise me?'

'Promise.'

'Rosie, everything's going to be okay, okay?' I said, taking both her hands. 'And I'm absolutely fine. We'll all sort this out and I promise you I am not hurt or unhappy. Lucy is a good person and they are a good team. Better than your father and me.'

'You're not angry at Dad. And at Lucy?'

I shook my head. 'No... not at all. Pleased, really. For him. And Lucy. I'm glad for them.'

'Mum, that's weird.'

'Well, I'm weird.' I smiled at her. 'For the first time in my life I am embracing my inner weirdness. You see, the thing is I don't mind. You are the one I am worried about here. But I think Dad might have found his soulmate in Lucy and that's a good thing...'

'I can't imagine Dad having a soulmate,' she said. 'He's not really the soulmatey type of person.'

'Your parents still can have the capacity to surprise you,' I laughed. 'I know my mother is still surprising me.'

'Mum, I was thinking. About Red.'

'Red?' Why was she bringing *him* into all this?

'What did he say when it all happened? Was he upset?'

'I didn't tell him.'

'What?'

I should have done, but I couldn't. It meant... we didn't see each other for all that time.'

'And he still doesn't know?' Her eyes were wide open. She was learning far too much about the lives of grown-ups today.

'No. I'm going to tell him. I think he deserves to know. He didn't understand why I just stopped contact...'

'And why did you?'

'I didn't know what to say... I suppose... I suppose I was depressed.'

She was silent for a moment and then she said, 'I get it. That makes sense.' She reached for my hand, *her* comforting me.

Both our phones rang.

'We've got a signal!' shouted Rosie, finally delighted about something. 'The WIFI has materialised!'

It was Michael on her phone.

* * *

Rosie nodded and cried throughout the whole conversation. I felt furious with Michael for upsetting Rosie like this. If you were going to have an affair, surely there were better ways of announcing it to the world than in the front pages of newspapers. Making a speech at Celia's party would have been preferable.

I checked *my* phone for messages. I had fifteen missed calls and texts messages. Clodagh had texted repeatedly.

The first one had been sent in response to mine from earlier.

Am alone in house with just a bar of Milka and a bottle of Baileys. All well.

But then her texts were charged with increasing panic as the news of the scandal spread.

Just seen papers. Call me.

Michael the Ken doll of politics? Surely some mistake!!!!!!

And:

Are you all right? Am now worried. Where are you? Get thee to a fecking signal.

And, there was a text from Red.

Let me know if you are all right.

For a moment, here in West Cork, I'd been beguiled by its magic. The cherry tree, the Sheep's Head, Finty's ramshackle caravan... but real life and all its dramas was waiting for both of us back in Dublin. We had to return and deal with it all. I could see why people ran off to West Cork, there was a sense that reality was suspended. But ours had to be faced. We'd go back to Dublin tonight and work out what to do.

Eventually, Rosie waved the phone at me. 'Dad wants to talk to you,' she said, wiping her eyes on her sleeve.

'I am so sorry.' He sounded like he'd been crying. 'I am so, so sorry. I don't know what to say and I wish I could deny everything, but I can't...' He stopped suddenly. 'Those feckers. This is what it was like for Diana, hunted by the paparazzi...'

'Michael,' I cut into to his ridiculousness. 'It's not the end of the world. We'll just make sure that Rosie is all right. The rest we can sort out.' I didn't feel furious any longer, just irritated and exasperated. My marriage had ended not by a dignified, mutual parting. A grown-up shaking of the hand, but in a tabloid exposé. It was a mess.

But what would happen and where would Michael and Lucy live? Would we be like one of those happy blended families, all sitting around the Christmas table, laughing away, Celia gazing at us all fondly, all *mater familias*? Oh God, Celia. What would Celia say?

'I just want to say how terrible I feel about this. I am so sorry. I have been such a coward and done it all so badly. I am sorry...' He began to cry.

'It's all right.'

'It's such a terrible thing I've done, I mean, you must be so hurt and Rosie...' He cried even more now at the thought of what he had done to his daughter. 'I've been so awful...'

'It's fine, Michael. I'm pleased for you.' *I'm free*, I was thinking. I was now free to do anything I wanted. Released from marriage to Michael. I should be thanking him. And Lucy.

'But Tabitha, I want to say, I never meant to hurt you. I really didn't.'

'I know, Michael, and you haven't hurt me.'

'It's such a betrayal, such an immoral thing to do...' He almost sounded disappointed as though his sex scandal wasn't quite as explosive as some other politician's. If you were going to be embroiled within one, you may as well make it a good one, as his mentor Bill Clinton might or might not advise.

'Michael, it's Rosie who is important here. It doesn't matter what you get up to...'

'But my bill for standards in public life!' he wailed. 'It's going to be voted next week. Europe is relying on me.'

'Well, you should have thought about that before you started shagging Lucy.'

'There!' He sounded triumphant. 'You *are* angry and hurt!'

'No, I'm not,' I insisted. 'Just irritated that all you care about it the SIPL thing. You're at the centre of a sex scandal. ... What about Rosie? Have you given her one moment's thought?'

'Yes, yes, yes, of course,' he said, dismissing me. 'But you know the worst thing is ...'

'What? Pestilence, plague, a swarm of locusts?'

'Well, I mean, *one* of the worst things' he said. 'I mean, up there with the worst things...'

'Go on, what is it?'

'There's a misprint in the order of business for the parliament. It says that the bill on Monday, the one that the whole of the parliament will be voting on, well, it says it's for... it's for standards of pubic lice.'

I began to laugh.

'It's not funny,' he said sulkily.

'Are you coming home? We're going to get on the road now.'

'Yes, we're taking the next flight home. I mean, *I* am taking the first flight home.'

There was something about Michael I was going to miss, but I twisted off my wedding ring and massaged the deep indentation, eighteen years I'd worn that ring but I slipped it into my purse. Even my finger looked relieved.

* * *

We had a long drive and it was already gone 11 a.m. and when we arrived at the caravan, Nora and Finty were still sitting outside, Nora wedged into the picnic chair, her legs propped up on another, bare toes waggling in the summer morning breeze. She looked exceedingly comfortable.

'Flapjack, Tabitha?' Finty gave Nora a wink. 'I made them meself,' he said, causing Nora to diffuse into giggles. And once she started, she didn't seem able to stop and then she developed hiccups.

'Mum,' I said. 'We've got to go. We've had some news and we just want to get back...'

'Whatever for?' she said, wiping her eyes and stifling her hiccups. 'What's the hurry?'

Rosie and I looked desperately at each other.

'Granny,' said Rosie bravely. 'It's Dad. He's in all the papers. The front page...'

'He's got himself caught up in something,' I stepped in. 'A scandal. And we need to be back. He's flying home and we thought we'd like to be there as soon as possible.'

'A scandal?' Nora said, her eyes like saucers. 'The only scandal he'd get into is if he couldn't find his vest of a morning.'

Now, it was Finty's turn to begin crying with laughter, he was on his knees, slapping the ground and wheezing. Rosie and I looked at each other, puzzled. What was going on? Had they taken leave of their senses?

'I'm sorry, Mum, but we've got to go,' I said, feeling like the only grown-up in the field. 'Michael's flying back and we need to be at home. I'll explain everything in the car.'

Nora carefully lifted her legs, one by one, off the chair and on to the ground. 'Chill Tab,' she said, exploding into laughter. 'Chill Tab!' she said again, giggling and spluttering.

Finty was now lying prone, convulsed by laughter, stuffing his filthy scarf into his mouth to stop the giggling.

'Mum...' I was cross now. 'Michael's had an affair. With Lucy. He loves Lucy.'

And this made her laugh even more. She fell onto the ground and lay supine, slapping the earth, tears pouring out of her eyes, crying with laughter. Finty, meanwhile, had managed to stagger to his knees, holding his stomach, as though his sides might split, tears of laughter pouring from his face. He rolled over onto his back, legs kicking in the air. For a dying man, he was showing remarkable signs of life. 'I love Lucy!' he shouted.

It dawned on me that there was something in the flapjacks that you might not give to children. Or sensible adults.

'Mum...'

Nora was now lying spread-eagled, gazing at the sky above her.

'So beautiful,' she said dreamily. 'So beautiful.'

'Come on,' I said, holding out my hand to pull her up. 'We're going. You coming?' She held my and Rosie's hand and we hauled her to her feet.

'Goodbye,' she said to Finty. 'Goodbye, bold Fintan.'

'Goodbye, Nora, sweet, beautiful Nora.'

'Thanks for the fun times.'

'Oh they were!' He smiled at her. 'And we'll have more of them.'

'That we will.'

'I'll see you in the big yonder. I'll see you in the Elysium Fields. And we'll hold hands and sing songs.'

'It'll be just like the Peace Camp,' said Nora, holding her face close to his. 'Just like the glory days.' She stood up and blew him a kiss.

'Just like them. But better. This time *I'll* bring the flapjacks.'

* * *

On the way home, Nora snoozed in the back of the car, me and Rosie in the front, talking quietly, as the black of the Irish countryside enveloped us. Eventually, from the back of the car, there was a voice. 'I am very lucky to have you two.'

'Hi Granny,' said Rosie. 'We're nearly home. And *we're* very lucky to have you.'

'You've slept the whole way,' I said drily.

'And now I'm awake,' she said. 'And ready for chats. I've been thinking about Rosaleen and how much she would have loved to have met you, Rosie.'

'She would,' I agreed.

'She was a very loving woman,' said Nora. 'One of those people who were happy out.'

'Like you,' I said.

'Me?'

'You're always happy,' I said. 'Even when there is no reason to be.'

'But isn't that a good thing?' said Rosie. 'You're making it sound like it isn't.'

'Well,' I said. 'It is and it isn't. You don't have to be happy about everything.'

'I'm not,' said Nora. 'There's lots of things I'm not happy about. Like developers and nuns and the Catholic Church and female genital mutilation and people who don't recycle and the fact that coffee is now a very complicated business altogether and all sorts. And selling school land. That kind of thing...'

I groaned.

'But,' she went on, 'caring about those things, waking up in the middle of the night worrying about those things, does not stop me being deep-down happy.' She paused for a moment. 'Promise me something, Rosie...'

'What is it, Granny?'

'That you'll follow your dreams, your calling, that you won't be bound up by convention or being *normal*, whatever that is. Just be you. That you will carry on caring about things, that you will be passionate and committed and stand up for what's right.'

Rosie nodded dutifully. 'I will. I promise.'

'Don't be boring,' went on Nora. 'Whatever you do. Don't be boring.'

'Am I boring,' I said, 'because I didn't hang out in fields or want a tattoo like the child you really wanted?'

'No, you're not boring, Tabitha,' she said. 'You're brave like Rosaleen, strong. Interesting. Good-natured. Smart. You have her look. In your eyes. And you have it too, Rosie.'

We were all silent for a moment. I was thinking of Rosaleen and Nora and me and Rosie, four generations of Thomas women. Life was nothing if not interesting. Life was fascinating, scary, frightening and wonderful, and I realised that I wouldn't change a single thing about the two women I was driving home. And I wouldn't change a single thing about my life if it meant that I wouldn't be here, right now, in this car, with these two. None of it. Not a thing. It was all over with Michael. And I was free. And Red wanted to talk to me. And I would have to tell him about the baby. And I didn't know what he'd say. But it was time for full disclosure. It was time to be honest.

'Tabitha?'

'Yes, Mum?'

'Can we stop for a moment? There must be a garage or something. I'm absolutely starving.'

Oh God. My mother had the munchies.

26

Once we were back in Dublin and we'd dropped Nora home (she was going straight, she said, for a lie-down), I'd just put the kettle on when we heard Michael's key in the door. What did one say to one's husband who has fallen in love with a (slightly) younger and (definitely) perkier woman?

He came into the kitchen and stood there, grey with worry, his eyes red as though he'd been crying all night. There was no sign of Lucy.

'Rosie?' he said.

'Yes?'

'Are you still mad at me?'

'Well I haven't had much time to *not* get mad at you,' she said. 'So yes, I'm still mad at you.'

'Cup of tea, Michael?' I said. 'We've just had such a long drive, I'm gasping. You?'

'I can't keep a thing down,' he said. 'Not even water. I had to sit next to a baby on the flight who cried the whole way from Charleroi. And I've got a splitting headache.'

'Granny Nora's got one of those,' said Rosie, giving me a look.

'Grown-ups really are not being the best role models lately to you, are they?' I said to her, as Michael sat on a chair and massaged his temples. He did look pretty green. 'You might be the only one among us who has behaved with dignity.'

'You're not doing too badly, Mum,' she said quietly, and gave my arm a squeeze. We waited for Michael to refocus on the room. I noticed he wasn't begging for forgiveness or following any of the usual errant spouse scripts. Even with his career in danger, he'd obviously decided that Lucy was for him.

'I'm so sorry,' he said, eventually. 'Oh Tab, I didn't mean this... any of this... it's awful... I am just so sorry... oh Tab, I can't believe I've done this... I didn't think I'd ever be one of those... politicians...'

'The sleazy kind?' I suggested, helpfully.

'Well...' he spluttered, not wanting to accept sleaziness but knowing his moral standing was rocky. 'I know how angry you must be...'

'Michael, it's...'

'You're probably fuming, wanting my guts for garters... you've probably got a little voodoo doll in a suit and you're going to stick pins into it...'

'Michael...'

He was examining my face. 'You look dreadful, so upset,' he insisted. 'It must have come as a terrible shock...'

'I'm absolutely...'

'Furious? Devastated? So you should be! What a thing to discover. Your husband having an affair with his secretary. Oh, Tabitha, I am so ashamed, so appalled, so horrified, to have put you through this. To have hurt you and Rosie so badly, to have destroyed your lives like this...'

'Hold on a moment...' I said. 'Michael...'

'You'll forever be known as Michael Fogarty's wronged wife. I can't believe I have done this to you, Tabitha, it was so selfish of me. How will you ever get over it? And my constituents! They will be devastated. I'll lose my seat, for sure.' His eyes were almost gleaming at the thought of his great fall. 'It's just that when you fall in love, passion gets in the way of everything. People get hurt. But... but sometimes, that's the way it has to be.'

I'd heard enough. 'Michael, please. Just listen. It's fine. Believe me.' I nodded, smiling, encouragingly. 'I'm really pleased for you. Really pleased. I can't talk for how Rosie feels about the matter, but for me, I can see that you and Lucy are meant for each other. I mean, she's such a marvel. And your constituents will get over it. They'll just go and vote for someone else. We'll all be fine.'

'What?' He looked shocked and almost disappointed I was taking it so well. 'Are you sure you're okay?' He looked at me sceptically, puzzled that I had taken his one chance to be a blackguard away from him. 'Rosie?' he said, the colour now fully drained from his face.

'I'll get over it,' she said.

'I just... we couldn't help...'

'Falling in love?' I prompted.

He nodded miserably.

'Michael, we can talk about this in detail another time but we need to get divorced and you need to move out as soon as possible. Now, in fact. And you and Lucy have my full and complete blessing as long as you do this as swiftly and painlessly as possible. For all our sakes.'

'Do I have your blessing as well, Rosie?'

She nodded. 'It kind of puts my messing up my Leaving Cert in the shade, so I'm not so disappointed. It's nice when your parents behave worse than you do.'

He gave her an agonised, tortured smile as though he had no idea if she was joking or not. She wasn't.

'Where is Lucy by the way?' I said.

'Outside. Waiting.'

'You'd better bring her in.'

* * *

When he returned with Lucy, she grabbed my hand, her eyes full of tears. They'd obviously both had a good sob about my awful plight on the journey home. 'I'm so sorry, Tabitha,' she said. 'I'm so sorry.'

'Lucy, it's fine,' I said briskly. 'Can we all stop saying sorry and be grown-up about this?'

'Yes, yes,' she said, sniffling and coughing 'I'm sorry... I mean...'

'Have you seen the headlines?' Michael said, taking a pile of newspapers from Lucy and putting them on the kitchen table. Finally, he had achieved one of the great tenets of being a politician – a sex scandal. Maybe even conventional people like Michael craved being at the centre of a drama sometimes. We're all human, we all need attention at times, I supposed. And you don't go into politics not to be noticed. And Michael had finally done it, nationwide notoriety. This was political gold. 'I'm notorious... I'll never be known for anything else.' He looked pretty pleased with himself, the rosy pinkness back in his cheeks.

'What's your mother going to say?'

The colour drained out of him again. 'Mammy... oh God.'

'We'll tell her together, Michael,' said Lucy, back to her marvellous self and taking charge, brilliantly, as she always did. 'She'll come round.' She smiled him a smile full of love and admiration and can-do while he looked at her with gratitude and I was reminded once more why they were so well suited. I had never looked at him like that. Ever.

'There's something else,' he said. 'Bigger than everything... *this* you won't be so happy about. It's something of a bombshell.'

'What now?' I imagined the worst. 'You've embezzled money? You're on the run?'

'Out with it, Dad,' said Rosie.

Lucy went over and took his hand.

'We're pregnant,' he said. 'Well, Lucy is. We only found out this week... and...'

'We're going to have a baby,' joined in Lucy. 'Tabitha... I'm sorry... we're really sorry...'

I held up my hand. 'Enough. Right... a baby,' I stalled.

'A baby!' said Rosie, looking shocked.

'You're going to be a big sister,' said Michael.

'I hope you're pleased for us,' said Lucy. 'It's all been such a rush and I am sure there were far better ways of announcing things.'

'Better out than in,' said Michael.

'Rosie?' I said. 'What do you think?'

She shrugged. 'I'm not sure,' she said, truthfully. 'I feel like we're on a twenty four hour news channel and everything is moving so fast. But I could get used to it,' she said. 'It might be nice. A little brother or sister. Someone who might actually get to Trinity.' She gave Michael a look.

'Well, it's a little soon for that, but perhaps, you never know, it wouldn't be too far from the realm of possibility.' *Now* he looked quite delighted with himself.

'Lucy, you sit down here and I'll make you some tea. You've been travelling all morning. There's a biscuit here somewhere. Or you can have some of Clodagh's Baileys,' I joked. 'She keeps a bottle here for medicinal purposes.'

'Just the tea,' said Lucy. 'I think I'll be off the drink for a while.'

My phone beeped while I was digging out the mugs and the milk. It was Red.

Are you home?

I quickly texted back.

Yes. Would you like to come round?

'My headache's gone, Mammy,' said Michael.

'Has it?' I said, automatically, just as Lucy said, 'That's good news, Michael.'

And then I realised that I was released by the horror of being called Mammy by someone who wasn't my child. Every cloud...

* * *

The ring of the doorbell, gave me an excuse to leave the kitchen for a moment. Would Red have come so soon? Would he mind walking into a family drama? It was Red. We stood there for a moment, smiling.

What a sight for sore eyes. Red looking beyond handsome, hair pushed to one side, his sleeves rolled up. For a moment, I didn't move, didn't know what to say. I was just so pleased and relieved to see him and wanted to put my arms around him and take a moment to remember what he felt like, to feel the heat of his body.

We stood there, looking at each other.

'Welcome to the house of fun,' I said.

He laughed. 'Shall I go and leave you all to it?'

'No. No, don't go. It feels right, somehow.'

'Listen,' he said, eventually. 'I just wanted to say, I'm still your friend. Always was, always will be. And I'm sorry for acting like a drama queen.'

'Drama king,' I corrected him.

'Drama *king*. How's Rosie?'

'A little bit dazed,' I said. 'But not doing too badly. Taking it in her stride.'

'And you? Are you okay?'

I nodded. 'Never better. It's like everything is the way it should be. Michael with Lucy. I'm glad for them. And they're here,' I nodded to the kitchen. 'They are in the kitchen with Rosie.'

'And you're not angry with him?'

I shook my head. 'Not at all. I don't even think I should be,' I said. 'I'm almost excited. Life just got interesting again.'

He smiled at me. 'And there was I thinking that I could swing in, my sword out and beat up paparazzi... or husbands...'

'I didn't know you were into physical violence,' I said. 'I thought you were a pacifist. I can see I'm going to have to change my good opinion of you.'

'Well, when I say beating up, I mean a bit of teeth baring or even a shaken fist.' He looked at me, one eyebrow raised, an amused expression on his face.

I love you Red Power, I thought, a huge smile spread on my face.

Behind me, in the hall, Rosie ran upstairs. 'Hi Red,' she said. And she gave me a special smile of encouragement and support, a quick nod, which gave me a lump in my throat. 'Everything all right?' I said to her.

'It can't get any worse,' she said. 'I'm going with the flow. Nobody's died.' She grinned. 'Yet. I'm going upstairs to phone Alice.'

'You know something, Red,' I said, refocussing, once I heard Rosie's bedroom door close. 'I'm quite impressed. I didn't think Michael had it in him. Adultery! And I thought he was a man who thought a sex scandal was only if you removed your vest and socks during sex.'

Red laughed.

'I'm...' How *was* I feeling? 'I'm actually *delighted*.' Yes that was it. Delighted and happy. Giddy with new possibilities and new adventures to be had. Rosie was going to be all right, I knew that. I'd be there for her with everything she needed and now Michael, God bless him, had fallen in love with Lucy, it meant there was nothing stopping me. I had been determined to stay in the marriage for the simple reason that I wanted my daughter to have a mother and a father in the same house. I'd been wrong, it wasn't any good having a mother and father who didn't love each other, who weren't even a team.

But somehow, now, life stretched out like a glittering and exciting carpet. Or like the 'Billie Jean' floor in the Michael Jackson video. Enticing and exciting. 'And Lucy's pregnant.' And then I realised it wasn't all going to be plain sailing, that I couldn't afford to be giddy and excited. I still had to tell Red about my baby. *Our* baby.

'Good grief.'

I could do with a hug, I thought, as I stood to one side to let him go past me, his jacket brushing my hand. *I could do with the biggest hug of my life. From you. I'd hold on and never let go.*

I pulled him by the arm, feeling his muscles beneath his shirt, into the kitchen. We bumped up against each other and there was a lightness, a giggling quality, a slight hysteria was infecting us.

'I hope you don't mind, Mrs... Tabitha,' said Lucy when we went into the kitchen, 'but I made the tea. I haven't had a decent one for two days. One thing I don't like about Brussels. The water. You can bring your tea bags but it's not the same.'.'

'Michael, you remember Redmond Power.'

'Ah yes,' he said, holding out his hand. 'Tabitha's old friend.'

'That's right,' said Red. 'I hope you don't mind me calling at this time...'

'Time of what?' said Michael. 'Time of me being a national laughing stock?'

'No!' said Lucy suddenly and passionately. 'You're not a laughing stock. You're still the same Michael Fogarty you ever were: upstanding, proud and principled. That's the Michael Fogarty you were, the Michael Fogarty you are and the Michael Fogarty you will be.' She looked quite hot around the collar. Everyone needed a Lucy on their team. Finally, Michael had the life partner he deserved.

I glanced at Red and he widened his eyes at this impassioned speech and I felt like I might laugh, from happiness, hysteria or knowing that Red 'got me', understood me.

'Lucy, this is Red... a friend of mine... And Red, this is Michael's...' Lucy's smile was rictus. 'Michael's *girlfriend* and mother of his unborn child.' I turned to Lucy. 'Is that all right?'

'Yes...' She hesitated. 'I think so. Well, it's factually correct, I suppose, but rather bald when you say it out loud.'

'Good to meet you,' said Red, shaking her hand. 'I recognised you from the newspaper.'

'Oh stop,' said Lucy, blushing. 'I'm am mortified. Mammy is furious. She says she can't face Mass today because of all the talk. Expecting... when I'm not married!'

Michael patted her on the shoulder, a look of resignation on his face as he realised his hours and hours of lovely sleep were about to be cut short.

'Everything's going to be all right, you just take care of yourself and that baby. Now,' I said, 'where are those Jaffa Cakes? Jaffa Cake, Red?'

'Tea, everyone?' said Lucy. 'Michael?'

'Would you make mine black?' he said. 'I think I've gone off milk.'

And while Lucy and Michael were whispering together, Red held out his hand and touched mine and my smile turned into a goofy, giddy grin. Red, meanwhile, was looking as goofy and giddy as me. This is how it used to feel, I remembered, this is how we used to be.

'Well,' said Michael, 'we're going to hit the road. We're going to stay in the flat in town. I'm going to take Rosie out for pizza tonight and we can talk about everything.'

Michael hung back a little when I saw him and Lucy off at the front door. This was my husband leaving me. Shouldn't it be more dramatic, a bit more *EastEnders*? Shouldn't I be crying? Or at least hitting the vodka? Or him?

'Thank you,' said Michael. 'Thanks for being so good about things... about everything.'

'It's all right,' I said. 'We're all human. Anyway, it's something of a relief, to be honest. We were never right for each other.'

'Well, thank you for trying, anyway,' he said.

'We both tried,' I said. 'We did it for Rosie.'

'A most noble cause,' he said and reached towards me and hugged me awkwardly and stiffly. We hadn't actually had such close physical contact in years, not since the last by-election and he was so overexcited he hugged all of us standing there at two a.m. I thought I was going to drop with tiredness, but he and Lucy were on cloud nine. Thinking back, I should have twigged something was up when he hugged all of us but not her. It was the classic putting people off the scent trick, but I was too tired that night to see it.

'Goodbye Michael, and good luck with your Standards In Pubic Lice thing,' I said. 'I mean public *life*!'

'I think that's over,' he said, sadly, looking not unlike a wounded lion, 'along with my career. And the milk scheme will never be a runner now. I was so sure they would be ground-breaking. They were going to make my name in Europe.'

'Well,' I said, 'you'll be known for adultery rather than public lice and milk. I think that is far more rock and roll, don't you?'

'Typical Tabitha answer,' he said. 'Everything amuses you.'

'Michael, I am not amused. Not particularly. But it's better to find humour in a situation like this, don't you think?'

'I suppose,' he said gloomily.

'Something tells me you'll be fine,' I said. 'When are you going to talk to your mother?'

'She's already called me. Several times. And on Lucy's phone. I'll call her. But all courage seems to have left me on that front. If she comes here, tell her I've escaped to Darkest Peru. Or Outer Mongolia. Well then...' He bounced on his feet again, from awkwardness or desire to get on with his new life, I couldn't tell. 'Thank you, Tabitha,' he said, 'you've been ridiculously understanding.'

'And you, Michael, have been ridiculous!' I said, but he didn't hear me as he was already jogging away.

'Coming, Mammy!' he called to Lucy. 'I'm coming!' And Lucy, standing by the ministerial car (Terry sitting in the driver's seat, eyes studiedly front), looked as if she didn't mind her new role at all. In fact, she was glowing with happiness.

I'd hardly had a chance to close the door when the doorbell rang again; it was Celia looking more than her usual uptight self.

'Where is he?' she said. 'And where is that homewrecker?'

'They've just this minute left,' I said, feeling a surge of irritation that Michael was on the run from his mother and had left me to deal with her.

'They've? You mean, Michael and... Lucy?'

I nodded.

'And *you* let them go?'

'Well, I have no choice.'

'Typical of you, Tabitha,' she said. 'You wouldn't fight a wet paper bag. Never mind your marriage, your reputation. You're happy, are you? Your husband swanning about with a young one, a girl half his age...'

'She's only ten years younger...'

'How am I going to live this down? The shame! Michael Senior, now he had a roving eye but it was never talked about. *Never.* That's what men do. Boys will be boys. But to get into the papers. I mean, this is a new low.' She looked as though she was going to collapse. Her voice wobbled as though she was about to cry. 'I don't know what to do.'

'Celia, come in. I'll make some tea.'

In the kitchen, Red was leaning against the work surface, drinking his tea.

'Celia, this is Red, a friend of mine. Red, this is Celia, my... mother-in-law.'

'Pleased to... whatever,' she said, the tragedy of her son, the adulterer, making her forget her manners. Something she would never have countenanced before.

'Listen, I'm going to go,' said Red. 'Leave you to it.'

'No you can stay,' said Celia, 'whoever you are. It's all common knowledge anyway. I am beyond caring. You may as well know everything. The whole world knows. We have no secrets, it seems. Out dirty washing hung on the line for everyone to inspect. Where's Rosie? I hope to God and all the saints she has been spared this shame. Though how we can keep it from her for much longer, I really don't know.'

'Celia, she knows. It was in the papers.'

'In my day, children did not know anything that went on in the lives of their elders. My own mother never, ever mentioned anything which was not suitable for small ears. It wasn't until I was married myself did she tell me about her health issues... down there. And my father, he was a rogue – aren't they all – but I heard not a dickie bird until he was long gone.' She sighed. 'How is she taking it?'

'In her stride, so far,' I said. 'We're all taking it in. But, Celia, I think that there is little we can do about it except wish them well.'

She looked at me as if I was from outer space. '*Wish them well? Wish them well?* What on earth for. Maybe you should hold a party and make a cake. Or move out of the house into the shed in the garden and let them have everything, why not? Let that little minx take everything! When I think of how nice I was to that girl. I thought she was good for Michael, someone he could trust and rely on. I had no idea she was feathering her nest, ready to pounce, the little magpie.'

She fell into the chair at the table and put her head in her hands. 'Imelda took great delight in showing me the article. The headline... oh...' She shuddered. 'I could see it in her eyes. Delight, ecstasy, pure pleasure! At my downfall. She's been waiting for this for years, she has. Since we were in school. She's always been jealous of me, just because I was good at spelling and had a long neck and a nice nose. And then when I married Michael Fogarty – senior – and she was stuck with Frank. Fat Frank we called him, secretly – her jealousy took hold. And now I am the mother of –'she coughed twice delicately, 'ahem-ahem Foggy.'

'Celia...' I stood there helplessly. 'You should talk to Michael, not me.'

'Oh, don't you worry,' she said. 'Don't you worry. I shall be doing more than talking to him, I can tell you. I shall be giving him a piece of my mind.'

Rosie came downstairs. 'I'm going out, Mum,' she said. 'Oh hello, Granny. I just want to go and see Alice... see how she's getting on.'

'Rosie,' said Celia. 'You shouldn't be visiting friends. You should be revising.'

'I'm not doing them,' she said. 'Not this year anyway.'

Celia looked as though she had vomited in her own mouth.

Rosie blundered on. 'I'm taking a year to reassess...' she said, speeding up, as Celia's face was a picture of someone witnessing untold horrors. 'I'm going to reapply to another college. Do something with English.'

'Not. Doing. Your. Exams? Not. Going. To. Trinity!' Celia's wild eyes swivelled to me. 'What is going on? *Somebody* FOR GOD'S SAKE tell me what's going on!' She focussed on Red, who was leaning inconspicuously on the edge of the kitchen counter. 'Can you tell me?' she charged at him. 'Do you know anything? Because it seems I am the last to know!'

Red shook his head.

But then she turned to me. 'And you're happy, are you, Tabitha?' she accused. 'You're *happy* about this? I might have known you'd scupper her chances, ruin her future.'

'Granny, please...' Rosie was on the verge of tears.

'Celia, it's all going to be fine,' I tried to explain. 'This year's been really tough on Rosie and she's seeing a counsellor to deal with anxiety... there was no way she could do the Leaving Cert.'

'*No way she could do the Leaving Cert?*' Celia repeated, utterly incredulous, looking as though she had swallowed a wasp. She began making weird throat-clearing sounds.

'Anyway,' went on Rosie, 'everything'll be lovely once the baby's born.'

'A baby? You're not... don't tell me that... surely you're not... you can't be...' Celia was white with shock.

'Not me, Granny. Dad and Lucy!'

Celia looked ready to faint. Her hand rattled her cup. 'Baby?' Her voice had dropped to a hoarse whisper. 'A baby.'

Time for the medicinal Baileys, I thought but then my phone rang.

'If it's Michael, tell him his mother wants a word,' warned Celia.

'It's not, it's Mary. I have to take this.'

'Tabitha.' Mary was crying. 'Tabitha. I'm in customs in Dublin airport and they won't let me through. I had my purse stolen in Dubai and I've lost my passport and everything. I'm so sorry to bother you, I know you've got enough on your plate because Mammy rang me about Lucy. She's mortified. Are you all right?'

'Don't mind me,' I said.

'I tried to call Red,' she went on, 'but there was no answer.'

'You were in Dubai?'

'Stopover. We were only there for three hours and I just wasn't paying attention. I was so caught up with...' She began to sob now. 'You've probably got enough to do but if you could get a message to Red, he might be able to come.'

'He's here with me actually,' I said. 'But what do you need me to do?'

'Would you mind going to my house. Key's under the geranium pot on the window beside the door. There's a copy of my passport in the filing cabinet in my office upstairs. Top door, marked Personal. They said they would accept a copy for now and then at least... at least we can go home. It's been such a long and exhausting week and we just need to sleep.'

We?

When I put down the phone, I turned to Red, 'we have to go to the airport,' I said. 'Mary's lost her passport. She said she tried to call you.'

He held up his phone. 'On silent. Sorry. The poor woman.'

'Do you know what's going on?' I said.

'I might do but I think it would be better if it came from her. Shall we go?'

'You're coming?'

'Try and stop me. Where you go, I go.'

'You'll find out,' he said. 'I'm coming with you.'

'That's a relief,' I said. 'I wasn't sure how to make you come otherwise.'

And after I had poured Celia another Baileys and left her sitting on the sofa, her feet up, ready for a little sleep, he took my hand and we ran out to his car.

'I had no idea your life was so exciting,' he said.

'It hasn't been for decades,' I said. 'I don't know what's going on.'

27

At the airport, Red dropped me off and went to park the car. Inside the terminal, I explained everything to a security guard.

'It's a friend of mine. Mary Hooley. I have a copy of her passport to prove she is an Irish citizen. I don't know why you didn't just ask her to speak. She's from Ballyjamesduff and she has the accent to prove it.'

He jerked his thumb. 'She's back here.'

He led me through a secret door, flashing and skimming his pass through a warren of corridors and electronic gates until he pushed open a door. And there was Mary, drinking a cup of tea, with another security guard.

'Cavalry has arrived,' said the first guard.

'We are so sorry to drag you all this way,' said the second guard. 'But with things as they are, you know, we'd get in terrible trouble, so we would. We can't let people through without passports. It's not like the old days when any Tom, Dick or Paddy would swan through passport control. Now, Mary here and the little lady can finally be away. They've had a terrible journey all the way from Beijing so they have. They're both fit to be tied.'

'Little lady?'

Mary was looking at me with big eyes, tears pooling. 'I've got her, Tabitha,' she said. 'She's here. My little angel is finally here.' She unpeeled the top of her coat to show me what was tucked inside. A tiny face, eyes closed, a thatch of black hair on her head. The sweetest little rosebud for a mouth. 'This is little Huan... my new daughter, adopted from China. I've waited so long for her but this time everything is all right... everything is just perfect.'

'Oh my God...' I looked at Mary with wonder. A huge smile of awe and amazement spread on my face, matching the one that had appeared on Mary's. 'You are a dark horse,' I said, bending over the tiny figure, nestled against her new mother. 'Hello Huan,' I said gently to the little black head. 'Hello little lady.'

'It means joy,' said Mary. 'Who would have thought that something so small could bring so much joy?'

She pulled her coat down lower so I could see Huan's tiny hands balled into fists, her bright intelligent eyes looking at me, wondering where on earth she was. She still had on a beautiful jade-coloured Chinese jacket and tiny little embroidered slippers.

'She's beautiful,' I said, overawed by this adorable baby who had travelled so far. 'Welcome to Ireland, little girl of happiness. You've come a long, long way and it's time to go home.'

* * *

We helped settle Huan into her new house, their house, making sure the heating was on and warming up Huan's cot – which Mary had bought before heading off – with a hot water bottle.

Finally, we drew up outside my house. We sat in the car for a moment, talking about Mary and Huan.

'So you knew everything?'

'Only some of it,' he admitted. 'I knew she was going through this long and arduous process, that she had travelled to China before and that it hadn't worked out. Frankly, I don't know how she kept it together, there were so many disappointments, near-misses... and then this happened. She got the call that there was a baby who needed a home and... well, she just had to leave. I think she talked to me because I was an outsider. No judgement...'

'I wouldn't have judged,' I said, quickly, defensively.

'We became friends,' he said. 'I think it was our shared love of Johnny Logan. And then going to see improving films together. She told me what exactly she'd gone through to get to this point.'

'A baby...' I said. 'There's nothing like a baby.' For a moment, I watched Red and wondered what he was thinking. He was looking though the windscreen at the road ahead.

'Would you have liked one?' I said, tentatively. 'A baby, I mean.'

He nodded. 'Yes.' He smiled. 'But with the right partner. Teaching has been a way of being around children, of being part of their lives but I would have wanted one I could call my own. If you're allowed to call them your own.' He turned to me, a wry, regretful look on his face. 'It never happened. And it's probably too late...'

I wasn't sure what to say in return as I thought about the baby – our baby. The baby we lost.

'I'm starving,' he said, suddenly. 'Would you like to go for something to eat? Maybe Rosie would like to come.'

'She's still in Alice's,' I said. 'And then going out with Michael. I hope he doesn't go on about trying for Trinity again.'

He smiled. 'Is she good at dealing with him?'

'Better than me,' I said. 'Fathers and daughters are different to wives and husbands. Daughters have more power than they maybe realise.

28

Red and I saw each other every night that week and we seemed to be finding our way back to one another. However there hadn't been the right time to tell Red about the baby. Perhaps I was scared that he might not want to see me again and I couldn't bear the thought of losing him.

We'd been for a walk to the harbour this evening and he'd come in for a cup of tea.

'Tab?' Red was leaning against the kitchen cupboards after we'd eaten and cleared up. 'Yes?'

'Why didn't you come to San Francisco? What happened? I wish I could just let the past be the past and not go on about it. We were both so young I know that, and it was so long ago but... but I just want you to tell me, give me a reason.'

I had to finally tell him my side of the story. I'd heard some of his, he didn't know any of mine. But he'd brought it up now.

'Red...'

'Look, Tab, there is something about you that makes me so happy, so deeply, incredibly happy, that I can't stop... and I wish I could. Because it is burning me up, it's stopping me from just getting on with my life. Moving on. I thought I'd done it, I thought I was okay. All healed and put back together once more and then I walk into your office and it's like I'm twenty all over again. And it's been so difficult. I am right back to where I started, when you... when you broke my heart.'

'Red, I'm so sorry...'

'Tab, just tell me, why didn't you come to San Francisco. Was I not good enough? Had you fallen out of love with me? What? Just tell me and it might help me. I'm not going to be hurt again, but I would know. And that would be so much better than not knowing. Because it's the not knowing that really killed me. Did you meet someone else? Was it Michael?'

I took a deep breath. I was scared of hurting Red but I didn't want to carry on withholding something from him that he had had a right to know years ago. *Here we go.* 'I was pregnant and I... and I lost the baby.'

Utter confusion and bewilderment filled his face, he shook his head, trying to put everything together.

'It was ours. I only found out the week before Rosaleen passed away. And it was such a lovely feeling,' I went on desperately. 'I had a whole week to start to think about the baby and how much I was going to enjoy being its mother. I didn't tell you because I thought it would be a really lovely surprise when I came over. I didn't want to tell you over the phone. It was impossible. And I liked just knowing it myself. God, that sounds selfish. But I didn't think it was a secret. I was going to tell you. I just wanted to tell you in person. And I was going to see you so soon. Not telling you seems like the most stupid and self-indulgent thing in the world now.'

He'd been silent for all of this, taking it in. 'Did you tell anyone?' he said, eventually.

'First just Rosaleen knew. And then... I told Nora.'

'And you didn't tell me?' His voice was quiet, urgent, his questions filling in the gaps of my story, as he mentally rearranged the piece to try and find some kind of coherence... a reason.

'I wasn't thinking clearly,' I said. 'If I did it all over again, I would tell you. But, Red, you've got to remember, I was going to be seeing you in ten days' time. It was my secret, but only for a little while. I thought I was doing the right thing.' He nodded slowly, as though he sort of understood. Or at least was trying to understand. But standing there, trying to explain myself, it seemed such a stupid and selfish thing to do.

'When did you lose the baby?' There were tears in Red's eyes.

'The day of Rosaleen's funeral, I went down to the Forty Foot. I hadn't slept at all and I thought I'd go down and have an early morning swim. And it was freezing. I mean, it always was, but it seemed particularly cold. And for the first time, it was like there was death in the air or something dark and horrible in the water. There wasn't, I know there wasn't. But I wasn't thinking straight. I don't know, it was a combination of grief and hormones or maybe I'm imagining it, I don't know. I can't say. It was just one of those things, I know now, but then I blamed the sea, blamed myself for going swimming...'

'Oh Tabitha.' And Red's arms were around me, pulling my body to his, holding me closer and tighter and more tenderly than I had been held in years. 'Oh Tab. I can't believe you went through that.' He pulled away, looking at me. 'I wish you had told me.'

'It felt like the deepest punch in the stomach,' I said, 'as though life, and me, and everything would never be the same again. I mean, I couldn't function. When I look back now, I just remember that I couldn't get out of bed. I felt unutterably changed, entirely different. I thought nothing could ever be the same again. I wasn't me. People lose babies all the time, don't they? Why did it affect me so badly? Why couldn't I have just got on with things, brushed it off. I could have flown to you in San Francisco and told you all about it and... everything would have been all right. But I couldn't. For some reason, I just couldn't. It just so seemed so silly to be mourning the loss of a baby I was too young to have, that I had never met, that I had only known about for a couple of weeks. It all seemed so stupid, something that no one would understand.'

'I would have understood,' he said. 'I would have been there for you, every step of the way.'

'There was so much to think about and the last thing I wanted to do was think. We'd lost Rosaleen, I'd lost the baby. Telling you was one thing I couldn't do. I couldn't have coped with your reaction, your sadness, your anger, whatever it might have been...'

'I wouldn't have been angry,' he insisted. 'I would have been there for you. Like I always promised I would be. But you didn't give me a chance.' There was silence for a moment between us. The clock ticking on the wall. The birds outside. 'I would have been Tab.'

I nodded, miserably. 'But I couldn't do anything. For weeks and months. I stayed in my room. I couldn't face anyone. I'd never experienced anything like that before. Maybe it was the combination of Rosaleen being gone as well, but it was like I had lost a part of me. No, not a part of me. It was like I had lost the most precious thing I might ever have. And I had been careless and stupid and lost it. I blamed myself. I didn't know where to begin to try and explain how I was feeling, but this beautiful thing, this lovely treasure inside me was gone.'

'Who looked after you?'

'Nora. She hung around for a few months. She was amazing, actually. I think it was some kind of breakdown. It's all a blur, really, and it took me years to get over it, completely. Even after Rosie was born, it took me time to bond with her. But slowly, I did. Slowly I got better.'

'I'm sorry you went through all that.' He took my hand and kissed it and then held it. 'I wish you had told me, given me the opportunity to be there for you...'

'Me too,' I said quietly. 'Me too.'

'Did Michael know about the baby?'

I shook my head. 'I never told him. He doesn't know about you or anything. Rosie knows, though. I told her the other week.'

'She's dealing with a lot lately.'

'Yes, yes she is.' I thought of Rosie and how much she'd been through. She'd be all right though, I was sure of it. She was made of strong stuff. Like her great-grandmother. Like her grandmother. Like her mother. She was a Thomas after all.

'It was horrible not knowing,' he said. 'You not taking my calls. I even sent Dad around to try and find out what was going on.'

'I know...'

He shook his head. 'You should have told me,' he said. 'Not because I had a right to know. That was your decision and I understand that. But because I was your friend. Your boyfriend. And I loved you. I loved you so much, Tab.'

'I loved you too,' I said. 'I'm sorry.'

We looked at each other. 'When did you meet Michael? God, that was horrible when I found out that you had got married. To Michael Fogarty. Jesus Christ!'

'A year later,' I said. 'He seemed to suit who I thought I was, what I'd become. I thought it was the right thing to do. And it meant I could try and have another child.'

He took my hand in his. 'I don't know what to say...'

'Nor do I.' His hand was warm and smooth. Just like I remembered. 'Why did you stay away so long?'

'You. I was hurt. Lonely. Angry. Sad. All of those things. You were gone. You were with Michael... you had Rosie.'

'Did you meet anyone?'

He nodded. 'A few really nice women. All of them, I realise now, reminded me a little bit of you. You know, something about their hair, or the way they used their hands or the colour of their eyes.' He shook his head, looking down. 'But I just couldn't get it together to be the man, the partner, they wanted, they deserved. I couldn't stop thinking of you. And I wanted a child. I really wanted a child, but it seemed so wrong to have one with someone I knew that I would never love...' He stopped again, as though he couldn't quite form the words. He cleared his throat. 'As much as you. I wish I had or could, and I tried, all these years to...' He stopped speaking. He was scanning my face.

'To what?' My voice was practically a whisper.

'To forget you, to find someone else to fall in love with. To move on.'

'Me too.' I blinked away my tears. 'I didn't forget you either. I thought about you every day. But I couldn't turn back time. I'd made all these decisions and then I had Rosie. It was too late. I wanted her to have a father and to have a normal home.'

'I don't regret all of it,' he said. 'I haven't spent the last 18 years wishing everything was different. I've been happy... I've loved living in the States, I have learned so much about the world. But I compartmentalised, you know? I kept you and Ireland and *us* tightly locked away. It didn't stop me from having fun and being happy and content, but it did stop me from being fully who I am...'

'Me too,' I whispered. 'Me too. That's how I feel. I wouldn't change a thing about Rosie, you know that. But I have felt the loss of you, the lack of you, for all these years. It's like I cut off my own arm, I know it sounds ridiculous, but that's what you were...'

'Your *arm*?' he deadpanned, defusing all intensity, and I laughed.

'My *right* arm, does that make it better?'

'A little.' He smiled at me.

'But it's true...'

For a moment, we stood looking at each other, the gulf of all those years we hadn't spent together, the fear of an unknown future, but the need to be close, to make up for lost time, the desire to touch each other was too much. And he felt the same. Strong arms pulled me into his chest and I fitted in exactly as I used to, my spot, tucked right in there, close to him, up against his body, the warmth of him.

'Tabitha...' His voice in my ear. 'I never stopped.'

And maybe it was the way he sounded, or the smell of him, the heat of his body, the memories of long nights and days in bed, but something burned inside me that hadn't for a long time. And it was Red who ignited me, always had... always would.

'Nor did I. I'm sorry, Red.'

'Me too,' he said. 'Sorry you went through that. But no regrets. You have Rosie and she is all that matters. You know, Tab?' He gave my forehead a little tiny kiss. 'You haven't changed.' And another one. 'Not one bit, not in any way.' Two quick ones, closer to my mouth this time. 'When I saw you again after all those years in your office, it was as though I had stepped back in time.' And again, on my cheek, edging closer. 'The way you spoke, the way you looked. Your beautiful face, your lovely voice... it was all I could do to stop myself from throwing myself on you and refusing to let go.' And he kissed me on the lips, a long and lingering and gloriously deep kiss. He was right, sometimes time does stand still, feelings can just stay there for years and years. There we were, Red and Tab. Together again.

And there was something I needed to say. 'I love you, Red.'

'And I love you, my darling Tabitha.'

Darling. It beat Mammy any day.

29

I'd finally made up my mind about the Copse. It was the last day of term and everyone was looking forward to eight weeks' holiday, but I had one last decision to make. I wasn't selling the Copse. Not to anyone.

Brian had repeatedly said the land was worthless, valueless, but it wasn't. It was priceless. I saw that. The protestors had made me see it, the children themselves. When I met Red and his class down there and seeing how much the children blossomed outdoors. They needed more than classrooms and playgrounds. Walls and tarmacadam. They needed nature, the trees, the butterflies. The squirrels. When I thought of Rosie and how academically focussed her life had become, I had realised very clearly, that we needed to be very clear in what we were teaching children. There was more to life than exams and achievement. There was living and being in the world. The natural world. Something that might build greater resilience and strength as they grew up. It was the chance to sit and stare, the opportunity to be in nature, to daydream and to think, to make daisy chains and plait grasses, to climb trees and to lie on your back and hear the birds sing. Being outdoors, away from books and screens and pressure, like Rosaleen in her cherry tree or Nora in the Forty Foot.

As I drove in through the school gates, the protestors were still set up. They wouldn't give up.

Nora was drinking a mug of tea. 'Last day!' she called, cheerily, utterly recovered from our dramatic trip to West Cork. There was the smell of sizzling bacon as Robbo fried it up while Arthur buttered the bread. 'How are you?' she said. 'What happened with Michael?'

'Well,' I said, 'he's moved into the flat in town, we're getting a divorce and Lucy's going to have his baby.'

She whistled. 'So he has lead in his pencil after all.'

'Mum! How's your headache?' I said, pointedly.

She ignored me. 'And you and Rosie?'

'Doing remarkably well.'

She smiled. 'Good. I'll go round and see her later. She's going to come for a swim with me. And what about himself?'

'Who?'

'Fella me lad,' she said. 'Redmond. Ah, you're blushing. So something has happened?'

'No nothing. Not yet. But I think it's all there. Us. We're still there, if that makes sense.'

'Good for you, Tabitha. You deserve a bit of good romance in your life after Mr Stuffed Shirt. Me, I've had too much, but you, you haven't had as much as you should.'

'Thanks, Mum,' I said. 'I think.'

Just then, Arthur handed her a bacon sandwich – she was a fair-weather vegetarian – and she waved it at me. 'And today's the day, you're making your big decision. You are not going to let me down, are you?'

'You'll find out,' I said as I drove off, my hand waving to her from my open window.

In the car park, Red was carrying Mrs Morrissey's bags into the school and he waved. With Red in the world, I felt I could do anything.

Mary was in the school office, tiny Huan in a Moses basket up against her desk. 'Tabitha!' she said in an urgent whisper. 'Where were you? Didn't you get my messages...?'

I checked my phone in my bag, it had been on silent. Thirty-seven missed calls.

'We've got the special assembly now... can it wait?'

She shook her head and motioned to my office with her eyes just as

Brian Crowley appeared from my door, his voluminous body eclipsing the light from the window, smiling his small-toothed crocodile smile.

'I hope you don't mind me waiting in your office,' he said, holding a sheaf of papers. 'But it's time to crack on. Get these babies signed. Last day of term and our man Freddie doesn't like to wait for too long.' He rubbed his hands.

'Tabitha...' Mary called.

'I'll talk to you in a moment, Mary,' I said as I followed Brian into my office. Through the window and past the school gates were the protestors. These people full of life and conviction, the opposite of Brian Crowley who was full of self-interest and self-gain. Robbo, I could see, was strumming away on his guitar, Leaf was holding her hands up as Nellie wound wool around them and Arthur and Nora chatted to a group of elderly neighbours. And across the school playground was a place which would outlive us. The Copse was full of birds and their nests, the caterpillars, the squirrels, the snails, insects. The daisies waiting to be made into chains, the twigs and branches ready to be made into dens. We needed to clean it up, tidy it up. A few benches and from September on, it would be part of the school playground. Our wild play area. A place of infinite learning. And I knew, if I sold to Brian and this Freddie, I would regret it for ever.

'Brian, we have our special assembly this morning, I was hoping to talk to you after it...'

He followed my glance out of the window. 'Those toe rags out there will have to go, cluttering up the school, that scruffy bunch of socialists and environmentalists...'

My phone flashed with a message, from Mary:

DO NOT DO IT.

And then another:

FOR THE LOVE OF FATIMA, STOP!

'Brian...' I tried to remain composed, 'one of those protestors is a retired professor, another is a daily churchgoer who volunteers at the homeless shelter in Dun Laoghaire five nights a week and the younger members are very impressive people, talented, hard-working and committed.' I stopped and gave him my hardest stares, 'And the fifth member is my *mother*.' He knew this, of course.

'Ah, do beg my pardon,' said Brian, with a most oleaginous smile. 'I had entirely forgotten, forgive my turn of phrase, it's just that they are persistent, aren't they?' He flashed me a tiny-toothed smile that looked entirely unapologetic. 'Oh well, they've lost, haven't they? They'll all have to go and find something else to protest about. Like banning all cars and making us all ride bikes or wear hemp clothes.' He passed me his fountain pen. 'Ready?' He slid the contract in front of me. 'And here's where it says land is *not* zoned for development... you should be pleased with that?'

> I, Tabitha Thomas, as head teacher of Star of the Sea National School, hereby declare, as patron and governor of the school, as guardian of its pupils and as de facto landowner of the school, its buildings and of the land surrounding it, that the half-acre site, hereby known as the Copse should be sold to...

'Brian...' I began.

'One moment,' he said, 'just sign and then we can have all the chats in the world and you can tootle off to the assembly or whatever it is.'

'Brian,' I said. 'I'm not going to sign. I don't want to sell. I don't care about the money. The school is actually doing all right, without iPads. We'll carry on with our cake sales and book clubs and cheese and wine dos and as long as the children are happy, that's all that matters.'

'What?' he paled. 'Have you gone mad? What authority do you have? This has been unanimously agreed by the boards of governors.'

'But it's not unanimous,' I said. 'There's me. I haven't voted but I have listened to all the arguments and have thought about it a great deal. We are not selling the Copse...'

'But what is Sister Kennedy going to say?' he said, sweat forming on his brow. 'She is not going to be happy, I can tell you that. She was saying how much she admired the plan and what a difference it would make to the lives of the children, computers and the like...'

SIAN O'GORMAN

'Brian, I don't care about what Sister Kennedy says.'

'Well!' he spluttered, outraged. 'I bet she would be interested in hearing your opinion of her,' he said, talking faster now. 'I bet she would like to know what you really think. As if she doesn't matter. An ex-head teacher of this very school and she doesn't matter! I've got a good mind to ring her straight away.'

There was a scrabbling sound from outside my door and a piece of paper was slipped under it. The word NO scribbled on it, layer upon layer of blue biro.

'Why don't you, Brian. But I'm the head teacher now and I am not selling. I have the final say.' I stood up and walked to my office door, my hand on the knob and, just as I pulled it open, there was Mary on her hands and knees.

'Lost your glasses again, Mary?'

'Paper clips,' she said, feeling around on the carpet tiles. 'I dropped some paper clips.'

'One moment, Brian,' I said, and Mary and I quickly ushered each other out of my office.

'What's going on?' I whispered urgently.

'He's going to *build* on the land. I know for sure he is. Whatever you do, don't sign.'

'I'm not going to, but how do you know?'

'Last night, I was taking my usual evening walk along the Colliemore Road, just down from the harbour. It's my constitutional. Well, it's ours now, mine and Huan's... sea air, you know...'

'Go on...'

'Well, I was sitting there, back against the wall, it's a lovely spot, and you really get a blast of evening sun. There's a large flat stone and you're kind of hidden away. It's sort of like meditating, in the moment or whatever they call it...'

'Mindfulness. Now, go on...'

'Anyway, so there I am, in my own world, pondering, as you do... when on the other side of the wall come two men...'

'Right...'

'So, I take no notice and they park themselves on the other side of the wall. And I've got my scarf tied on my head. My woolly one, tied under my chin. So, I'm in disguise...'

'And?'

'I recognised Brian Crowley's voice immediately. You know, that throat-clearing thing he does.' She then did a pitch perfect impersonation of the sound. 'And *his* boomy voice that would carry right over the Irish Sea to Wales ... and I heard every word ...'

'Go on...'

'The other fella was Freddie Boyle, the so-called pig farmer. Mr Good Samaritan himself. Now, this Freddie is a very large man, and he says, "when is that fecking teacher going to make up her mind?" Except he didn't say fecking. And Brian tells him not to worry and it's in the bag. And then Fat Freddie gives this huge laugh, a chortle really...'

'A chortle?'

She nodded. 'And says they've got it for a fecking song, except again they used the other word. Twenty grand, said Brian, and we're going to make 100 times that, once the apartments are sold. So, at this point, I am rigid and pressed against the wall, not daring to breathe and praying Huan won't wake up, ears straining.'

'I wasn't going to sell anyway,' I said. 'But it's good to have suspicions confirmed.'

A cough and we both looked up, startled. Brian was standing at the door of my office. 'Why don't we have a nice chat about everything? I think you just might be tired. You've had a long school year. The protest must have been such a strain,' he wheedled. 'They've put some real pressure on you, haven't they? Why don't we take a deep breath and just have a nice little chat?' He glared at Mary. 'Just the two of us...'

'One moment, Mr Crowley,' commanded Mary, pulling herself up to her full height. 'Will you hold on for one moment please? Ms Thomas and I are discussing something of utmost importance. And it cannot wait.'

'What are you discussing?' he said, suspiciously.

'We need to discuss changing from Barry's teabags to Lyons,' she said, desperately. 'It's a big decision and very urgent.' We looked at each other, panic in our eyes.

'Well, if you call that urgent, then obviously you haven't spent any time in the private sector. *This* is actually urgent. Ms Thomas? The papers? Can we get on? Let's have a nice chat and we can get it all sorted out in a jiffy. I now you are a sensible woman. And the fairer sex aren't normally known for seeing sense, but I am sure that you can be persuaded to do the right thing.'

'It's all right, Mary,' I said, straightening up. 'We can decide about the teabags later.'

I followed him back into my room where he flung himself down in the chair, his giant bottom hanging over the edge of the seat. I remained standing, my hand resting on my desk to give me stability and to make sure I felt as strong as I needed to be.

'Brian, I would like you to leave my office immediately and if you do not hand in your resignation as a member of the board by the end of the school day, I will begin a thorough investigation into this proposed deal.' I was bluffing, but I kept my face straight and my voice firm. And I seemed to have hit a nail on the head.

'What?' He tried to laugh. 'What are you saying?' But then he stood up, angrily, his chair falling back. 'You know you are the same as that lot out there.' He jabbed his thumb in the vague direction of where Arthur, Leaf, Robbo, Nellie and my mother were. 'I thought you were different. Married to Michael Fogarty. But that's obviously gone to pot. Foggy and the secretary. What a cliché. Ha!'

'Good day to you,' I said, standing up and walking to the door and opening it where Mary had been hovering. 'Mr Crowley?' I held out my arm towards the door to Mary's office. He left, reluctantly, and as he walked past, he pushed us with his shoulders, jostling us. We watched as he walked down the corridor to the main entrance. But then he turned and called back.

'Fuck you Foggy!' he snarled, his little crocodile teeth bared at us.

Mary and I looked at each other, open mouthed.

'Oh my word,' said Mary, shaking her head.

'Lucky escape,' I said. 'Now, you have to tell me everything. But first of all, tea. Six sugars. Anything to stop the shaking. And then I have a couple of phone calls to make before the special assembly.'

* * *

The girls all filed into the hall. Huan, who was in a sling wrapped around her new mother, had become quite the star attraction in school, all the girls gathering around wanting to look at this baby who had lost her birth mother but had found a new one in Mary Hooley. There was excitement and chatter in the air.

On stage behind me, were Red's drama group, one of the children in a red curly wig, the others dressed as raggedy orphans.

'And now,' I announced, 'on stage, is the Star of the Sea drama group with songs and selected scenes from *Annie*!'

We all joined in with the final rousing reprise. '*Tomorrow! Tomorrow, we love ya tomorrow!*'

Red gave me a big thumbs-up as we all sang lustily, fuelled by the thought of the long school holidays, the sunshine and golden days ahead.

'*You're only a day away... tomorrow, tomorrow, we love ya tomorrow, you're only a day awaaaaaaay!*'

I stood in front of the school.

'Thank you girls, for that wonderful production there. I can see we have a few budding actresses on our hands. Now, before we say goodbye for the summer holidays I have something to say. You see, girls, sometimes life can get difficult. Things can happen in school or at home and they are not easy to deal with. But we are here, not just to teach you but to support you, to take care of you. So always come to us and tell us how you are feeling. We are on your side.'

I looked around at the faces of these lovely girls, all of them listening intently to every word. 'You don't have to tell me now, but does anyone have anything they are dealing with that they are finding difficult?'

One hand crept up slowly, then another, then another... until there were twenty or so small hands in the air.

'From September, we are setting up the Feelings Club. Once a week, you can meet and you can talk about what is going on at home or at school or in your life generally. Anyone who wants to join the Feelings Club, let your teacher know. By the way, you can still join even if you are not ready or not able to speak. Just come along anyway. Okay?' I peered around at them, their lovely innocent faces. 'And I have another announcement. It's about the Copse...' There was silence in the hall, a collective intake of breath. My mind went back to that day when I had made the children cry. I could see their little faces, wondering whether I was about to tell them that the bulldozers were arriving in the morning. The squirrels about to be squashed, the snails trod on, the birds homeless?

'I would like to tell you all now,' I announced, 'that, it is *not* going to be sold.'

There was a huge cheer. The children began hugging each other and dancing about. And instead of dying down, the cheering went on and on. I looked around the room and all I could see were smiles.

'Okay, okay...' I tried for quiet. 'Right, this is what is going to happen. It's now going to be called the Peace Garden. And over the holidays the protestors and me - and anyone else who wants to volunteer - are going to clear it of the nettles and brambles. We are going to make sure that any animals are not disturbed. We are going to put in benches and a picnic table. And it's going to be a place of peace and tranquillity, where you can enjoy the wildlife, the view of the sea and take a moment to yourself. It's going to be a place for quiet reflection, for everyone, you, the teachers, your parents, your brothers and sisters. It's going to remain a very special place. How does that sound?'

There was more cheering and shouting. 'Star of the Sea, Star of the Sea, Star of the Sea...' someone began chanting. 'Star of the Sea, Star of the Sea...' And they all joined in.

'Let's go outside,' I shouted, 'and tell the Squirrel Savers they have won! We've all won!'

The whole school surged after me as we marched out of the hall, down the corridor, out the door and across the playground. 'Star of the Sea, Star of the Sea, Star of the Sea!'

Barry Whelan, the news reporter was outside, the camera on us as the river of a school poured out of the gates. I hadn't thought he'd get down to us so quickly.

Barry thrust a microphone right underneath my chin.

'The board of governors have come to a decision. The Copse will not be sold. I wanted our children to have access to computers. As a school, we needed money to buy them and cake sales and raffles don't bring in enough. Selling the land was what we believed would have been to the benefit of the children. However, I know now it isn't.' A song from my distant past swum into my consciousness and words babbled forth. 'You see,' I went on, 'I believe that children are the future, we are going to teach them well and let *them* lead the way! So, we will now not be selling the land. It is to be turned into a Peace Garden for the use of pupils, teachers and parents, anyone who wants to enjoy a moment of wildlife and tranquillity.'

The children began cheering again. *Star of the Sea, Star of the Sea*... And then the protestors who had been hugging each other, even Nellie had put down her crocheting to hug Robbo, they began with the chant as well. And then we all did. *Star of the Sea! Star of the Sea!*

* * *

Mary and I were tidying up the office, doing a last sort out before the long summer holidays. Huan was still in her Moses basket, fast asleep. Mary tucked the blanket around Huan, who still had the little Chinese jacket on, making sure she was warm and comfortable.

'Tabitha, I am so sorry. My own flesh and blood. Lucy carrying on with Michael' Mary reddened. 'What can I say? I feel ashamed because she is my cousin. Carrying on like that. There are far more decent ways to behave. Her Mammy has refused to leave her bed since she heard the news. Lucy's on her way up there today.'

'I've been thinking, though, Mary. That even decent people act *un*decently sometimes. None of us are perfect. I've made a hash of things in my life. There are many things that if I could go back, I'd do them differently.'

'You're right,' agreed Mary. 'It's a right of us all to behave like complete eejits at times. I told my own mother about Huan when I picked her up in Beijing.'

'What did she say?'

'Shocked would be an understatement,' she admitted. 'But even before we said goodbye, I could hear her coming round to the idea. Who could resist a baby?'

'Just think, Mary, if you hadn't disobeyed your mother, you'd be in some convent somewhere. Can you imagine?'

'And I wouldn't have Huan. I wouldn't have my...' she tried out this new word on her lips. 'I wouldn't have my *daughter*.'

'They're good things, daughters,' I said. 'Obviously, I'm biased.' I smiled at her. 'But they are pretty cool.' I thought of Nora, Rosie and me and of Rosaleen and the four mighty Thomas women. Mothers and daughters, grandmother and granddaughter. Such wonderful things to have and to be.

* * *

That evening, Rosie and I sat down in the living room, mugs of tea in our hands, to watch Clodagh's last ever news broadcast. You would never have thought it was her swansong. She calmly and smoothly ran through the news, the face and voice of Ireland.

We were watching as Clodagh deftly fielded a debate between the owner of a huge chicken farm in Monaghan and a member of the union for farm workers, she then moved neatly into a report from America, looking at Irish emigres.

'To the seaside village County Dublin of Dalkey, now,' she said...

'This is it! Oh God...'

Rosie grabbed my hand. 'They surely won't be mean like last time, will they...?'

'The environmental protest at the Star of the Sea school came to a close today when the school principal announced that the plot of land at the centre of the protest would now not be sold. But there was an unusual domestic drama because the head teacher and one of the protestors are mother and daughter... Our reporter Barry Whelan went to see what was going on and if old hurts had been healed...'

We watched as the sea of children filled the camera, all of them chanting. And there was me, in the front, looking slightly manic, it has to be said. My voice sounded shaky enough and I could barely remember saying any of what I said.?

I was surrounded by children the whole time, with their arms around my waist, my hands on their heads, all their faces smiling and happy. The other teachers were in the tumble of humans, all of us one big wonderful community. I spotted little Donna, a junior infant, who has Down's Syndrome, holding Red's hand, the biggest grin on both of their faces. There was Mary with Huan in one arm and holding another child's hand with her free arm. 'Three cheers for Ms Thomas!' Red shouted, and the children, buoyed up on natural excitement and enthusiasm – and the thought of the long school holidays – cheered.

'Mr Brian Crowley, the head of the board of governors, expressed his opinion as to the decision made by principal Tabitha Thomas...'

There was footage of Brian walking along the street. 'I don't have a comment to make except to say how disappointed I am and that this is the wrong direction for the school.'

'There have,' continued Barry Whelan, 'been allegations as to impropriety regarding the behaviour of a member of the board of governors, a Mr Brian Crowley, which the Gardaí say they are taking very seriously and anyone else connected to the school are not related to these allegations. A statement from the Dun Laoghaire Gardaí Station say that they are gathering information and will report back as soon as possible.' There were shots of the Copse. 'Ms Thomas has promised that the plot of land will be turned into a Peace Garden, a place for children, and, she says, teachers and parents, to find peace and quiet.'

And then there was me again speaking to Barry. I couldn't for the life of me remember saying any of it. 'We are all under tremendous pressure,' I said, slightly breathlessly, my eyes wild, 'and we need to give ourselves the space to reflect. Time out, if you will.' Rosie squeezed my hand. 'Our children,' I went on, 'know that they have not only the academic support and good teaching in our school but also the emotional support. We are a school which is not just chasing good exam results but happy and contented children. Mental health, happiness, pleasure and joy and the simple things in life have always been a part of our ethos, but today I am saying that it is the core of who we are as a school. I say to all our parents, that they are welcome to use the Peace Garden whenever they wish. They are part of our community too.'

'As to the domestic drama, all seemed to be resolved...' said Barry, cueing a shot of my mother and me hugging.

'I can't remember hugging her,' I said to Rosie. 'We don't hug. We're not huggers.'

'Well, apparently you are. The camera doesn't lie.'

I tried to think. Nellie and I had definitely hugged, and Arthur had gone in for one. Robbo had practically squeezed my insides out, the opposite to Leaf's limpid but well-meaning hug.

It was coming back to me now. 'Come here.' Nora was standing there. 'Just come over here.'

And we hugged, tears in my eyes, tears in her eyes – the woman who never cried. A swirling dream, the noise of the children cheering.

'You did it,' said Nora. 'I knew you would. That's my girl.'

'It still would have been far easier if you hadn't been protesting, wouldn't it?'

'Yes,' she said, 'but it wouldn't have been half as much fun.'

'I thought I was doing the right thing,' I said. 'I really did. I thought I was being the best teacher I could be, giving the children something we all thought they needed.'

'Fresh air and exercise. The best medicine there is,' she said, smiling, delighted with another triumphant protest. 'We've all discussed the summer, helping get the Copse ready. Robbo's even cancelling going to some music festival so he can help out. We'll have it bramble-free in no time.'

'Thanks Mum.'

'Now, one thing I need to say. Rosie is a credit to you. You're a natural mother. I wish I was more like you.'

'Really?' This was my mother. Being nice to me. Tears prickled in my eyes.

'And another thing...' she said.

'Please stop. I'm more comfortable when you are being rude and dismissive.'

'It's just that... Rosaleen would have been so proud of you. And you're just like her, you know that. You remind me of her every day. And you know that cutting, the one you took from Rosaleen's cherry tree. Well, once it grows a bit, it's going to be planted in the Peace Garden. What do you think about that?'

'That's a perfect idea.'

On television, we were back to the studio now and Clodagh was smiling. 'What a great story,' she said. 'Good things do happen to the best people.' And she winked.

'Did she just wink?' said Rosie.

'I think so...'

'And now,' said Clodagh, on screen, 'with the weather is the ever-lovely Bridget O'Flaherty...'

And there was Bridget, looking sexier than ever. Her dress was leather – or pleather, it was hard to tell under the studio lights – with a zip that went all the way from top to bottom.

'Clodagh... thank you...' She smiled at the camera. 'But I'm not going to do the weather right now. You all know what it has been like where you are. Let's just say that it will be more of the same tomorrow. But what I do want to do is pay tribute to Clodagh Cassidy who has been presenting this very news bulletin for the last ten years. And, guess what folks, today is her last day...'

The camera panned to Clodagh who was holding her earpiece with one hand, as though someone was shouting into it, and also trying to remember she was on camera and that it was a good idea to smile. So she did.

'And I'll be taking over from Clodagh. From Monday, I'll be your new news reader and I'm going to make sure that all of you get your fix of the headlines and that we have a bit of fun too. Life isn't all doom and gloom, is it?' She smiled broadly at the camera, giving it a cheeky wink. 'See you all here at six o'clock on Monday.'

Panning out, we saw Clodagh who was gesturing to someone off-camera. 'Thank you, Bridget,' she said recovering herself. 'And I wish you the best in your new role.'

My phone beeped. Red.

Are you watching? She's some mover.

I texted back:

And she was interested in you. You could have been Mr Bridget O'Flaherty.

And then it beeped again.

You're my type. Meet me at the bandstand at 8 p.m.?

Another beep.

Forgot to say, I love you.

BEFORE

Waiting for Red at the bandstand on the pier in Dun Laoghaire. I am twenty-one years old. I'm wearing jeans and his jacket that I'd been wearing for months now. And there he is, wearing an old navy fisherman's jumper, his hands in his pockets and he is looking around, at the boats bobbing beside the pier, tied to their buoys, the seagulls ahead, the skittering clouds. It's a beautiful evening. And then he sees me, and his face breaks into the most beautiful smile, and I can feel it inside, happiness exploding like a firework in my chest. Red Power. The man I love, the man I want to spend the rest of my life with. And he begins to run towards me. And that's all I want, everything I love. As the great seer Johnny Logan would say, 'we'll always be together, forever in love...'

* * *

And here I am eighteen years later, older and not particularly wiser. But as soon as I see him, I feel the same. It has never gone away, those feelings, I never stopped loving him. I just learned to pack them up and not to look at them.

He's sitting on the steps of the bandstand and when he sees me, it's the same smile and I smile too and he stands up and waits for me and I break into an awkward little skip and then next minute his arms are around me and it's him. It's Red Power and we're us again and there are fireworks. We never went away. We just... we just had some other stuff we needed to sort out. But it doesn't matter, none of it matters, because nothing has changed, we are still the same.

'I wish I'd known that you and Michael weren't happy,' he said, holding my hand. 'I would have rescued you from Fuck Me Foggy, ridden up on a white horse. Or my bicycle or whatever, and taken you away.'

'It was so stupid. All of it. But I have Rosie and I wouldn't change an ounce of her. Not one thing. I would do it all again, just to have her exactly the same as she is. She's been the most wonderful thing that has ever happened to me.'

'I'm going to apply for the position to be the number two best thing.'

'You don't have to apply.'

He smiled at me. 'Let's never let that happen again, all right. Let's always be Red and Tab or Tab and Red. Let's be us forever. Deal?'

'Deal. So, I heard from the department that if you want, you can stay another year in Star of the Sea. We'd love to have you, if you stay... Or maybe you'd like to go to the other school. It did sound like a good offer.'

'They wrote to me too,' he said. 'And I would like to have another year being around you. I'd like a lifetime of being around you. So, I'm going to stay.'

'I was hoping you'd say that.' We grinned at each other.

'You're the reason I stayed away for so long. I came back because Dad had been ill... but I hadn't ever stopped thinking about you. I hadn't ever moved on...'

'Nor me...'

'I was curious, you know. I wondered how your story, your life was turning out. The one that got away. Or ran away.'

'And then you came to the school. Was that a coincidence?'

He shrugged. 'Kind of. Who knows? I saw it advertised and I knew it was your school. I had known that by a very rudimentary Google search. And something made me apply... and then I was in. I think... I think I just wanted to make sure you were all right, that life was working out for you. I needed to know you were happy and I would have been fine with that.

Wished you well and then maybe I would have settled down with someone. But...'

'But what?'

'You didn't seem happy, deeply happy. Not really. That first day we met in your office, it was like a light had gone out... I wanted to be there for you, sort it out. I didn't know what to do... But as far as I knew, you were happily married.'

'And then my life began imploding,' I said. 'Did you, by chance, have anything to do with that?'

'What? Your husband running off with his secretary, your mother organising a protest outside your school?' He shook his head. 'If only I had such powers, I would have put them to better use.'

'Like what?'

'Like the two of us flying on a magic carpet to the terrace of a palazzo on the Grand Canal in Venice to drink Bellinis.'

'The last one's possible,' I said. 'Rosie's even saying she thinks she will be able to go away with her friends in a couple of weeks. She's even thinking of getting a summer job and...'

'And what?'

'I think she'll be okay,' I said. 'I'm so proud of her.'

He smiled. 'So Venice?'

I nodded. 'Oh God yes!'

'However,' he said, 'I can't do the magic carpet. Would Ryanair be an adequate substitution? I'll book it tonight and find a palazzo fit for you.'

'On one condition,' I said.

'Anything.'

'That you don't do any Johnny Logan songs in Venice.'

'What? But that was going to be the big moment, when I get dressed up in a white suit and be Johnny. I thought that would clinch the deal.'

'Deal?'

'I'll just have to think of another way to get you to marry me.' He smiled at me. 'But we can talk about that another time.' He took my hand again and kissed it. 'Oh Tabitha Thomas, what a spell you cast on me.' He held me tightly and I clung on.

'Dad's poetry was reviewed in the New York Times yesterday,' said Red.

'He's delighted. Peggy and the poetry gang are going to have a special party. You'll have to come.'

'Of course. What did the review say?'

'*A talented voice singing new songs of Irish freedom...* something like that anyway. Dad has it cut out. The book should do well.'

'That's amazing,' I said. 'When can I buy a copy?'

'It's being launched next month. Now, you know he is giving every penny in royalties to the school...'

'What?'

'He doesn't want it. For the school coffers, he said. Tab,' he laughed at my shocked face. 'He's an old communist He doesn't want to make money out of art. He wants the school to have it.'

'I don't know what to say...'

'Allow an old man the feeling that he might be doing some good.'

The full-length of the pier, we walked with arms around each other, as though we were one person, and talked and talked and talked. Just like we used to, as though nothing had happened except for a couple of weeks away. And the seagulls soared along with our hearts and love and life was in the air.

* * *

I woke really early, thinking of all the people in my life that meant so much. Rosie, Rosaleen, Red... and Nora.

She'd be on her way to the Forty Foot right now for her daily dip. The early morning sun predicted a hot summer's day. The sky was Aegean blue, there was a warmth already to the developing day. The rare, perfect Irish summer weather.

What was she always saying, that I should join her? And I thought I never would again. But suddenly I wanted to. Now, it seemed like the very rightest thing to do. Quickly, I gathered some things together. My suitcase was at the end of the bed packed for Venice. Red and I were flying off for two nights that afternoon, and Nora was going to be looking after Rosie. She'd promised me she was going to be all right. And later in the summer, Rosie and I were going to Paris. Just the two of us. I couldn't wait.

But as I tiptoed past Rosie's room, her door suddenly opened. She was standing there in her pyjamas, yawning. She eyed by bag with my swimming things in. 'Where are you off to?'

'The Forty Foot. For a swim.'

'Really?'

'Yeah, I thought it would be nice.' I tried to sound as though it was the most normal thing in the world. But I was scared. What if it was too cold? What if I had forgotten how to swim? But really, deep down, I was worried, afraid for myself. Would it bring back memories I'd rather forget or should I just feel the fear and swim anyway? 'Would you like to come?'

She suddenly smiled. 'Why not? I'll just grab my things.'

We drove to the Forty Foot, through the quiet and silent streets, only a few hard-working early birds on their way to the Dart or retired folk coming back from the newsagents, papers under their arms. We saw Nellie Noonan and I tooted my horn and waved to her out of the open window. She peered at us and then waved back. 'Beautiful day!' we heard her shout.

'Did you hear about Clodagh?' I said. 'She's been offered a new presenting gig. It's called *Clodagh!* with an exclamation mark. It's a serious political interview programme.'

'Even though it's got an exclamation mark in the title?'

'Viewers love them, apparently. According to Clodagh. The person not the programme with an exclamation mark. Nicky, her agent, got her a massive wodge for it. Apparently, some people value brains and experience.'

We parked beside the beach at Sandycove, just close to the Forty Foot. There were other daily dippers at the swimming hole.

'And *I* forgot to tell you about Bridget,' said Rosie as we began walking. 'It's not going well. She froze last night when she was interviewing the Minister for finance and didn't know what to say. It was in all the papers this morning. She's sacked her mother as her agent. And she says she wants to leave broadcasting and become a dog groomer.'

We had reached the Forty Foot and found a space in one of the changing areas. Rosie stood, looking out to sea, her hands shading her eyes.

'Can you see her?' I said as I struggled into my swimsuit.

'That's her.' Rosie pointed to the red dot far out and began to get undressed. 'There she is. Do you see her, all the way out there?'

'Actually, you go in. I'll stay and watch. I'm not feeling too well.' I had decided that I was going to sit this one out. I'd confront my phobia of the sea another day.

'Mum,' said Rosie, firmly. 'We're both going in. It'll do us good. My counsellor said I should do more exercise, be outdoors more often. So here I am. I haven't swum in the Forty Foot for years and I'm not going in without you...'

Rosie was my inspiration, I realised. Without her, I was nothing. She'd been through so much and if she could face her life head on, so could I. We held hands as we walked down the steps roughly carved out of rock and into the icy water. 'Jesus!' I yelped.

'Don't be a baby,' said Rosie. 'I'm going in.' She plunged in, diving down into the water, so I could see her shape under the surface, like a mermaid, her long hair streaming out behind her. 'Come on,' she said, when she re-emerged, 'just dive in.'

And I did, not as gracefully as Rosie, but I swam down until I could touch the bottom and submerged by the water, seaweed and rocks clipping my toes. For a moment, I opened my eyes and all I could sense was peace and gentleness and that I was safe. To my spirit guides, Rosaleen and the baby I had lost, I said, thank you. Thank you for everything. And I pushed my way back to the surface.

'That's better.' Rosie was treading water. 'Now let's swim to Granny.' She was so brave, my daughter. So strong. You could learn just as much from your child – if not more – that they learn from you.

And I had forgotten what swimming in the sea was like, even on a still day like this, the water felt powerful, the bump-bump of the undulations stronger and the peaceful feeling was still with me, as though it alone was keeping me afloat. On we went until I could see that Nora had spotted us. She was floating on her back but squinting at the two of us.

'Granny!' shouted Rosie. 'It's us!'

She narrowed her eyes even further, trying to see us and then she realised who it was. And a huge smile broke over her face, her arm stretched up in a wave.

'What took you so long?' she said when we were closer. 'I've been waiting ages.'

'Your invitation never arrived,' said Rosie, paddling up to her. 'Must have got lost in the post.' The two of them had the same grin, I noticed. I'd never realised that before, how much Rosie looked like Mum. And like Rosaleen. And like me.

'Finally, you made it,' Nora said to me when I reached them. The three of us doggy-paddled around in the water. 'I never thought I'd see the day.'

And there was something about Nora or maybe it was always there and I had never seen it, or maybe I had chosen not to see it, but she looked, dare I say it pleased to see me.

'I've been watching Howth Head,' she said, pointing to the headland on the other side of Dublin bay, and I was wondering if they still had the goats.'

'The goats?' Rosie doggy-paddled herself around so she was looking out to see past the little fishing trawler that was chugging in the distant, past the ferry that was bringing people either home or away.

'Goats, that's right. They have goats on Howth Head and your great-grandmother brought me to see them once when I was a little girl. And there they were. A herd of them. Nibbled my cardigan they did. Did you ever see them, Tabitha?'

'No... but Rosaleen once brought me to see a horse race,' I told them. 'On Barley Cove strand, in West Cork. They used to do it every year apparently. She went there when she was a girl and so she brought me. Did you go, Mum?'

She nodded. 'Oh yes, she loved West Cork, it never lost her, that love for it. The place was in her bones, in her heart. When she was exiled – that's what she called it,' she explained to Rosie, 'she would seek out all the West Corky things she could, like goats, or she'd buy eggs that were sent up from Bantry every morning or she would read the stories of Flannery Vickery. He set all his novels in West Cork. Made her feel less homesick.'

Rosie flipped over to float on her back and then Nora did and then I followed, the three of us floating, looking up at the cloudless blue sky.

And then I felt Nora's hand grab mine and we held on and it didn't feel awkward or weird. It felt nice. And then I found Rosie's hand in the water and the three of us joined, like a chain of paper dolls, three generations of Thomas women. A trio of pirate queens. Rosaleen would have been happy to see us like this, I thought, and if she was up there, she would be looking down at us, pleased and proud. We might just be all right, I thought. Everything might just be all right.

MORE FROM SIÂN O'GORMAN

We hope you enjoyed reading *Mothers and Daughters*. If you did, please leave a review.

If you'd like to gift a copy, this book is also available as an ebook, digital audio download and audiobook CD.

Sign up to Siân O'Gorman's mailing list for news, competitions and updates on future books.

https://bit.ly/SianOGormannewsletter

Another heart-warming book by Siân O'Gorman, *Life After You*, is available to order now.

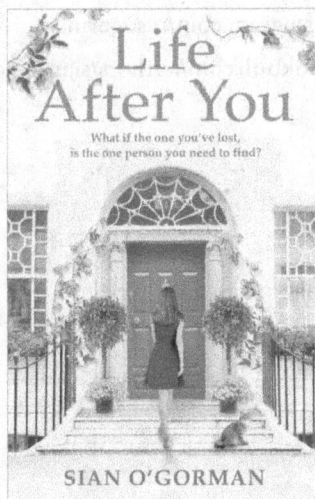

ABOUT THE AUTHOR

Sian O'Gorman was born in Galway on the West Coast of Ireland, grew up in the lovely city of Cardiff, and has found her way back to Ireland and now lives on the east of the country, in the village of Dalkey, just along the coast from Dublin. She works as a radio producer for RTE.

Follow Sian on social media:

facebook.com/sian.ogorman.7

twitter.com/msogorman

instagram.com/msogorman

bookbub.com/authors/sian-o-gorman

ABOUT BOLDWOOD BOOKS

Boldwood Books is a fiction publishing company seeking out the best stories from around the world.

Find out more at www.boldwoodbooks.com

Sign up to the Book and Tonic newsletter for news, offers and competitions from Boldwood Books!

http://www.bit.ly/bookandtonic

We'd love to hear from you, follow us on social media:

facebook.com/BookandTonic

twitter.com/BoldwoodBooks

instagram.com/BookandTonic